RICHARD MAPLES gradu
College, Winchester and ha
graphy and Historical Metho
taught History at O and A Le
currently Head of History at

MARK WRIGHT obtained
Politics from Sunderland Polyt went on to take an MA in Historiography and Historical Method at Thames Polytechnic, specializing in English radicalism. He has taught History to O and A Level privately and in Adult Education and is currently employed as an editor in educational publishing.

Adrian Cox

key facts

GCE A-Level Passbooks

APPLIED MATHEMATICS, E. M. Peet, B.A.

BIOLOGY, H. Rapson, B.Sc.

CHEMISTRY, J. E. Chandler, B.Sc. and R. J. Wilkinson, Ph.D.

ECONOMICS, R. Maile, B.A.

GEOGRAPHY, R. Bryant, B.A., Ph.D., R. Knowles, M.A. and J. Wareing, B.A., M.Sc.

MODERN BRITISH AND EUROPEAN HISTORY, R. Maples, B.Ed., M.A. and M. A. Wright, M.A.

PHYSICS, J. R. Garrood, M.A., Ph.D.

PURE MATHEMATICS, R. A. Parsons, B.Sc. and A. G. Dawson, B.Sc.

PURE AND APPLIED MATHEMATICS, R. A. Parsons, B.Sc. and A. G. Dawson, B.Sc.

GCE A-Level Passbook

Modern British and European History

R. Maples, B.Ed., M.A. and M. A. Wright, M.A.

key facts

Published by Charles Letts and Co Ltd
London, Edinburgh and New York

The authors are grateful to Lane Pics for permission ro reproduce the cartoons on pages 204, 211, 242 and 258. Acknowledgement is due to the Longman Group Ltd for permission to use the diagram on page 247. The diagrams on pages 145, 228, 230, 234 and 236 are taken from *Industry and Empire* by E. J. Hobsbawn (Pelican Economic History of England: 3, 1969), copyright © E. J. Hobsbawn 1968, 1969 and are reproduced by permission of Penguin Books Ltd.

Diary House, Borough Road, London SE1 1DW

Printed 1985
Made and printed by Charles Letts (Scotland) Ltd
ISBN 0 85097 634 0

Contents

Part 2: Modern British History

Guide to Using this Book

Our chief aim in producing this book has been to assist students to study for A-Level History in a more effective manner. We would hope that users of the book start their revision early enough to make best use of the material it contains, but even if readers start their revision quite late, the book will still be of assistance.

It would have been impossible to cover every available option or avenue of study in a book such as this, neither would it have been realistic to cover every 'historical fact' relating to the topics we have chosen. What has been done is a result of analysing current British and European History syllabuses at A Level for the very popular period after 1815. While the topics chosen provide an outline and analysis of events and ideas in the nineteenth and early twentieth centuries, do not be fooled into thinking that you can get away without some knowledge of events and movements in the late eighteenth century in Britain and Europe, or of contemporary events in the rest of the world. A wide reading of texts is essential; mere 'facts' are not enough – what is necessary is an analysis of these facts. An extensive bibliography has been provided at the end of the book and, although it is unlikely that you will read every book on the lists, you should at the very least try to read one or two in each section for the area you are studying. Remember that the ideas are as important as the events, and you should try to gain from your reading an understanding of the ideological movements which have done much to shape British and European history throughout this period. So, democracy, nationalism, socialism, communism and fascism are all central to any study of the late nineteenth- and early twentieth-century British and European history. Likewise, you should have an understanding of the prevailing social and economic conditions.

Each chapter includes a brief introduction to the topic which will give background information. This is followed by an account and analysis of the events and ideas within the topic and will give guidance on various avenues of research and reference to current historical thinking. Each chapter is concluded by a summary of the important aspects that you should cover and questions you should be asking yourself in the light of your studies.

The reading lists for each topic at the end of the book are designed to provide a balanced source of reference material. Some of the books are essential and you should try to purchase these for yourself. Other material will only be available through reference libraries or through inter-library loan.

A number of maps, diagrams and cartoons have been included to highlight points in the text – you should study these carefully and re-read the relevant text, especially where this relates to complex issues such as territorial changes.

You should at all times try to gain both an understanding of a particular topic and an understanding of contemporary events. It is therefore important to cross-reference your studies, e.g. if you are studying British foreign affairs, you should try to read the chapters of the book dealing with the foreign policy of Britain's rivals in order to gain an overall picture.

With effective study and revision, you should have few problems with the examination. Examination technique is covered in the section on page 261.

Introduction to A-Level History

The study of history at A Level should, it is hoped, be interesting and rewarding, but, equally, it is an area in which certain demands will be made of the student. An interest in history is an obvious prerequisite of the course, but to ensure maximum success, you must be clear about the level and type of approach required and about the qualities for which your examiners will be looking. Clear, concise English is an obvious requirement, as is a sound grasp of facts and chronology, but history at A level is more than just recall, though, for many of you, this will be the starting point.

Historical analysis

Having provided yourself with the necessary factual and chronological information, the temptation is to answer the question with a simple narrative response. While this might be acceptable at a lower level, A-level study requires you to display powers of analysis. It is not enough to be aware of the events pertaining to a particular period or topic; you must be able to analyse it within the context of the question asked. Such a skill will not come immediately, but will develop with practice and experience.

Each essay question will present a situation in which you are asked to recall information, but, more importantly, you will be expected to discuss, compare, contrast, judge and justify. The narrative element of your essays will be important in communicating your ideas, but the analytical content is far more significant. An A-level essay with little evidence of analysis will score poorly because it has failed to meet the requirements of the course. All the A-level boards stress the importance of analysis over simple narrative, and some, like the Joint Matriculation Board, specifically state that only 45 per cent of the marks awarded for an A-level History answer will be given for knowledge and 55 per cent will be given for the ability to assess evidence and to select and organize material.

Your skills of analysis must develop as the course progresses, together with your ability to understand the demands of A-level questions and the opportunities they provide for displaying these powers.

Assessment and empathy

A-level History, by definition, requires an advanced understanding and the ability to make assessments. For instance, it will not be enough simply to be aware of Palmerston's actions in the field of foreign policy; you will need to be able to gauge their significance and effect and to consider the alternative possibilities at any particular juncture. For a single event or piece of legislation, you should be aware of the contributing factors and able to assess their significance. Similar considerations apply in broader questions covering a period of change, but even greater care must be given to the question of context.

In studying History, we run the risk of interpreting events with retrospective bias. What happened was not inevitable and, at the time, may have been seen as an unlikely outcome. Equally, actions which today we would find abhorrent and morally inexcusable were deemed not only acceptable, but even just. The way to cope with this problem is to seek to empathize with the leading characters and to see the situation from their point of view. Harsh judgments on people and events will sometimes be justified and necessary, but, more often than not, they are a result of failure to take account of historical perspective. By seeking to empathize and by considering each development as only one of a number of possible outcomes, you will not only guard yourself against 'historical inevitability' but, in doing so, will produce a more credible assessment.

A question of language

Although History may not yet have reached the level of jargon of the Sciences, it does require an understanding of some technical terms. Broad concepts such as 'liberalism' and 'nationalism' are open to serious misuse and, when you use them, you must define and back them up with appropriate examples. Precise positions or statements of political development such as 'absolutist' or 'semi-constitutional' also need to be fully understood in the context of the question and must be used accurately when you are describing a given political situation. The fact that West Germany is known as the German Federal Republic and East Germany as the German Democratic Republic perhaps best illustrates this point with regard to our Western definition of the term 'democracy'.

Synthesis

When you have mastered the problem of historical analysis, feel competent to provide a fair assessment and are confident in handling historical concepts, your final problem is that of synthesis. All the hard work you have done so far, using textbooks and documents and doing background reading, must now be channelled towards achieving examination success. In short, you must, in a limited period of time – usually no more than three hours – be able to provide a synthesis of your work in the form of a number of selected essays.

By synthesis, we do not simply mean preparation leading up to your final exam, though that is part of it, but, rather, the constant awareness that your studies must be geared towards giving you the greatest chance of examination success. A-level examiners marking hundreds of scripts will be impressed with the student who displays the capabilities already mentioned and who has the flexibility to mould his/her knowledge and use his/her analytical abilities to produce a relevant answer to the question posed. Knowledge of the relevant events will, of course, be important, but awareness of historical perspective and of the factors influencing the events will be invaluable. Equally, the examiner will be impressed by your knowledge of the many points on which modern debate is focussed and by your ability to argue for one side against the other, illustrating the strengths and weaknesses of the arguments.

You should, therefore, be aware of the need for synthesis throughout the course, so that when you need to review your studies in preparation for the exam, your knowledge will be as deep as possible and flexible enough to cover most, if not all, possible lines of enquiry.

Conclusion

At the start of your A-level course, your abilities will probably be limited to the simple narrative response required at O level. From such a standpoint, the skills outlined in this introduction may seem quite daunting. In reality, however, through normal hard work, cross-referencing and attention to content, your historical essay-writing will develop. Your task is to realize the demands which will be made of you and to progress as rapidly as possible to the point where the skills required are second nature to you.

Part 1

Modern European History

Chapter 1
The Concert of Europe: International Diplomacy, 1814–25

Introduction

Europe at the beginning of the nineteenth century was a continent with a strange dichotomy: divided by national ambitions yet sharing in its overall social outlook a relative homogeneity. The former had created turbulence and conflict which dated back to at least the French Revolution and which would continue to plague the continent into modern times, despite all attempts at unity. Culturally, though, Europe was still united to a considerable extent. The ideas of the eighteenth-century Enlightenment had ignored international boundaries, and the scientific discoveries and general philosophy of the period were truly international.

However, as the age of Enlightenment was replaced by Romanticism, the pressures of change were mounting. **Rapid economic development**, the **rise of the new social classes** and the **growth of class conflict**, the development of **new political ideologies** and the **rise of nationalism** were collectively to herald the emergence of Europe into the modern age. That this passage has not been easy is clearly indicated by the political struggles that have rent Europe since this time as the powers of continuity and change have struggled to shape the development of Europe to their chosen ends.

The Empire of Napoleon, which the other powers of Europe were in the process of dismantling, was, ironically, a time of considerable European unity. This unity had been imposed within the Empire, and outside it had been maintained through the alliance of the major powers in opposition. With the Empire's demise, these powers now sought to **return Europe to equilibrium**, to achieve a 'Concert of Europe'.

They had already shown this willingness for joint action by the provisions of the **Treaty of Chaumont** (March 1814), under which Austria, Great Britain, Prussia and Russia bound themselves to **overcome Napoleon**, to guarantee both his **exile** and the ensuing **territorial settlement**, and to **stay in alliance for twenty years**. Upon the success of this action, they further agreed to **restore the Bourbon dynasty to France** on the abdication of Napoleon, which occurred in April, following his departure for Elba.

International government

Having defeated Napoleon, the victorious powers were now faced with the problem of reconstructing the map of Europe that he had so drastically changed. Their central objective was that of **re-establishing a balance of power**, but beyond this, each of them had differing aims and influences to take into account.

Russia, under Tsar Alexander I, sought a **liberal settlement**, but combined this with a desire for **reward** for Russia's primary role in bringing about Napoleon's defeat. Thus, the ideal settlement for Alexander I was a **firm but fair treatment of France**, and the **creation in Poland of a satellite kingdom** which would provide a useful buffer zone and a place for the Tsar to satisfy his reformist ideals. To obtain such a satellite kingdom would, however, require **Austrian and Prussian consent**.

For **Prussia**, led by Frederick William III, Russian aims in Poland were permissible, as Prussia's aim was the **annexation of Saxony**, whose unfortunate ruler, Frederick Augustus I, had been made to pay for his loyalty to Napoleon. Such a move would significantly add to the power and wealth of Prussia but would obviously invoke considerable **opposition from Austria**.

Austria, which had suffered badly under Napoleon (being defeated on four occasions and forced to come to terms with the Emperor) had entered the final struggle against Napoleon very late, when his defeat seemed almost assured. Under the guidance of Chancellor Metternich, Austria was the power with the most conservative outlook seeking the '**just equilibrium**'. There was no room for liberal sentiments, merely a desire for balance. **France was not to be destroyed**, but equally the **territorial expansion of Russia and Prussia was to be guarded against** because either would upset the balance.

Great Britain, like Austria, sought a return to a balanced Europe, but for different motives: it wished to **avoid continental intervention** and required a **stable market with which to trade**. The continental system applied by Napoleon had clearly illustrated the dangers to Britain of a Europe dominated by a single power. Britain was not overtly opposed to the extension of Austrian control in Italy or to Prussian expansion in north and western Germany, but did **oppose Russian expansion** (especially at the expense of the ailing Ottoman Empire), and continued **French control of the Netherlands**.

With these objectives in mind, the allies concluded the **First Treaty of Paris** in May 1814. France was treated with as much consideration as possible. Despite the fact that it had forced its will on continental Europe, it was allowed to **keep its army**, **no reparations** were demanded, its **boundaries** were defined as those existing in **1792**, not 1789, and it was allowed to **retain the looted art treasures** of Napoleon. France lost to Britain only its **colonies of strategic importance**: Malta, Tobago, St Lucia and Mauritius, but retained the commercial wealth of its other colonies. Overall, the settlement for **France** was more than generous, and was aimed at making the accession of Louis XVIII and the progress of France back to international legitimacy as rapid and as easy as possible. Meanwhile, the allied powers also began their efforts to patch up the map of continental Europe, announcing their intention to **create a large Kingdom of the Netherlands**, to recognize the independence of Switzerland and to realign the local frontiers of Germany and Italy – all of which was to be discussed at a congress in Vienna later in the year.

The Congress of Vienna

The Congress which duly convened in Vienna in September 1814 was to be both the culmination of the wrangling over the settlement of post-Napoleonic Europe, and the first of what were intended to be regular consultations. Although almost every European nation was represented, in reality the settlement was the result of negotiations between the **five major powers**. France was reluctantly admitted following Talleyrand's demand for the 'sacred principle of legitimacy' – the idea that Louis XVIII, who was the legitimate French King and had never been at war, ought to be represented at the Congress.

Metternich, with the assistance of his able secretary Gentz and a bewildering assortment of Austrian officials, set the scene in a diplomatic chess game lasting nine months and culminating in the Treaty of Vienna. Metternich's desire for **order and balance** was shared by Britain's representative, Lord Castlereagh, but although Russia and Prussia also sought a return to stability, they desired some **reward** for their involvement in defeating Napoleon. This conflict of interests did not help the course of the discussions – in fact, towards the end of 1814, it seemed possible that the differences might actually lead to renewed conflict. By 3 January 1815, the situation had become so serious that Talleyrand was able to convince **Austria and Britain** that they should join with **France** in a **secret defensive alliance to resist the claims of Russia and Prussia**. In retrospect, however, in a Europe tired of confict, war was a highly unlikey outcome, and a compromise was reached. Only Talleyrand was completely satisfied by this outcome and wrote to tell Louis XVIII that 'France is no longer isolated in Europe'.

Talleyrand's observations, however, proved rather untimely, as in March 1815 Napoleon decided to re-enter the arena of European affairs, at Cannes. With a handful of men, he rapidly progressed to Paris where, by popular acclaim, he replaced Louis XVIII. The allies who had seemed at loggerheads now acted with complete unanimity, regrouping their forces for a new campaign. In the event, a single battle, that of **Waterloo** (18 June), was enough to shatter Napoleon's dream and force him again into exile, this time on the lonely South Atlantic island of St Helena. France's punishment was also harsher. The allied powers, alarmed at how easily French aggression was renewed, imposed on France under the **Second Treaty of Paris** (November 1815) a **war indemnity** of 700 million francs, **military occupation** by 150 000 men under the command of Wellington, and the **return of the art treasures** looted by Napoleon – that strange oversight in the first treaty. But, even so, France was not overly punished, **losing only minor sections of territory and retaining Alsace and Lorraine**, which Prussia in particular demanded.

Predating both the second Treaty of Paris and Waterloo, however, was the **Treaty of Vienna** (9 June 1815), the compromise settlement of the allied powers. To maintain the all-important 'balance of power', each of the powers was to **regain the equivalent of the territory it held in 1805. Russia** thus settled for a **Polish kingdom**, later known as Congress Poland, (which included Warsaw, but was not as large as the ancient boundaries), to which the Tsar then duly granted a constitution. This acquisition, together with the large Russian army of nearly a million troops, **worried Metternich and Castlereagh**, but was a concession they were forced to make. In compensation for the loss of Warsaw, **Prussia** received **two-fifths of Saxony**, together with a **large area of the Rhineland**, **Westphalia and Swedish Pomerania**, which, although smaller in terms of area, was German in blood and speech. In tidying up, **Sweden** (which had lost Finland and the Aland Isles following the Russian invasion of 1808) was given **Norway**, and **Denmark**, in compensation, received the small duchy of **Lauenburg**.

Austria and Britain, in order to thwart Prussian and Russian ambitions, **strengthened the territories of Germany** by reorganizing them into a **confederation** composed of thirty-nine sovereign states. Austria remained the dominant power but its aim – as ever – was **balance**. Only in **Italy** did Austria seek to gain territory, **recovering Lombardy and acquiring Venetia**, but with the sole aim of securing balance and stability. Other Italian measures included the **creation of a stronger Piedmont**, the **restoration of the Papal States** and the **introduction of a Bourbon monarchy in Naples**, all of which reaffirmed Metternich's contention that Italy was 'a mere geographical expression'.

The **fear of French aggression dictated the joining of Holland and the Austrian Netherlands** into a Kingdom of the Netherlands under the House of Orange. Castlereagh reinforced this by restoring **Java** to the new state and lending it two million pounds to fortify its frontier. The **neutrality of Switzerland was recognized, Spain and Portugal regained their old borders**, and in this way the map of Europe was redrawn.

There remains considerable debate about the chief aim and the success of the Congress of Vienna. Was it an attempt at **restoration**, or was it a **return to reality** after the revolutionary attempts of Napoleon to impose order on Europe? Neither seems totally satisfactory, for a total restoration was impossible, as astute statesmen such as Metternich and Castlereagh realized. The keystone of the settlement was the **principle of legitimacy**, tempered by **negotiated compromises** and the need for the **mutual compensation** of the victors, set against the background of an overall desire for the re-establishment of the balance of power.

The Congress of Vienna and the ensuing Congress System were successful in that there was no great war in Europe for almost a century and no war of any significance until 1853. Admittedly, Europe was weary of war after the struggle against Napoleonic domination, but Vienna was a true congress where the concern was for the **future of Europe**, not for revenge but for **restitution**. That France was permitted to be present at the Congress is proof enough of this desire, and it is unfortunate that the same motives did not reappear over a hundred years later at Versailles!

The chief shortcoming of the Congress of Vienna was its **failure to take account of national self-determination**, as the treatment of

Norway, Finland and Belgium clearly demonstrated. However, given that its aim was to restore order, and that it was framed by monarchs and statesmen accustomed to eighteenth-century diplomacy, it is not surprising that it failed to meet the emerging demands of the nationalists and liberals of the nineteenth century. Its final epitaph must therefore surely be the length of time for which its influence was felt, ensuring the **minimum of dissatisfaction** amongst the major powers and bringing about what can be seen in retrospect as the most durable peace of modern times.

The alliances

The need for **more concrete guarantees of the safety of Europe** resulted in the formation of two further alliances in 1815. **The Quadruple Alliance**, concluded in November 1815, bound the four allied powers to **maintain by force for twenty years** the arrangements made at Chaumont, Vienna and Paris and to **meet periodically 'for the maintenance of the Peace of Europe'** – the so-called **'Concert of Europe'** as it became known. Serious rifts were later to arise amongst the signatories as to **what constituted a threat to European security**. Was, for instance, an internal revolt a legitimate or reasonable cause for intervention? In particular, **Castlereagh**, while keen to safeguard the international settlement, **did not wish to see Britain involved in the internal affairs of any of the continental powers**, not even France.

It was Britain, too, who refused to join the other alliance floated at this time, the **Holy Alliance**, created by Tsar Alexander I following his religious conversion by a mystical occultist. Alexander I urged his fellow monarchs to sign an undertaking to rule by the 'precepts of that Holy Religion', but on a more pragmatic level, the Holy Alliance was a **general union of sovereigns against revolution**. Its wording was so vague and mystical as to render it harmless enough for most European monarchs to sign (the **exceptions** being **Britain**, the **Pope** and the **Sultan of Turkey**) and for Talleyrand to label it a 'ludicrous contract'. But **Metternich**, who was always keen to further his policies, saw that it was potentially useful to him and amended one of the clauses to imply that signatory monarchs would render assistance in putting down internal disturbances, which gave the Alliance a sinister overtone.

The Congress System

The first Congress to take place as laid down in the Quadruple Alliance occurred at **Aix-la-Chapelle** in November **1818**. By this time, France, under the administration of the Duc de Richelieu, had paid off the indemnity imposed in 1815 and now took its place at the Congress with the other powers. In recognition of this return to international legitimacy, the **troops of occupation were withdrawn** and France was invited to join a **Quintuple Alliance** to preserve peace. At the same time, however, the Quadruple Alliance remained in force and new provisions concerning the defence of the barrier fortresses in the Netherlands were added. The real result of Aix-la-Chapelle, however, was to indicate that, once the threat of French Imperialism was removed, the **common purposes of the allies were rapidly being overshadowed by conflicting interests**.

The attempt of Tsar **Alexander I** to create a more **'solid guarantee' of support for legitimate government** met with considerable **British opposition**, and later, as this moved beyond the preservation of balance towards intervention for self-interest, **Metternich, too, opposed it**. For an autocratic Tsar this might be legitimate, but not for the parliamentary government of Britain. Similarly, when Alexander I proposed organized intervention to aid the King of Spain in regaining control of Spain's South American colonies, Britain again influenced the Congress to refuse such an appeal and gained Metternich's support through his desire for diplomacy rather than force.

The forces of **nationalism and liberalism** were, however, still fermenting in Europe, and in January 1820 they surfaced again when the ineffectual King of Spain, Ferdinand VII, was forced, following a military revolt, to regrant the **liberal constitution that Spain had enjoyed** in 1812. Alexander I was horrified and immediately called for the assembling of another Congress to review this development and to seek the repression of liberalism, by armed force if necessary. **Castlereagh**, feeling challenged by Alexander I's interpretation of the obligations of Vienna, issued a state paper in May which clearly declared Britain's position. In a key phrase he stated that 'when the territorial balance of Europe is disturbed, she [Britain] can interfere with effect, but she is the last government in Europe which can be expected or can venture to commit herself on any question of abstract principle'.

By the time the Congress actually assembled in **Troppau** in October 1820 (moving on to **Laibach** in January 1821), **Naples**, under the equally inefficient Bourbon King Ferdinand I, had also been forced to grant the Spanish constitution, and was followed in August by **Portugal**. Now not only **Alexander I** but also **Metternich** felt the need for action of some kind. Since Castlereagh had already made Britain's position clear, he, together with France, sent only observers to the Congress. The remaining powers – Russia, Austria and Prussia – now debated what action they should take. Initially, Alexander I was almost pushed by his adviser, Capodistrias, to recognize the need for reform, but an untimely revolt against excessive military discipline by the **Semënovsky guards** in Russia convinced him that he should take a more conservative line. Consequently, in November, they issued a joint declaration that they could **never recognize the right of a people to restrict the power of kings**, which Castlereagh promptly labelled as 'destitute of common sense'. By March 1821 Metternich, backed by Russia and Prussia, and commissioned to suppress revolution, had moved Austrian armies into Italy, **destroying the constitution** first of **Naples** and then of **Piedmont** which had unexpectedly revolted in March. The original kings were once again reimposed, but the **cracks in the alliances** were by now considerable.

Metternich had skilfully **used Russian support to safeguard Austrian interests in Italy**, but when, in March 1821, a revolt broke out in Greece against the Turks, he quite naturally saw the **danger of Russian support for the Christian Greeks against the Moslem Turks**. In the hope of preventing this, he summoned what was to be the last real Congress, which met at **Verona** in October **1822**. Both **Austria** and **Britain** wished to **discourage Russian intervention**, but more significant for the Congress system itself was the fact that, following Castlereagh's suicide in August, Britain was now led by **George Canning**. Castlereagh may have been wary of the Congress System, but Canning was to prove instrumental in its destruction. By the time of Canning, the threat of French imperialism, which had lain as a shadow on Castlereagh's policy, had been removed, and he **saw no need for international government** except to deal with specific matters such as a treaty or peace settlement. He was suspicious of the collusion of powers, particularly when most of them were autocratic, and undoubtedly felt that the **wishes of the smaller powers were overriden** by the system. His policy is clearly illustrated by his statement 'every nation for itself and God for us all'. Although tempered by British interests, his policy towards **South America**, firstly through the **Polignac Memorandum** (which guaranteed French non-involvement and British protection), and then his support for the **Monroe Doctrine** (which opposed colonialism in South America), are yet further indications of Canning's desire for natural development and his opposition to international collusion.

When the Verona Congress actually met, however, the **Greek question had been largely solved**, following the extraction of a promise from the Turkish government that it would institute reforms, and the unwillingness of Alexander I to act in isolation. **Spain**, however, remained a problem, and since July France had been talking of possible intervention. Canning instructed Wellington, the British representative at the Congress, to state that **Britain would not intervene**. This statement **signalled the end of the Congress System**. France intervened in April 1823 on the pretext of danger to France, but no further united action took place. Proposed Congresses in 1823 and 1824 failed to materialize, due largely to Canning's refusal to attend, and when in 1825 the other four powers actually met in St Petersburg, the result was inconsequential deadlock and the end of the Congress System.

The Metternich system

The master strategist of European diplomacy was undoubtedly Metternich. He championed the cause of **conservatism**, combining a controlling influence over the divergent parts of the Austrian Empire with a concerted antagonism to liberalism and nationalism throughout Europe. As far as foreign affairs were concerned, the achievement of a durable balance of power and of the various safety factors (e.g. the Quadruple and Holy Alliances) had both secured and enhanced Austria's position in the European power area. Domestic policy equally required balance and careful manipulation, and it was here that Metternich devised his famous system.

The Austrian Empire was composed of numerous nationalities loosely administered and defying unity, so Metternich's system worked on the principle of **'divide and rule'**. The new **German Confederation** not only provided a barrier to Prussian extension but, as Metternich realized, was also **open to Austrian influence**. Consequently, when Metternich proposed the **Carlsbad decrees**, which laid down regulations for controlling the press and universities, the German confederation not only passed them but convinced the Prussian King, Frederick William III, of the inadvisability of granting even a limited constitution. Metternich's case was strengthened by the murder of the right-wing journalist **Kotzebue** by a left-wing student, which he was able to present as evidence of fermenting trouble.

In **Italy** too, the policy of divide and rule was implemented by means of the various **Hapsburg princes** and Metternich's **exhaustive diplomatic network**. Italian administrators found their careers frustrated, **foreign troops** such as the Hungarians in Lombardy thwarted popular sentiment, and **careful alliances** made any unified opposition almost impossible. However, Italy had enjoyed an enlightened period under Napoleon's rule and was to prove more intransigent than Germany, resisting the formation of an Italian confederation and being far more wary of Metternich's manipulation.

Just as the failure to reckon with growing nationalism brought about the decline of the Congress System, so, too, it was one of the chief shortcomings in Metternich's policy of repressing liberalism. Nevertheless, given the disparity within the Austrian Empire, Metternich's achievement in the sheer act of holding it together for such a long time, is extremely impressive. However, his inflexibility and **inability to adjust to the changing political demands** were eventually to bring about his own downfall and the decline of the Empire he cherished.

Summary

The attempts at international government in the period following the Napoleonic wars are admirable in many respects. Through considerable negotiation, a generally acceptable policy was agreed upon and the map of Europe was redrawn in a peaceful and orderly manner. Admittedly, the smaller powers of Europe and the interests of nationalism and liberalism were sometimes overridden, but a lasting peace was largely achieved, and little more could realistically have been expected given the nature of the major powers involved, the inherent incongruities within their union, and the development of a Congress System geared towards maintaining the status quo. The fact is that peace was achieved and maintained, and the machinery for consultation between the powers had been shown to be both available and successful, given the desire to make it work.

Chapter 2
Restoration and Revolution 1815–48

Introduction

At Vienna and the subsequent Congresses the political map of Europe had been restored, tailored and manipulated with the central aim being to re-establish order. However, order was to a large extent reliant upon the **maintenance of stability**, and unfortunately for the great powers, the beginning of the nineteenth century was to see the growth of **divergent political thought** through the pressures of **liberalism** and **nationalism** that sought change and, when they were repressed, revolution.

Nationalism and liberalism

Although the Congresses had achieved a great deal, the settlement created by them faced the greatest threat not, as they had feared, from the individualistic policies of the signatories, but from the **growth of popular movements**. The success of the **American Revolution** and the disruption and upheaval caused by the **French Revolution** had shown the power that such movements could command. Now, in the middle years of the nineteenth century, these powers were once again to rise to the surface, to challenge the status quo.

The driving forces behind the growth of these popular movements were the twin ideals of nationalism and liberalism. **Nationalism** had been a potent influence in Europe since the Middle Ages, but it did not become a genuinely popular force until the French Revolution. The basic motivation for nationalism was that of a **desire for independence and unity, through a common sense of cultural community** – common institutions, traditions, language, customs and so on. It could be achieved through either **evolutionary or revolutionary developments**, or a combination of the two. In the French Revolution the sense of national unity was combined with the political ideals of liberty, equality and fraternity, but then Napoleon was subsequently able to command similar, if not stronger sentiments while exercising dictatorial control. Nationalism could spring up through **subjugation and resistance** or through a **realization of common culture**. Such motivations would manifest themselves most clearly in **Italy** and **Germany**, being fuelled by the observations of philosophers such as Herder, who, in trying to make the Germanic peoples aware of their cultural heritage, developed the idea of each nation possessing a ***Volksgeist***, a spirit or soul which expresses its individuality. The challenge and threat of becoming part of Napoleon's Empire appeared, in retrospect, to have done much to crystallize the ***Volksgeist*** in Germany and to allow similar nationalistic ideals to flower in Italy, once Austrian control had been removed.

The other important political ideal was that of **liberalism,** which, like nationalism, also had its immediate roots in the French and American Revolutions. Its concern was with the question of human rights and liberties but, like nationalism, its features were dependent on the **nature of the state** in which it flourished. Generally, liberals desired a **firm statement of the basic rights of individuals, to limit the extent of executive power**, to obtain **representative government**, and to have the security of an **independent judiciary**. Within this, however, were moderate liberals who sought only a **limited parliamentary democracy** where power would devolve from the aristocracy to the middle classes, while democratic liberals wanted nothing less than **universal manhood suffrage**. Not surprisingly, the existing ruling system had a heavy bearing on where these types of liberals were to be found. Thus the more extreme liberals were found in the more advanced western European countries, along with more advanced sub-division of liberal thought. For example, in Britain, economic liberalism developed with leading figures such as Adam Smith arguing the case for freedom from government restrictions and regulations in trade and industry.

The ideals of nationalism and liberalism thus posed a not inconsiderable threat to the carefully-balanced map of Europe, and more so because in this early period they were ideals that invariably went hand-in-hand. Liberals were usually nationalists and nationalists usually liberals. The more absolutist powers of Europe were now to be shown the dangers of ignoring these ideals and of presenting themselves as immovable barriers to the forces of change.

France from Restoration to revolution

The re-establishment of the Bourbon monarchy in France had not been implemented without misgivings both on the part of the French people and the victorious powers, but each had little alternative and at least the **Royal Charter of 1814** had created what, on the surface at least, was one of the **most advanced continental constitutions**. Under its provisions the King had sole executive power but shared the legislative role with a chamber of peers and a chamber of elected deputies. Those eligible for candidature were males over forty worth a thousand francs in direct taxes. The voting qualification extended to males over thirty worth three hundred francs in direct taxes.

The Charter was, however, a **compromise** and as such would rely upon the goodwill of the interested parties. This, though, was unlikely, for both right and left found the compromise unsatisfactory. For the right, the **returning émigrés** and rural nobility were dismayed at Louis XVIII's willingness to accept the charter and even more so at his use of former Napoleonic ministers such as Talleyrand and Fouché. Together with **the Church** they sought to wreck the charter and to **increase their power at the expense of the King and constitution**. They became known as the **Ultras**, and influential amongst them was the King's own brother, the Comte d'Artois, together with Polignac, Montmorency, Chateaubriand and Villèle.

Equally, the left or **independents** had little love for a system that restored a Bourbon monarchy of which it had struggled so hard to rid itself. The activities of the ultras should have been enough to unite them, but they were **unable to agree** amongst themselves over exactly what course of action to follow and exactly what should replace the constitutional monarchy. Only a centre group known as the **constitutional royalists** accepted the charter. They were moderates who saw, in the provisions it laid down, the hope for concord between monarchists and constitutional democrats, but they were too few in number and lacked the necessary influence to prevent the eventual collapse of the Restoration.

The period following Napoleon's Hundred days revealed the potential threat of the ultras as they took advantage of Napoleon's failure. In a move known as the **White Terror**, Napoleonic generals and officials were executed, imprisoned or dismissed, with the popular hero Marshal Ney figuring amongst the victims. In the first elections that followed the actions taken against these officials, the **ultras dominated the first chamber of deputies**, but Louis XVIII, showing some political insight, appointed a **cabinet of moderates** under the Duc de Richelieu. This insight was rewarded when the 1816 elections produced a **majority for the constitutional royalists**, and in this period of co-operation France returned to stability both internally and in terms of international recognition. The following few years, though, saw this trend continue with the political character of the chamber swinging to the **left**. This created considerable alarm which reached its height in 1820 with the **assassination of the Duc de Berry**, son of the Comte d'Artois.

Richelieu tried to bring the extreme factions in the chamber together, but in late 1822 he was forced to resign and the period of **Ultra rule** began, highlighted by France's incursion into Spanish affairs in 1823 to restore the Bourbon King of Spain.

In 1824 Louis XVIII died and was succeeded by the Comte d'Artois who took the throne as **Charles X**. Not surprisingly, ultra rule continued, and in the period that followed concerted attempts were made to **restore royal, noble and clerical power** behind a facade of pomp and ceremony. Through these actions and the ineptitude of at best mildly capable ministers and officials, Charles antagonized the people and by 1827 the **unpopularity of the government** was clearly revealed through the gains made by the independents. He dismissed Villèle who had been an adequate, if unexciting Prime Minster, and after a period of using the moderate Martignac, threw sense and caution to the wind and appointed **Polignac**. Polignac's unsuitability, was highlighted by his religious fanaticism; he was also totally unpopular and out of touch with public opinion. His advice to Charles was to **suppress the forces of criticism**, which led to the publication of the **Four Ordinances** aimed at ending opposition. By the Ordinances, newspapers were limited, the new chamber was dissolved before it met, the number of deputies was cut, and the electorate was reduced by 75 per cent.

The King, oblivious to the popular dissent against these policies, was totally unprepared for the **revolt** which they created, but others, notably **Talleyrand** and **Thiers**, moved quickly to take advantage of the situation. With the best units of the army engaged in Algiers, the King's forces were quickly overcome and the **Duc d' Orléans, Louis Philippe**, was persuaded to take the throne in what is often referred to as the **July Monarchy**. The tricolour was accepted as the flag of France and, with the situation well beyond recovery, Charles and his son fled to exile in England.

Louis Philippe's accession was a return to the road of compromise, but it was a **compromise** that was **acceptable to both the French people and the other powers of Europe**. The new King seemed well qualified for the task of satisfying the different factions, being both Bourbon and a former revolutionary, and this was fortunate, for a delicate line would have to be followed to ensure peace and order. Almost immediately, voting qualifications were lowered to **double the size of the electorate** and, as further proof of his allegiance to the interests of his people, Louis could be seen regularly parading himself around the streets of Paris. The **glory of France was highlighted to promote French unity** and this even went to the extent of bringing Napoleon's ashes back from St Helena to rest in an enormously impressive tomb at Les Invalides. However, behind the screen of unity and compromise there was still **disquiet**. The King was suspected, not without good reason, of wishing to **increase his power** at **the expense of the constitution**, and his Parliament was seen as a **corrupt** body whose aim was to increase the fortunes of the businessmen. Thus the stability of Louis Philippe would depend, to a large extent, on his ability if not totally to satisfy his critics, then at least not to antagonize them.

1830: the seeds of discontent

The overthrow of Charles X in France sent waves across Europe. One of its early effects was to ignite the **growing hostility between the Belgians and the Dutch**, whose union had been created at the Congress of Vienna as a barrier to French expansion and who were divided by religion, language and the question of representation at the higher levels of government. The revolt started with rioting in Brussels on 25 August. The Belgians initially sought administrative separation, but the actions of William I (trying and failing to take Brussels by force) led to the formation of a provisional government which, on 5 October, proclaimed **Belgian independence**.

William I appealed to the powers to intervene, with the astute observation that the action **threatened the Vienna settlement**. **Louis Philippe**, new monarch of the nearest of these powers, was in the difficult position of **wishing to remain popular at home** yet **not wanting to upset the other powers** (who viewed French interest with suspicion) while at the same time desiring a **return to stability**. In the event the situation was resolved by the new British Foreign Secretary, **Lord Palmerston**, who was **determined to stop any possibility of French expansion** yet was **sympathetic to the cause of Belgian nationalism**. The Belgian National Congress actually favoured a French prince as King (the candidature of Louis Philippe's son, the Duc de Nemours, was suggested) but, pressured by Palmerston and the other powers, they eventually relented and accepted **Leopold of Saxe-Coburg**.

Leopold proved to be an excellent choice. He was an avowed **liberal**, he managed to **popularize his accession** and produced a settlement known as the **'Eighteen Articles'** which proved acceptable both to the great powers and the Belgian Congress, though not to William I. Consequently, **Dutch troops once again invaded Belgium**, and

Louis Philippe grasped the opportunity and replied by driving them out with French troops which occupied Brussels. The fears of French influence in the proposed independent state were once again aroused, but Louis Philippe was aware of his vulnerability and withdrew his forces rapidly. Later in 1831 – 32 they did return, but only to combine with British forces and finally expel the Dutch from Belgium.

The settlement was now almost complete, but it would take until 1839 for the independence of Belgium to be totally guaranteed, the final act being the **Treaty of London**. This was to become famous in 1914 as the scrap of paper that would bring Britain into World War I, but at the time the Treaty and Settlement were more notable for highlighting the **dangerous position of Louis Philippe** in international relations, and the **success of Palmerston** in establishing an independent constitutional monarchy.

While the overthrow of Charles X and the cause of Belgian independence had succeeded, **the cause of national self-determination suffered setbacks in Poland, Italy and Germany**. Here, under the control and influence of more autocratic powers, liberal activity was deemed extremely unhealthy. In **Poland** the revolt in 1830 was significant in that it prevented the Tsar from taking any direct action in the Belgian problem, but given Poland's sensitive territorial position and the limited nature of the revolt, its failure was far from surprising. The revolt was initiated by junior army officers who took control of the Warsaw garrison and forced the few Russian troops to leave Poland. However, this military coup **did not make the transition into popular revolt, nor did it elicit the help of the powerful aristocracy**. Thus, while it troubled the Russians militarily it had little chance of permanent success. Polish forces were able to hold off the Russians at first, while a moderate government was formed under Czartoryski, but military defeat at **Ostroleka** was soon followed by the collapse of the rebel government. Consequently the rule of Russia returned, and the Poles, who had appealed forlornly for assistance in their fight for independence, suffered another national humiliation.

In **Italy**, too, the chances of success against the might of the Austrian Empire required careful consideration; the overall objective being that of **timing any move to coincide with trouble for Austria in another area**. A young lawyer from Modena, Enrico Misley, had devised such a plan for the creation of a **kingdom of Central Italy under Duke Francis of Modena**. The plan was originally meant to be implemented while Austria was preoccupied with Greece, but the accession of Louis Philippe raised hopes with the suggestion of possible French assistance being given by the French Foreign Minister, Sebastian. Founded on hope rather than anything concrete, a series of revolts broke out, but the plan was **betrayed** by both Duke Francis and Louis Philippe, who gave Metternich a free hand to deal with the problem. Metternich was subsequently able to send troops to crush the revolts and restore the legitimate rulers. Thus Italian nationalism received another setback.

Similarly in **Germany** the actions of the Poles and initially the French inspired **local revolts**, forcing out the ruler of Brunswick and imposing liberal constitutions in Hanover, Saxony and Hesse-Cassel. As elsewhere, however, even fairly moderate gains produced a hostile reaction, and in 1832 Austria, working together with Prussia, forced the Diet at Frankfurt to pass **acts re-establishing repressive measures throughout German states**. These measures were extended even further in 1834, and with these, even the pessimistic Metternich felt that the threat of immediate revolution had passed. In a sense, of course, he was correct, but the spectre had only been delayed; it had not been dealt with.

The revolutions of 1848

The events of 1830 had revealed the existence of revolutionary under-currents in Europe, but in 1848 the worst fears of the extent to which these could reach were acknowledged by almost all European governments and earned 1848 the title 'the year of revolution'. Exactly why these dramatic events took place in 1848 is a source of considerable debate and, obviously, what was true for one country was not necessarily valid for the next. What happened in 1848 was that a **number of different factors combined to create conditions that were conducive to change**. The authorities were caught unawares, but equally so were the leading revolutionaries who, in numerous instances, were far from the centres when the revolts broke out. In retrospect, 1848 proved to be one of the high-water marks of the union between liberalism and nationalism, though there is no evidence of the belief in a European-wide conspiracy, held at the time. The fact that the *Communist Manifesto* was published in January 1848 is due to coincidence rather than conspiracy. The period was also one peppered with **agricultural and economic crises**, and this affected almost all of Europe, creating in the masses a **greater susceptibility to ideas of social and political change**. Thus, when in January 1848 the King of Sicily,

Ferdinand II, was **forced to grant a constitution**, it set off a whole wave of revolutionary fervour that had a domino effect spreading across the whole of mainland Europe. The targets of these revolts were either **oppression by the ruling establishment**, as in Naples, or **oppression by a foreign power**, and their general aims were greater democracy and independence.

The revolutionary impetus had begun in **Italy** with the success in **Sicily** and was followed by the granting of constitutions in **Piedmont**, **Tuscany** and **Rome** where nationalist groups such as Mazzini's 'Young Italy' agitated for change. The real international urge to revolution, however, was provided by the **fall** first of **Louis Philippe** and then of **Metternich**. In **France**, while there was growing discontent, the fall of the monarchy was due almost overwhelmingly to its own **incompetence**. A period of dull government had made the people look back to the glories of the revolutionary period and, since they were forbidden to hold public meetings, it became the practice to hold political banquets. The practice was relatively harmless, but when Guizot decided to ban a Paris banquet, the mob rose to protest. Louis Philippe responded by dismissing Guizot and appointing a moderate chamber. The mob, however, did not subside and the opposition, now able to express itself, spilled on to the streets. In the rioting that followed, fifty-two rioters were shot and the National Guard began to defect. Louis Philippe, apparently tired of the strain of holding power, abdicated.

France now had to choose between a regency and a republic but, with the mob still active, monarchical rule was rejected and a **provisional government** was formed with notable **republicans** such as Lamartine, Blanc, and Ledru-Rollin which was to make way for the **republic**. However, it was one thing to topple Louis Philippe but another to form a credible government able both to rule France and have wholesale popular support. The provisional government was quite obviously an uneasy alliance and, although political and social measures were hastily passed, the people were suspicious. The **'national workshops'**, one of the major socialist measures set up to deal with unemployment, provided in effect, **little more than poor relief** and, while **universal suffrage** was a considerable achievement, it **did not create a politically-aware electorate**. Subsequently, after the **April elections** the radicals found themselves decisively beaten at the polls. Of the 900 seats, the moderates took 500, the monarchists 300 and the radicals a mere 80. The radicals refused to accept this and raised the mob to try to overthrow the government, but this time the National Guard supported the government and the attempt failed, with key figures, such as Blanqui and Barbés, being imprisoned. Even worse for the left, with financial ruin facing France, the government closed the 'national workshops' in late June. The response was rapid, as the Paris mob put up barricades to force the government either to relent or collapse. Neither occurred, though, and after four days of fighting (in which over 1500 died and 12 000 were imprisoned) order was restored. The republic had survived, but in its mildest form and with a **legacy of class division** from the **June days** that would return to challenge it when the time was right.

In **Germany**, where **economic distress** had already led to food riots the previous year, the revolution in Paris gave the opposition the courage to act. Demonstrations occurred both in the towns and rural areas, and in smaller states liberal ministers began to be included in the government. In the Austrian Empire similar unrest was occurring. **Frederick William IV** sensing the danger, albeit rather late, summoned the United Diet on 14 March. He offered **internal reforms, new liberal ministers and a reorganization of the German Confederation**. Through the pressure of the mob, however, he was **forced to go even further**, adopting the **new German flag** of black, red and gold, allowing **universal suffrage** and promising to **merge Prussia into a united Germany**.

A liberal government under Ludolf Camphausen was formed but, as in France, the **diversity and radical nature** of some liberals meant that **continued unity against oppressive regimes was difficult to maintain**. The mob, while a useful instrument for bringing about change, was not always so easy to disarm and satisfy and represented to some liberals a worse danger than oppression. The **Prussian National Assembly** that had been elected by universal male suffrage proved **too radical even for the moderate liberals** and, as the recession gave way to economic recovery, Frederick William IV took the initiative. In November he appointed a Conservative cabinet. Then, as the rebels' unity degenerated into disagreement, he dissolved the National Assembly and decreed his own constitution for Prussia.

In the rest of Germany a similar unifying body, the *Vorparliament*, had been created which met at Frankfurt with 500 representatives from the parliamentary assemblies of the separate German states. Here, as in Prussia, **moderates and radicals clashed**. However, even when the radicals, under the leadership of Struve and Hecker, withdrew in protest, the body **achieved little of note**, quite simply because it was in a political void. What the exercise did provide, however, was concrete evidence of a desire for German unity and also of the importance that Prussia would play in orchestrating such a move, should it ever come about.

Of all the great powers **Austria** was the **most susceptible to unrest**, since it was stretched to maintain order even in times of relative peace. The troubles in France and Prussia therefore spelt trouble in an Empire of such diverse nationalistic and liberal groups. In **Hungary**, Louis Kossuth seized the initiative to demand the **abolition of serfdom** and the **granting of a constitution**. These demands were echoed a few days later in **Bohemia**. In Vienna itself the liberal opposition took to the streets and, as order appeared to be disintegrating, Emperor Ferdinand took the popular step of sacrificing **Metternich**, who was forced to resign. Metternich's fall, like that of Louis Philippe, had the effect of **accelerating the revolutionary fervour** and convincing the subject races of the Empire that they really could achieve national unity.

The **problem of maintaining liberal cohesion** against the old repressive regime in the Austrian Empire was, however, as much a problem as elsewhere. It was further complicated by the fact that, while **Hungarians** and **Czechs** sought independence from Austria, so did **Serbs**, **Croats** and **Slovaks** in Hungary and Bohemia. As the revolts appeared to reach the point of anarchy, the tide began to turn, with the defeat of Czech revolutionaries in Prague by Windischgrätz and the success of Radetsky in defeating the Piedmontese troops in Milan marking the start of the reversal. Also, rather fortuitously, Kossuth, blinkered by his desire for independence, forced the Croat leader Jellačić to seek aid from the Emperor. This led to Austria declaring war on Hungary in October. Meanwhile in Vienna, radicals had sensed the change of mood and had taken charge of the city which the Emperor had left in May for the relative safety of Innsbruck. In their fervour the radicals murdered the Minister of War. However, the end was drawing near and two armies, under Windischgrätz and Jellačić, converged on the city, forcing its surrender.

For **Austria** the revolt was over. Prince Felix Schwarzenberg was appointed Chief Minister and, ignoring the revolutionary Ministry and the Austrian Reichstag which had been set up under the constitution forced by the rebels, he restored government and order. To further aid the renovation of the powers of the Empire, the aging Ferdinand abdicated and was replaced by his nephew, Franz Josef. What remained now was for the Austrian will to be reimposed throughout the Empire. In Italy, Radetsky had already begun to suppress the Italian revolutionaries with the defeat of Charles Albert at Custozza and, when he repeated this feat in March 1849, the Italian revolt was all but finished. Charles Albert abdicated in favour of his son Victor Emmanuel II. With the fall of Venice and Tuscany, Austrian rule returned.

Hungary, under the nationalistic leadership of Kossuth and the brilliant military defence of Görgey, caused the Austrians a considerably larger problem. With their forces committed in Italy and the Hungarians more solidly behind the cause than any other revolt, the **Austrians were forced to seek external aid** and found it in **Russia**. The Tsar, for various reasons (among them the threat of possible Polish revolt), provided Austria with a Russian army of 140 000 troops under the command of Paskievicz. Not surprisingly, with these extra troops, the Hungarians were finally defeated. However, the defence of Hungary had been spectacular, especially in consideration of the resources available to the Austrians. Now in defeat, Hungary was to suffer firstly the **brutality of Austrian reconstruction** and then the return to **reactionary administration**.

The revolutions of 1848, in terms of their main objectives, **failed**. Of the absolutist powers that the revolutionaries wished to overthrow only Louis Philippe and Ludwig I of Bavaria had been forced to abdicate. As to constitutional change, the area of Europe that enjoyed the greatest degree of democracy was north-west Europe, Britain, Belgium and the Netherlands, which had not experienced revolutionary risings. The Hapsburgs and the Hohenzollerns remained, and the cause of national unity had not been successful in a single instance.

The revolutions had brought about change, however, and post-1848 Europe lay in the shadow of the experience of 'the year of revolutions'. In concrete terms, the major result of the revolutionary wave was the **abolition of serfdom** and the **relaxation of restrictions on the personal freedom of peasant and worker**, but every state that experienced a rising was marked in some way. In **France**, **universal suffrage** and the principle of **popular sovereignty** were firmly established. In **Austria**, the cautious policy of Metternich gave way **to more open involvement in international affairs**. In **Italy**, the **seeds of nationalism** lay waiting for the right opportunity. In **Russia**, the

momentum for reform and modernization began and in **Prussia and Germany** the realization dawned that something **more than liberal government would be required to unite the Germanic people**.

Summary

The revolutions of 1848 severely disturbed the fabric of European political and social life to such an extent that European monarchs and governments would **never again be able to rule with purely absolutist powers**. Subsequently, they would attempt to combine those aspects of constitutional democracy that they believed they could control, though as the unification movements of the nineteenth century would indicate, they would not always succeed. However, perhaps the greatest effect of the revolutions' failure was to reveal the **potential destructiveness of nationalism** and to highlight the fact that **liberalism was not necessarily the path to national unity**.

Chapter 3
The Eastern Question

Introduction

A constant source of concern and diplomatic activity during the nineteenth century was the fate of the once-powerful Ottoman Empire. Originally a problem because of its expansionist policies, it now posed a threat, in its decay, to the peace of Europe.

Background to the problem

The **Ottoman Empire** in the sixteenth and seventeenth centuries had threatened Europe because of its **strength, commitment and organization**. By the nineteenth century, however, Turkey, far from being feared as an aggressor, was commonly referred to as the '**sick man of Europe**'. The Sultan could no longer adequately control his territories or, more importantly, his subject peoples. **Nationalism**, a potent force throughout Europe, was dangerous within an empire that, while officially Mohammedan, contained a large **Christian** minority. The Sultan, like other absolutist rulers, was **not prepared to introduce reform**, which he saw as a sign of weakness, and instead he tried to **maintain his rule through repression and acts of great brutality** which, it was hoped, would crush any opposition to his rule.

This action, though, far from achieving order, further convinced the subject races of the **need for independence**, which led to the **Serbian rising** in 1804. The major internal threat, however, would come from the **Greeks**, who combined both **nationalism and Christianity** with their ancient heritage. And, of course, success by one nationality would act as a spur to the others, amongst whom the Romanians and Bulgars were the most populous.

A crumbling Turkish Empire racked by internal revolt was enough of a problem in itself but, worse, the size and position of the Empire **involved almost all the great powers**. Austria and Russia had a direct concern, as they both bordered the Empire and shared a similar sprinkling of subject races, and Britain and France, through colonial and maritime concerns, also had declared interests. The main concern, however, was with **Russian expansion**, a concern which generally united at least two, if not all, the other interested powers. Of particular interest was the **fate of Constantinople** and the surrounding **Balkan territories**, for it was considered, not without good reason, that **if Russia made substantial**

gains it would **upset the balance of power**, endangering not only **central Europe**, but **France's influence in the Mediterranean** and even **British influence in India**.

The Greek Question

Though Serbia, following the 1804 revolt, was struggling to maintain independence, it was the Greeks who were to cause the greatest challenge to the Turks and who, in doing so, were to present the greatest problems for the major powers. The **Greeks** comprised not only a **distinct national group** but also had the further strength of **religious difference**. Awareness of their **individuality** led to **nationalistic desires**, and both were reinforced by a growing movement for Greeks to appreciate their **ancient heritage and culture**. This culminated in 1814 with the foundation of the **Philiké Hetairia** to press for the liberation of Greece.

In **1821**, following pressure from the Philiké Hetairia, the **Greeks rebelled**. The Turks, with scant regard for caution, retaliated by executing the Patriarch of Constantinople, and a bitter struggle ensued. The Russians, given a free hand, would undoubtedly have liked to have gone to the aid of their fellow Christians, but **due to pressure from the other powers** – particularly Britain – Russia **remained an observer**. However, in 1824 the situation was radically changed when the **Sultan requested aid from Pasha Mehemet Ali**. The Egyptian leader sent an army under the command of his son Ibrahim, and it seemed as if the Greek revolt would be finally crushed by this efficient force.

The **Russians**, under the new Tsar, Nicholas I, decided that **intervention was necessary to save the Greeks**. The **British**, fearful of what this might lead to, decided to **act with Russia** in an attempt to force Turkey to accept Greek autonomy. To this the two powers agreed, signing in April 1826, the **St Petersburg Protocol**. The force to be used was implied rather than proposed but, with little Turkish response, a more aggressive stance was taken in the **Treaty of London** in July 1827. By this treaty Britain and Russia, now joined by **France**, agreed that if Turkey refused an armistice they would threaten to support the Greeks. The threat, however, went unheeded and in October the **Battle of Navarino** occurred, at which the joint British, French and Russian squadrons destroyed the Turkish and Egyptian fleets.

It seemed as though Britain had averted the threat of unilateral action by the Russians, but in April 1828, with the Turks still refusing to accept the situation, **Russia declared war on Turkey**. The revolt now appeared to be on the point of becoming a major crisis in which only Metternich could find satisfaction, but fortunately sanity prevailed. The Russians who, not surprisingly, **defeated the disorganized Turkish forces**, did not use the opportunity to press for territorial gain in Europe, and the **Treaty of Adrianople**, signed in September 1829, provided the basis of a final settlement. Under this, **Turkey accepted the Treaty of London** by which **Greek autonomy** was recognized and **Russia gave back to the Turks their conquests in Europe**. The threat of the now independent Greece becoming a Russian satellite concerned Britain, but while Greece remained weak, the overall aim of its policy was the **maintenance of independence**. The Greeks had rid themselves of Turkish overlords: they did not want to replace them with Russians.

Continuing crisis 1831–41

One of the more lasting aspects of the struggle for Greek independence was the **change in Russian policy towards Turkey**. The traditional policy of expansion towards Constantinople was reassessed following the Russo-Turkish war and found to be detrimental to Russian interests in the area. A committee appointed by the Tsar came to the conclusion that, contrary to previously held beliefs, it was **in Russia's interests to preserve the integrity of the Turkish Empire.** The reasoning behind this was that Russia had treaty rights and influence with Turkey and that, **if independent Balkan States were formed, a unity of policy and influence would be difficult – if not impossible – to maintain**.

The strength of this new policy was clearly revealed in **1833** when **Turkey requested Russian assistance**. This request came as a result of aggressive action taken by **Mehemet Ali** who had not been paid or compensated for his assistance to the Sultan in attempting to suppress the Greek revolt. As a result of this failure to get satisfaction from the Sultan, Mehemet Ali sent his son, Ibrahim, to invade Syria, which rapidly fell. Worse for the Sultan, the main Turkish army was utterly defeated at **Konieh** and the whole of Asia Minor appeared to be under threat. The Sultan appealed first to Britain but, when he was refused by Palmerston, he turned to Russia. A naval squadron positioned itself off Constantinople and six thousand Russian troops took up positions on the eastern shores of the Bosphorus, with the result that the threat all but disappeared. The move, however, caused great **consternation in the rest of Europe**, and pressure was rapidly put on the Sultan, which resulted in Syria being ceded to Mehemet Ali. The Russo-

Turkish collusion, however, did not just melt away for, before Russian troops withdrew, the two powers signed the secret **Treaty of Unkiar Skelessi**. By the provisions of this Treaty, which gradually became clear, Russia and Turkey were to **provide each other with mutual assistance in the event of being attacked**. In Turkey's case, this was to consist of the closing of the Dardanelles to foreign warships.

The Treaty of Unkiar Skelessi created much **suspicion** amongst the other powers. In particular, Britain and France viewed the Treaty as putting Russia in a position to dictate policy to Turkey. For the **French, the fall of the Turkish Empire might provide territorial gain** and was possibly an attractive option if Russian expansion could be prevented, but for the **British the threat of Russian expansion was to lead to a concerted policy of maintaining the Turkish Empire as a barrier**. The **Austrians**, until now interested observers, were also brought into action, feeling that **the new Russian commitment to maintain the status quo in the Balkans was identical to their aim**. Consequently, in September 1833 the **Münchengrätz Agreement** was signed, by which Russia and Austria agreed to **maintain the Ottoman Empire** and to **consult with each other** over what action was to be taken if partition ever became inevitable.

In April 1839 all these carefully-laid positions were sent toppling when the **Sultan decided to take direct action against Mehemet Ali**. The precise motive behind this decision remains unclear, but the military step taken was to **attack Ibrahim's forces in Syria**. As before, the Turkish forces proved no match for the Egyptian army which crushed them at **Nezib**, and to complete the disaster for Turkey, on 1 July, the Sultan died, leaving the throne to a sixteen-year-old boy who became Mahmud II. In response the entire Turkish fleet sailed into Alexandria and surrendered.

It would be difficult to imagine a worse situation, but perhaps it was the gravity of this state of affairs that forced decisive action. **Palmerston**, now **committed to maintaining the Turkish Empire, sought to unite the powers in action to achieve this end**. **France**, however, had **territorial ambitions** in the area and was not interested in defeating Mehemet Ali. Palmerston tried to coerce the French but failed, so he revived what was in effect the Quadruple Alliance of 1815, which now set out to deal with the Egyptians. The French, angered by Palmerston's actions, made warlike noises, but Palmerston had calculated correctly that they would not risk action by themselves. In the Mediterranean, **British forces landed in**

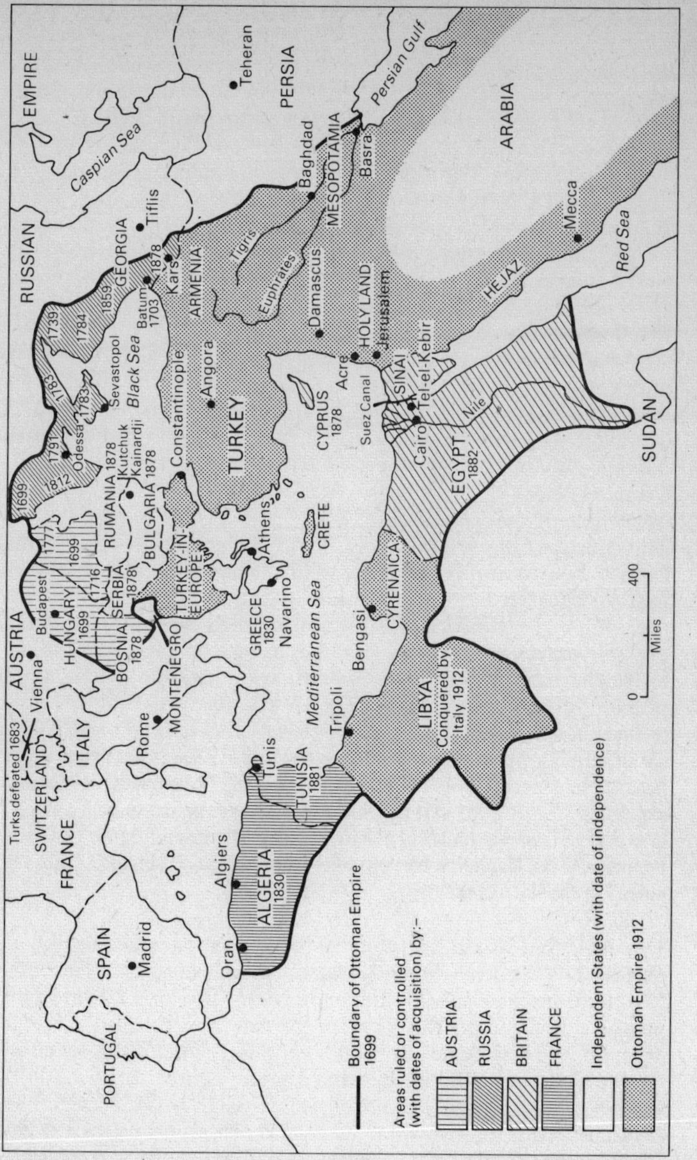

Figure 1. The Eastern Question. The map shows the decline of the Ottoman Empire from the late 17th century to the early 20th century. It is important to understand the aims of Turkey's rivals and the various reasons for the attempts to ensure the survival of the Empire.

Syria; Beirut and Acre were taken and **Mehemet Ali was forced to accept the provisions of the Treaty of London** (July 1840) by which Syria, Crete and Arabia were restored to Turkey along with her fleet, and Mehemet Ali was confined to the hereditary Pashalik of Egypt. To complete the territorial settlement and calm the international disruption, a convention was held in July 1841, the **Straits Convention**, in which the great powers (once more including France) agreed that **the Straits (the Bosphorus and Dardanelles) were to be closed to all foreign warships in time of peace**.

The Crimean War: causes

Although revolts had broken out, and the major powers had been under threat, the concert of Europe was still intact and operational in 1850. The Eastern Question still remained unsolved, however, and in 1854 it was to erupt and severely damage, if not destroy, the Concert with the outbreak of the Crimean War.

The causes of the war were bound up in the **unstable nature of the Balkans**, but ostensibly the single major factor was the question of **Russian influence** in the area. For the Russians, the Balkans represented both an opportunity and a threat – an opportunity for possible **expansion** and a threat in that **nationalism could slowly spread to Russian territory**. For the **Austrians,** who had for a long time prevented Turkish expansion, Turkey's demise presented the new **problem of who would fill this power vacuum**. There was no obvious satisfactory option, though **least attractive of all was the extension of Russian ambitions**. The **British** were equally **suspicious of Russian expansion**, fearing an **upset to the balance of power and to their colonial interests**, a fear which was mirrored by the **French** who had obvious **interests, in the Mediterranean** but also in **championing Christian access to places in the Holy Land**.

The crisis that would lead to the war arose about the question of **religion**. The French, who had a **tradition as protector of Christians in the East**, had, under Louis Philippe and then Napoleon III, brought pressure to bear on the Turkish government to allow greater access to the **Holy Places** – Jerusalem and Bethlehem. Subsequently, the Roman Catholics had been given control of these holy shrines, ignoring the claims of the Russian-backed Orthodox Church. The Tsar, who had **considered himself the defender of the Christians under Turkish rule**, saw this, not unnaturally, as a **challenge to his influence**. Fearful of what such a concession might further lead to, he sent Prince Menschikov to demand **custody of the keys to**

the Holy Places and recognition of Russia's claim to represent and protect the Christians in the Balkans.

The Tsar acted as he did because he thought that Britain would accept that Russia was only reasserting its rights as indicated in the **Treaty of Kutchuk Kainardji** (1744) and that the French equally would accept that their attempt to gain influence in the area had failed. He believed that Austria would provide positive support as repayment for Russian assistance in Hungary in 1848 and because Turkey had recently been threatening an invasion of Montenegro. These calculations, however, were seriously wrong. The **British Ambassador**, Stratford-de-Redcliffe, **encouraged the Turks to resist Russian demands**, viewing them as a prelude to Turkey coming under Russian domination. The French, also alarmed, **sent the French fleet**, and in June this joined forces with the **British Malta fleet** off the Dardanelles in Besika Bay. The **Austrians** made it clear they **could not countenance Russian actions** and turned to Britain and France to seek a peaceful solution.

The Russians, while becoming aware of their isolation, had not helped the situation when, in June 1853, the **Russian army had all but declared war on the Ottoman Empire** by crossing the Pruth and occupying Moldavia and Wallachia. In a last-ditch attempt to avoid war, the powers called a conference at Vienna and drew up a compromise solution known as the **Vienna Note** which recommended that the **Sultan** should remain faithful to the spirit of the Treaties of Kutchuk Kainardji and Adrianople and **consult both Russia and France before instituting any changes**. The compromise was **acceptable to Russia**, but the **Turks**, revelling in the power the situation had given them, **rejected it**, asserting the Sultan's right to rule as he thought fit. A period of frenetic diplomatic activity followed, but on 4 October Turkey went further by **declaring war on Russia**. Russia, unable to avoid conflict, returned the compliment by declaring war on Turkey on 1 November.

The Crimean War: escalation and events

Upon the declaration of war, the **combined British and French fleets had entered the Bosphorus**, although not without considerable deliberation. It was still hoped that a diplomatic solution could be found, but Turkey once again provided another turn in the crisis when a **Turkish squadron was sent into the Black Sea**, only to be destroyed at **Sinope**. **Public opinion**, particularly in Britain, put tremendous pressure on the government to act, and in January 1854 the combined fleet passed through the Bosphorus into the

Black Sea, with the aim of **containing the Russian fleet** at Sebastopol. Nicholas I, presented with demands that his fleet should take no further action, withdrew the Russian ambassadors from London and Paris, and, following his rejection of an ultimatum to evacuate Moldavia and Wallachia, Britain and France declared war on 31 March. **Britain, France and Turkey became allies** officially on 10 April, and ten days later **Austrian and Prussian neutrality was assured**.

The scene was now set for hostilities to commence, but, as if to signify the mismanagement of the affair, the British and French soon found themselves **fighting for objectives they had already achieved** in August at Vienna. **Four points** were put forward as the basis of a suggested peace: (1) the abolition of the Russian Protectorate of the Danubian Provinces; (2) free passage of the mouth of the Danube; (3) revision of the Straits Convention; (4) the renunciation by Russia of the exclusive protection of the Sultan's subjects. These demands in total were unacceptable to Russia, but she did comply with an Austrian request to evacuate Moldavia and Wallachia and in doing so she complied with the terms of the ultimatum of February 1854 which had been the reason for the declaration of war by Britain and France. Thus, by August, it appeared that the **reasons for war had disappeared**, but, driven by both **public opinion** and the **momentum of proposed conflict**, the war began.

Allied troops had been stationed initially at **Varna** on the Black Sea coast to protect Constantinople, but, with Russian evacuation of the area, fighting focussed on the **Crimea** and in particular the strategic naval base of **Sebastopol**. This area and base had not played any direct part in the crisis until this date, but the removal of the Russian fleet would undoubtably improve Turkish security. What followed, however, was a catalogue of **ineptitude, mismanagement and failure**.

The central aim of allied policy was the **capture of Sebastopol**, yet they were unable to implement effectively even such a simple objective. Landing in September 1854 and gaining control of the area to the north of the town, they inexplicably circled it rather than advancing to capture it, with the result that it took a year to besiege Sebastopol. The navy, too, complicated matters for themselves by sinking Russian ships in the mouth of Sebastopol harbour. Allied ships thus prevented their own entry to positions from which they could have been used to bombard the town. In the ensuing struggle, disease and climate claimed more men than the actual fighting, and the famous battles of **Balaclava** and **Inkerman** are remembered not for their military skill but for the ineptitude of the military command exemplified by the charge of the Light Brigade.

The most dramatic changes took place not on the Crimea peninsula but in the **diplomatic scene**. In December 1854 **Austria joined the allies** and in January of the following year **Piedmont** sent 15 000 troops. More significantly, however, 1855 saw the return of **Palmerston** to power and the death in March of Tsar Nicholas I. His successor, **Alexander II**, was more ready and able to consider peace, and with the fall of Sebastopol and the threat in November of direct Austrian involvement, he concluded an **armistice** in February 1856.

The Crimean War: settlement and results

The war had been costly in terms of lives: the Allies had lost over 160 000 men and the Russians double that number. Its results in comparison were negligible, and the **Congress of Paris** dealt only partly with the war settlement, its other concern being that of **relations between the great powers**. By the settlement, Russia was forced to give up southern Bessarabia, which was annexed to Moldavia and Wallachia. Wallachia and Serbia were to be allowed to maintain only light warships to patrol their coasts, and access was thrown open to all merchant shipping. The Danube similarly was declared an area of free navigation, and a more wide ranging '**Declaration respecting Maritime Law**' was signed which laid down codes of conduct, especially in wartime.

The overall aim of the settlement was to **stabilize the region** and to **re-establish the status quo**, but while successful in the **short-term**, in reality, it failed. Turkey may have been saved, but she remained weak and reliant upon the support of friendly powers. The cause of national self-determination had been slightly advanced as the future Romania took shape, but the moves were diplomatic rather than far-sighted. In terms of the Concert of Europe, the great powers may have **seemed to act in unison** to protect the Vienna settlement, but, in reality, they had all been **motivated by self-interest**, and the cracks that appeared now were to widen as the century progressed.

Of the victors, **Britain** had achieved its aim of **saving the Turkish Empire**, although this had been seen to be only a **stop-gap answer to Russian growth**. Further, the fighting had revealed the **backwardness**

and inefficiency of the fighting forces, and of the **lack of medical provision** available for them. **Napoleon III** gained much **personal prestige** from what was a victory, whatever the cost, with the added honour of hosting the Congress that settled the war. Finally, **Cavour** was able to gain the international spotlight for **Piedmont** which, though seemingly a small reward, was a step on the road to Italian unification.

For **Russia** the settlement was a **humiliating limitation of its rights** and one which it would spend many years trying to undo. The Holy Alliance had obviously been shattered by the war but, more than this, the **customary friendship between Austria and Russia was damaged beyond repair**. **Austria** had mistakenly believed its future interests to be with France and Britain, but events were to prove this to be a serious miscalculation.

Summary

The Eastern Question was a complex problem which proved to be beyond the limited influence of the Concert powers. The Concert failed to prevent the war, and its failure created the situation after the Congress of Paris in which the **maintenance of the status quo ceased to be an obtainable objective**. Britain grew wary of European involvement, Russia looked to its own internal problems, and in the resultant power vacuum the seeds of nationalism would once again germinate.

Chapter 4
The Unification of Italy

Introduction

The Vienna settlement which had achieved stability in 1815 had been shaken by revolutionary movements in 1830 and more seriously in 1848, and had seen its unity of policy severely challenged during the Crimean War. Russia had at first seemed the greatest victim of these events, but the passage of time revealed this to be Austria, for within the space of twenty years it was to lose control over both Italy and Germany as they achieved unification.

The Risorgimento

The experience of Italy under Napoleonic rule had given Italian nationalists a vision of what unity could achieve. The return of Hapsburg rule after the Vienna settlement made these objectives seem difficult to obtain, but, as events in 1830 and 1848 had shown, the **seeds of unity** were present. Italy, like Greece, had an ancient and glorious past, and the term **Risorgimento** referred to the movement for rebirth or resurgence. It dated back to the eighteenth century, but as a powerful impetus to unification it became most influential after 1814. The **Risorgimento** described the **sense of national consciousness** that steadily grew during the period and was exemplified by such fervent nationalists as Mazzini, founder of 'Young Italy'.

However, not everyone had the vision or desire to see a united Italy, and to many contemporaries there appeared to be more obstacles than points of common interest. Italy was, for example, not only divided into **seven separate states**, but within these existed **strong regional loyalties, different levels of political freedom** and a whole range of **divergent interests**. **Napoleon**, though, **had shown that unity of rule could be achieved**, and while benevolent foreign domination was unacceptable to individual Italian states, in Napoleon and then Austria they had found a **common enemy** to unite them. Individually, they could hardly hope to defeat Austria, but collectively they would pose a more credible threat.

To hate Austria was one thing, but the degree or nature of collective opposition was another. Austrian rule might be unacceptable, but **what was to replace it? Would a united Italy be a republic, a monarchy, or a federation?** Each suggestion had its plan of action, but each carried limitations. The idea of a republic created through a popular uprising, while the most romantic, ran the not inconsiderable risk of alienating the support of the middle classes and of proving difficult to control. The confederation of states under the suggested leadership of the Pope was workable but the papacy had not shown itself capable of, or sympathetic to, the idea of unification. This, therefore, left the idea of a **unifying monarchy**, the suggestion being the King of Piedmont. Although not totally satisfactory, this became the acceptable solution.

Cavour

The failure of the 1848 revolution was a setback for Italian nationalism. Austrian rule seemed as secure as before, and many of the nationalist leaders, among them Garibaldi and Mazzini, had been forced to flee abroad. Yet the revolution had left in its wake **Piedmont**, which remained outside Austrian control and which had **retained its constitution**. Piedmont, under its King, Victor Emmanuel, had resisted the pressures put upon him to withdraw the constitution, and in doing so he not only **secured his own independence** but had **presented himself as a candidate for the monarch of a united Italy**. Victor Emmanuel, however, was not a great statesman, and the key figure behind the leadership of Piedmont for united Italy was **Count Cavour**.

Cavour was a convinced liberal, a businessman and a firm believer in constitutional liberties and procedure. A widely-travelled and knowledgeable figure, he became Prime Minister in 1852 and began to transform Piedmont into a powerful and influential state able to lead the rest of Italy. Through previous experience, particularly the failure of 1848, Cavour saw it was **unrealistic to expect that Italy could deliver itself from Austrian control**. The belief of previous revolutionaries and Charles Albert that 'Italy must win her own salvation' was discarded, and instead Cavour actively **sought the support of Britain and France**. **Britain** assisted with **trade and finance** but, while the British supported the idea of national self-determination, it was clear that they **would not provide military aid**. It was thus to **France** that Cavour began to look.

The Crimean War had not only transformed relations between the powers, it had also provided Cavour with the **opportunity to press Piedmont's claims for international recognition**. Thus, while the 15 000 troops sent to the Crimea had little effect on the final outcome, they provided Cavour with **a seat at the Paris Congress** and the **opportunity to seek France's aid**. Fortunately for Cavour, **Napoleon III** was not adverse to involvement in Italian affairs, having spent his youth in Romagna and seeing in such an involvement a chance for yet greater glory. He was also greatly assisted by the fact that Russia and France were more likely allies after the Crimean War than Russia and Austria.

French involvement

Napoleon III was willing to assist Italian unification, but he needed to be certain that the danger of such an undertaking was reduced to a minimum. The question of **Russian response** to such a move resulted in a meeting between Napoleon III and Alexander II at **Stuttgart** in 1857 at which it became clear that **Russian aid to Austria was unlikely**, but still Napoleon III would not commit himself. In January 1858, however, Napoleon III was finally convinced when an Italian nationalist, **Felice Orsini**, attempted to assassinate him in the cause of Italian liberation. Napoleon III had Orsini executed, but at the same time he authorized the publication of Orsini's appeal to him to free Italy.

Cavour wasted little time in obtaining positive results from this change of mind, and in July 1858 Napoleon III and Cavour met at **Plombières**, where a **secret agreement** was drawn up. By the terms of this treaty **France was to assist Piedmont to annexe Italy north of the Appenines, in return for which France was to receive Savoy and Nice**. The territories of central Italy were to be combined, with the exception of Rome, into a **central kingdom**, and **southern Italy was to remain largely the same but with the ruling dynasties replaced**. As a further enticement, Princess Clotilde, Victor Emmanuel's fifteen-year-old daughter, was to be married to Prince Jerôme Bonaparte, the Empress's cousin, and with this the alliance was completed. It was now up to Cavour to **provoke a war with Austria**, which proved to be exceedingly easy. It was clear to all observers that war was highly likely, with both Piedmontese and French troops mobilizing, but equally both **Russia and Britain urged mediation**. The Austrians, however, throwing caution aside, sent an **ultimatum** to Piedmont, demanding that it demobilize. Now, with the excuse of Austrian aggression, war began in April 1859.

The inability of Austrian diplomacy to prevent the war was now matched by the ineptitude of its military commanders, who inexplicably delayed their assault until French troops had arrived. In June the French and Piedmontese forces entered Lombardy, and there followed two significant battles, at **Magenta** and **Solferino**, at which the **Austrians were defeated** and driven back to their border fortresses. Napoleon III, however, now began to have reservations about his involvement in Italy, for a number of reasons. The Austrians, although defeated twice, remained **a potent force**, and it appeared possible that they **might be joined by Prussia**. Further, Italian nationalists were not abiding by the terms agreed at Plombières, and Napoleon III, wary of where this might lead, contacted Franz Josef to **arrange an armistice**. The Austrians were quite willing to come to terms, and in July Napoleon and Franz Josef met at **Villafranca**. Under the terms of their agreement **Lombardy was ceded to Piedmont**, an **Italian confederation** was to be supported under the titular presidency of the **Pope**, **Venice** was to remain with Austria, and the **rulers of Modena, Parma and Tuscany were to return**, though not by force.

Cavour had resigned when Napoleon III's betrayal became apparent, but events in Italy did not follow the plan laid down at Villafranca. The inhabitants of Modena, Parma, Tuscany and Romagna fiercely **resisted the attempts of the two Emperors to force the return of their old rulers** and came out in favour of **union with the kingdom of Victor Emmanuel**. At the same time, Napoleon III found he needed something more tangible from his excursion into Italian affairs than just battle honour. Consequently, in March 1860, Napoleon III came to an **agreement with Cavour**, who had now returned to power, by which **Nice and Savoy were ceded to France**, and **Romagna, Tuscany, Modena and Parma became incorporated in the North Italian Kingdom** under Victor Emmanuel. The whole of northern Italy, with the exception of Venice, was now **united**, and Cavour must have anticipated a gradual extension of this influence when the opportunity arose. That opportunity, however, was to come much sooner than Cavour expected.

Garibaldi

Cavour represented the organized and calculated pursuit of Italian unification. A similar aim, though using different means, was envisaged by the more romantic revolutionaries Mazzini and Garibaldi. In the north, Mazzini's supporters had been silenced by the **need for collective action under the leadership of Piedmont**, but in the south it appeared possible that a **republic** might be formed. In the end it would be seen that the influence of Cavour and Piedmont would not allow such a development, but equally it was not, at this time, believed that the **overthrow of the Kingdom of the Two Sicilies** was a possibility. The Bourbon King Francis II might have been unpopular but his overthrow was both seen as difficult and carried with it the risk of an adverse French reaction. The person who was to prove this analysis to be incorrect was **Garibaldi**.

Garibaldi had been a sailor by profession, but a leader of forces in Latin America and in the Roman Republic of 1848. He set out in May 1860 with over one thousand men to aid unrest in **Sicily**. His men, kitted out in red shirts, landed at Marsala and within two months, against all predictions, had control of the entire island.

Encouraged by this success and ignoring instructions from Victor Emmanuel to the contrary, Garibaldi now crossed into mainland Italy, and by the beginning of September he was able to enter **Naples** in triumph. Cavour, amazed at Garibaldi's success, now began to see it as a threat, for a number of reasons. The problem of **how much control Piedmont could exert over Garibaldi** had already been highlighted by his move to Naples, but there was also the **danger of unleashing republican sentiments** and of **involving the French**, who had troops garrisoned in Rome. With Mazzini and his followers ready to exploit the situation, and armed with an awareness that the sentiments of southern Italians would be more difficult to gauge, Cavour decided to **intervene directly**. Using the pretext of risings incited in the Papal States, he moved Piedmontese forces along the Adriatic coast, entered the Papal states and defeated the Papal army at **Castelfidardo**. Piedmontese troops then continued south and linked up with Garibaldi who, after a slight delay, surrendered his conquests to Victor Emmanuel and then unselfishly returned to his island home in Caprera. Plebiscites were held in Sicily, Naples and the Papal States in October and November 1860, and in the following March, **Victor Emmanuel became King of the new Kingdom of Italy** with the constitution that Piedmont had gained in 1848.

Unification completed

By 1861, Cavour had managed to galvanize Italian nationalism and patriotism so far as to form a geographical unit that lacked only Venice and Rome. His success within the space of ten years had been achieved with a very small loss of life and through a **masterly exploitation of the balance of power**. Unfortunately for the new Kingdom, Cavour died in June, just when his perception and quality of statesmanship were most required. The constitution, admirable as it was, had a very **restricted franchise**, and the *Risorgimento* came to be regarded as a **middle-class movement in what was a largely peasant society**. This factor and the **divergence of the previously separate states** made Italy more of a loose confederation than a solid political unit.

Figure 2. The Unification of Italy including the Italian gains of Tyrol and Istria in 1919

The completion of this stage of Italian unification had been a magnificent achievement, but **Venice** and **Rome** remained outside. Venice lay in Austrian hands and Rome was under the protection of French troops. The new Italy was not in a viable position to have taken on either of these powers alone, and was forced to wait until circumstances would be conducive to such moves. In the case of Venice this happened in 1866 as a result of the **Austro–Prussian War**, and for Rome it occurred in 1870 when French troops were withdrawn due to the **Franco–Prussian War**. Thus in 1870 Italy finally became a geographical unit with a single government whose capital was now in Rome.

Summary

The unification of Italy showed both the strengths and weaknesses of nationalism and of the political reality that such movements required to achieve success. Cavour, Mazzini, Garibaldi and Victor Emmanuel all played important parts in organizing and orchestrating Italy's unification, yet the key to its success lay in **Austria's inability to govern effectively** and in the **exploitation of Napoleon III's desire for glory**. Yet, as popular a movement as it was, Mazzini's republican ideals had little hope of success, and even Garibaldi's Redshirts were mainly students and professional men. The **unification was a success for the middle-class Italian nationalists**. For the peasants, unity brought a change of government, but little else.

Chapter 5
France 1848–70

Introduction

The fall of Louis Philippe in 1848 left France with the problem of what should follow; a regency or a republic. The regency was rejected through mob pressure and the republicans prevailed. The radical nature of the republic, however, aroused fears of a return to chaos, and, following limited but bloody street fighting, the political initiative passed to the right and centre in the guise of General Cavaignac. His rule, although a military dictatorship, was solely aimed at producing a **practical republican constitution**. This was duly and rapidly arrived at and, although it was a mixture of other existing constitutions, it proved acceptable to the populace. Under its provisions there was to be a **single legislative chamber** of 750 members elected by **universal suffrage** for three years, and a **president** elected by **universal suffrage** for a term of four years. However, the amazing result of this election, when it was held in December 1848, was that Napoleon Bonaparte's nephew, Louis Napoleon became President.

The legacy of 1848

Although Louis Napoleon had been elected President in 1848, polling almost three times as many votes as his opponents, it was not his first attempt to gain power. In 1830 at the age of twenty-two he had taken part in a coup that was a dismal failure against the Papal government in Rome. Following this he turned his attention to France, where, by a law of 1816, the house of Bonaparte was banned, and made two more unsuccessful attempts to seize power from Louis Philippe. The first in 1836 at Strasbourg achieved little, and the second at Boulogne in 1840 led to his capture and imprisonment in the fortress of Ham. From here he escaped in 1846 to England, from where he returned in 1848.

In these formative years Louis spent much of his time propagating the **legend of Bonapartism** while at the same time managing to support the ideals of **nationalism**, **liberalism** and **order** through his writings *Napoleonic Ideas* and *The Extinction of Pauperism*. Through careful exposure of these virtues, Louis became first a candidate in the parliamentary elections of 1848 and then a presidential candidate. His success was largely due to the fact that he **appealed to almost every section of the electorate**, because of his **name** and the **stability** it seemed to represent and also because the alternative candidates, among them General Cavaignac, had limited popularity. Louis may not have had his uncle's genius, but his name evoked **memories of French glory** at a time when the French were becoming tired of mediocrity.

From Republic to Empire

Louis' use of the Napoleonic legend had been instrumental in sweeping him to power, and once in power it seemed unlikely that he would willingly abide by the constitutional stipulation of only one term in office. Nevertheless, he proceeded at first with great caution. He toured the country, building up his popular support, and, having gained this security, he appointed a **conservative cabinet** and installed troops in Paris to forestall any adverse reaction. Further, to the horror of republicans, in June 1849 Louis sent a French army to Rome to restore Pope Pius IX and thus **destroy the revolutionary Roman republic**. Limited rioting followed, but Louis had little trouble in maintaining order.

The **conservatives** were under the illusion that they could use Louis to further their own ends, but Louis had appointed them and could equally dismiss them, as in fact he did in October 1849. The chamber, rocked by this setback and alarmed by increasing republican victories in by-elections, was panicked into altering the voting qualification thereby **reducing those eligible to vote by almost a third**. Louis realized the propaganda potential of such a move, and on 2 December 1851, the anniversary of Austerlitz, Louis carried out a **coup d'état**. Saint Arnaud and his troops controlled Paris, **martial law** was imposed, **universal suffrage restored** and a **plebiscite** was taken. The stunned republicans attempted to mount opposition, but they were hopelessly out-manoeuvred and, in the street battles that followed, they were quickly overcome.

Through the new constitution Louis created a **presidential dictatorship** but one which had the backing of over 90 per cent of the electorate. Under its provisions Louis had his **term extended to ten years** and his powers widened to include the **right to institute martial law** in any part of the country, **command of the armed forces**, and **control over foreign policy**, including the **ability to declare war**. There were to be **two chambers** to replace the existing one: a **senate** of 150 members selected by the President with the sole function of **reviewing constitutional violations** and a ***corps législatif*** which was only able to **vote on new laws without discussion**. The officers of the chamber were to be **named by the President** and he was to become the arbiter of justice as well.

A year later on 2 December 1852, Louis took the next logical step, and, following another **plebiscite**, the republic became an **Empire**. Now, as Emperor, Louis Napoleon III (accepting the Duke of Reichstadt as Napoleon II) had **revived his uncle's glorious past and gained wholesale popular support**. To complete the parallel he gained an Empress in January. She was Eugénie de Montijo, a Spanish noblewoman, and, in 1856, she dutifully bore him a son who became the Prince Imperial.

Imperial rule

Napoleon III's position in 1852 was very strong. He had overwhelming popular support, as indicated by the plebiscites; he was heralded as having brought back **order and stability**; his intervention in Rome, and the Falloux Law, had won him the strong **support of the Roman Catholics**. This broad base of support gave him a mandate for firm action, as he had shown after the coup d'état in 1851 when 10 000 of his opponents were transported to Algeria. The administration was **highly centralized**, with the Minister of the Interior exercising power through the prefects in the *départements*. **Press censorship** in both Paris and the provinces made sure that criticism of the government was controlled. **Government interference** took place in political clubs, education and in the nominations for elections.

However, Napoleon III was aware that a far more effective form of control was to unite **the people in the spirit and achievements of the regime**. Influenced by the industrialist theories of Saint-Simonians, Napoleon sought to encourage **financial prosperity**. A major problem appeared to be the availability of credit, and so Napoleon encouraged the **development of commercial banks** such as the Comptoir d'Escompte. Further, in 1852 he issued a charter to a joint-stock investment bank, the **Crédit Mobilier**, which channelled capital into industry, and to the **Crédit Financier**, which specialized in investments in real estate. In fact, the **money market** became so stimulated that it began to challenge London as a financial centre.

As well as monetary improvements, the period also saw considerable **economic growth**. The **railway system**, which amounted to only 1800 km in 1848 was expanded and made more efficient, and **coal, iron and steel** production all rose considerably. **Agricultural**

production, while not receiving the same degree of attention, also improved through government stimulation. Even the lot of the ordinary working people was improved by **mutual benefit associations** and limited **slum clearance**. On a wider scale, Napoleon III became a supporter of **free trade**, and in 1860, through the **Cobden – Chevalier Treaty**, France and Britain agreed on a **general tariff reduction**. Similar agreements with other European countries followed in the next few years.

Finally, like all dictators, Napoleon needed public evidence of his glory and achievement to compensate for the loss of liberty. **Land reclamation** and **forest conservation** took place in the country, but his greatest success was the **reconstruction of Paris**. In the space of twenty years under the careful supervision of Baron Haussmann the capital was transformed from a medieval city into the most modern and organized city in Europe. Wide boulevards, huge public squares and parks made it the envy of other powers, but behind the magnificence lay the ulterior motive of making central Paris accessible to modern cavalry and artillery and the streets more difficult to barricade.

Foreign policy

For France to regain her former glory Napoleon III would have had to challenge the settlement of 1815. Yet such a challenge would have had to be approached carefully, for the name Bonaparte instilled considerable suspicion, despite the new Emperor's assertion that 'the Empire means peace'. A policy based purely on aggression, however, was unlikely to succeed, not only because of the joint allied action it was likely to stimulate, but also because Napoleon III did not possess the military genius of his uncle. If gains were to be made and France's international reputation rebuilt, it would therefore be through **diplomatic** rather than military efforts.

The basic diplomatic aim of Napoleon III was undoubtedly to **break up the Concert of powers** and to **take advantage of the disagreements** that would follow. However, beyond this, he was also anxious to maintain **friendly relations** with **Britain** and also with **Russia**, where he believed there were considerable commercial opportunities for France. It was ironic, therefore, that Napoleon's first major excursion into foreign affairs in 1854 saw these secondary objectives compromised when he joined Britain and Turkey in a **war against Russia**. The involvement (which is dealt with fully in Chapter 3) came as a by-product of French championing of

Roman Catholic interests in the Holy Land, but the results proved most fortuitous for France. Napoleon III was **no longer isolated** – he had gained the alliance of **Britain** and almost of **Austria**. As a result of the war, the **Holy Alliance was destroyed** and the **Concert of Europe was shattered**. The Peace of Paris in 1856 which concluded the war was presided over by Napoleon III, and only four years after he had become Emperor it appeared that France had regained its international credibility.

In **colonial affairs** success also followed. **Algeria**, gained during Louis Philippe's reign, was developed; in West Africa the colony of **Senegal** expanded and the port of **Dakar** was created. In East Africa, **Somaliland** came under French control in 1862 and was followed in the same year by **Madagascar**, and, of course, throughout most of Napoleon III's reign the **Suez Canal** was being built by French engineers. In the Far East, **Cambodia** and **Cochin-China** came under French influence. Britain also had interests in the Far East, so the wealth and commercial potential of China were opened to European exploitation.

After the Crimean War, however, Napoleon III managed tc destroy the success of his early years through a series of **ill-fated ventures that once again isolated France**. The first of these came in 1859 when he decided to **revive French interest in Italian affairs** (see Chapter 5). The possible rewards were territorial gain and a client state in the Italian peninsula which would be favourable to the French. The venture, however, had the conflicting effects of giving Roman Catholic support to the Pope (1849) and of encouraging republicanism. It had the added danger of upsetting not only Austria, but also Prussia. In the event, although Napoleon III gained **victories at Magenta** and **Solferino** and won the territories of **Nice** and **Savoy**, the **diplomatic damage** was considerable. **Austrian hostility** was understandable, but because of the hastily-arranged peace at Villafranca, Napoleon III upset Cavour and other Italian nationalists. Worse still, under the impetus he had created, Italian unification achieved a **unitary monarchy** rather than a four-state confederacy. French gains in the process led to the **cooling of its entente with Britain**, and his sympathetic **support of Polish rebels** in 1863 managed to **alienate Russia** and thus leave France isolated once again.

Abroad, too, success was mingled with disaster. The extension of French influence in Africa, China and Indo-China led Napoleon III to **dabble unwisely in the politics of the New World** and, in particular,

Mexico. Here, through the twin pressures of glory-hunting and fears of anti-clerical policies by the Mexican leader Juarez, Napoleon III sent almost 40 000 troops. By 1863 they had captured Mexico City, whereupon they proclaimed the Hapsburg Archduke Maximilian Emperor. The throne was never very stable, requiring the backing of the considerable French military presence, and it came under **fierce pressure from the United States** in 1865 when the Civil War ended. The Americans protested that French action was in contravention of the Monroe Doctrine, and, wary of the developing events in Europe, Napoleon III bowed to the pressure, withdrew his troops and left Maximilian to end his brief reign in front of a Mexican firing squad. The glorious success of the early years was now only a memory. Isolated, Napoleon III and France were to pay the ultimate price for this failure (see Chapter 6, The Unification of Germany) as Germany gained its independence at France's expense.

The 'liberal empire'

Napoleon III had come to power through the diversity of his appeal and had remained in power through political exploitation of this appeal, as against the viable alternatives. Dictator though he was, he had been **wary of losing popular support** for his actions. Thus the changes in 1851 and 1852 had been accompanied by plebiscites. The elections of 1857, in which the large towns returned republican candidates, had given an indication of developing dissatisfaction, and in November 1860 Napoleon III responded by introducing **liberal changes**. Now the Senate and *Corps Législatif* were to **vote a reply to the Emperor's address** at the beginning of each session, to **scrutinize the budget** and to **publish** a record of their debates.

The reasoning behind the changes is difficult to assess, for, although he paid close attention to public response to his measures, he still commanded considerable support. One of the elements of his early appeal was the liberalism he expressed in his writings, but it seems more likely that this was simply a **pragmatic response** to the opposition created by his exploits in Italy, the free trade policy and the roots of republican feeling. Added to this, Napoleon III's **health** was giving cause for concern, and through benevolent control he obviously hoped to be able to prolong Bonapartist rule. Whatever the reasons, though, the relaxation of control continued. In **1864**, workers were given the **right to strike**, and in **1867** both houses were given the **right to cross-examine ministers**. Also, in **1868** the **press laws were relaxed**, allowing the publication of over a hundred new newspapers which gave voice to opposition demands.

The major change, however, came in the **Chamber** itself where, due to the lessening of government control, **republican representation grew**. In response to this, in July 1869 by decree of the Senate the *Corps Législatif* was given the right to **initiate legislation** and to **choose its own officers**. Napoleon III dismissed his own ministers; in January 1870 he made Émile Ollivier his Prime Minister and asked him to form a government. The **right of constitutional reform was now passed from the senate to the *Corps Législatif*** and the people were asked to endorse in a **plebiscite** all the constitutional changes which had taken place since 1860. The result of this was a 7½ million to 1½ million endorsement of the Emperor's policies but, unfortunately, while the domestic scene had been defused, Napoleon III's **meddling in foreign affairs** was about to bring about his downfall, not on constitutional issues, but on the battlefield.

Summary

Napoleon III ruled France for over twenty years, progressing from **President** to **Dictator** and then to **liberal Emperor**. In this time, opposition to his rule and policies did exist, yet neither he nor his popularity were ever seriously challenged. Even in 1870, only months before France's humiliation at the hands of Prussia, the people overwhelmingly endorsed the constitutional changes he had implemented in the previous decade. His downfall came not as it had to his predecessors, through France's internal revolt, but through his inability to apply the same insight and expertise in the field of **foreign policy**.

Chapter 6
The Unification of Germany

Introduction

The 1815 settlement had created a German confederation of thirty-nine states in which Prussia and Austria vied with each other for influence and thus control. The idea of a united Germany was fed by romantic nationalism and liberal sentiment; it aimed at unification, either through Prussia or Austria, or regardless of them. The 1848 revolution had seen both Prussia and Austria threatened by the Frankfurt Assembly's ideas for a united Germany, but in the end with the Assembly's failure came the realization that **one of the two powers would be needed to achieve unification**.

The German dream

The failure of the 1848 revolution was a bitter blow to German nationalism, for it had revealed the inability of the people to solve the problems of German unification by themselves (see Chapter 2). Worse still, **Frederick William IV** had refused the crown of the united Germany offered to him and had taken rapid steps when the opportunity occurred to dismantle the constitutions set up in 1848. Yet, as time was to prove, the **destiny of Germany lay in the hands of Prussia** and not of Austria. The reasons for this were dictated largely by geography. **Austria**, it was true, had the **controlling influence over the German confederation**, but it had **greater interests outside** the German sphere – its Slav, Italian and Hungarian minorities. Further, the Hapsburg rulers had **no desire to relinquish these territories**, so the movement for the ***Grossdeutsch*** or greater German solution floundered.

Prussia, on the other hand was quite obviously a **solely German power** and had been influential in developing **economic interdependence** between Prussia and the other German states. In 1818 internal tariffs within the Prussian state were abolished, and in 1834 the ***Zollverein*** or customs union was formed. Through this the **economic affairs of the German states were linked**, with only a few states remaining outside. Of these the most important was **Austria**, which **failed to realize the significance of the development** until it was too late. Thus German nationalism, unable to realize a union which included Austria, turned to Prussia for the achievement of unification, the ***Kleindeutsch*** or lesser German solution.

The rise of Prussia and Bismarck

Although Prussia was undoubtedly a **weaker** power than Austria after the 1848 revolutions, its **prospects were, in many ways, far superior**. The dissension that was to split the Austrian Empire would come largely as a result of nationalism aggravated by years of repressive central control. The **Prussian Constitution**, diluted by Frederick William IV, was certainly far from what many liberals had desired, but at least the populace felt it had some say in the formation of the government. Further, in Prussia, unlike the Austrian Empire, some liberals saw in the **existing government** an alternative – if less attractive – road to national unity. Heinrich von Treitschke was one of many moderates who came to accept that despotism was acceptable if it led to national unity.

Economically, too, Prussia was far stronger than Austria. Economic expansion, of which the *Zollverein* was a dramatic reflection, was progressing at a rate that would push Germany to challenge Britain as the world's leading industrial nation. The **acquisition of the Rhineland in 1815** had been of key importance, but equally the extensive **railway network** and active **government encouragement**, through its highly efficient civil service, accelerated this growth. As the country prospered so too did the people, in particular the **middle classes** and the **landowners**, for both industrial and agricultural production grew rapidly. The effect was thus to **link the interests and allegiance of these important groups with the welfare of the state**.

The importance of this duality of interests was illustrated clearly by the **constitutional conflict** which existed from **1862 to 1866** and which saw the rise to power of Otto von Bismarck, the architect of the path to unification. In October 1857, Frederick William IV had a stroke which led to his brother William becoming first Regent and then King, on his death in 1861. The new monarch, **William I** was initially thought to be a liberal sympathizer, but it soon became clear that his views were not markedly different from those of his brother. Before long he clashed with the Parliament, the *Landtag*, over the enlargement of the army (50 per cent) and the extension of national service to three years rather than two. In 1862 the Landtag refused to approve new taxes to meet these costs.

The King, unwilling to yield but nonetheless contemplating abdication, looked for a new Minister to find a way to deal with the problem. The man he chose was **Bismarck** who, having been

Prussian Ambassador to the German Diet and to Russia, had made a name for himself as a strong **monarchist and opponent of liberalism**. Called back from his appointment in Paris, Bismarck assumed the presidency and for four years ruled Prussia **without the co-operation of Parliament or a constitutionally sanctioned budget**. The basis of Bismarck's rule was that when the Crown and Parliament were in conflict, there was no higher authority which could resolve the dispute, and, as government was required, the Crown was forced to govern in the absence of agreement. The liberals, dependent on Prussian prosperity, unsure of their support and cowed by the thought that their actions would be illegal, meekly accepted Bismarck's interpretation. With the constitutional problem neutralized, Bismarck now turned his attentions to foreign affairs.

Schleswig–Holstein and the defeat of Austria

The cornerstone of Bismarck's involvement in foreign policy was the question of **isolation**: Prussia must not be isolated, but, to ensure the defeat of its enemies, they must be kept apart. Thus, for Prussia to obtain the territorial advancements it required, Bismarck had first to lay the groundwork to ensure the safety of any action. Quite obviously **the real barrier to Prussian expansion was Austria**, and because he had been Ambassador to the Diet at Frankfurt, Bismarck had clear knowledge of Austro–Prussian rivalry. Any action against Austria would be helped by **Russian neutrality**, which was likely because of Austrian neutrality in the Crimean War. Bismarck, however, did not wish to take any risks and **won over Russian friendship** by refusing access to foreign troops sent to assist in the Polish revolt. **French neutrality** was also essential, but when he failed to gain adequate support from Napoleon III, Bismarck chose to **ensnare Austria by first seeking its assistance**.

The issue which presented Bismarck with this opportunity was the question of **Schleswig–Holstein**. These duchies were held by the Danish Crown but were inhabited by Germans. The relationship between the duchies and Denmark aroused nationalist feelings on both sides, and when in 1863 **Denmark moved to annex Schleswig–Holstein** the Germanic confederation moved to oppose this. Bismarck saw in the dispute the chance to **obtain Schleswig and Holstein for Prussia**, but in the first instance he **proposed joint action with Austria**, which he induced to sign an alliance with Prussia in January 1864. Rapid military action took place in the face of mild protests by Palmerston, but by June the heavily outnumbered Danes had been forced to make peace. By the **Convention of Gastein**,

Denmark was forced to surrender sovereignty of Schleswig, Holstein and Lauenburg to Prussia and Austria. **Austria** took over the administration of **Holstein** and **Prussia** that of **Schleswig**. The Germanic Confederation, which Prussia and Austria had claimed to be representing, was completely ignored.

Having gained Austrian assistance, Bismarck now sought to **neutralize** its influence in Germanic affairs. Again the base requirement was for Austria to be **isolated**. **Russia remained anti-Hapsburg** and sympathetic to Prussian expansion following Bismarck's support of Russia at the time of the Polish revolt. **France's neutrality** was obtained following a meeting at **Biarritz** in October 1865 and **Britain's non-intervention** all but guaranteed following Palmerston's failure to stop the original taking of the duchies. The final move in Bismarck's plan was made in April 1866 when a **secret alliance** was concluded between **Prussia** and **Italy**. Through this, Italy pledged itself to join Prussia if war broke out with Austria within three months, with Venetia as Italy's reward for this support.

Bismarck's isolation of Austria was complete. He now required an **opportunity to take action against Austria without upsetting or invoking a joint European reaction**. The issue was fairly easy to engineer, it concerned the administration of **Holstein** which Bismarck challenged as being detrimental to Prussia's interests. Austria, diplomatically weak and seemingly isolated, was forced to mobilize its forces and, in its fear, to conclude a **treaty with France** whereby French neutrality was obtained in return for the surrender of Venetia to Italy and a promise of the creation of a new Rhineland state.

On 15 June Prussian forces attacked, led by Moltke. The rest of Europe, in particular Napoleon III, expected an evenly-contested war in which Austrian experience would finally win through, but instead, within three weeks the Prussians had decisively defeated the Austrian army at **Königgrätz** (Sadowa). This had been achieved despite the crushing defeat of the Italians at **Custozza**, and was largely due to the **excellent planning and organization of the Prussian forces**. However, Bismarck did not wish either to destroy or humiliate Austria, and within seven weeks of hostilities a settlement was reached known as the **Treaty of Prague**. The peace preliminaries had been arranged at Nikolsburg a month earlier, and under these **Prussia gained Holstein, Hesse-Cassel, Hanover, Nassau and Frankfurt**, with all other states north of the Main becoming

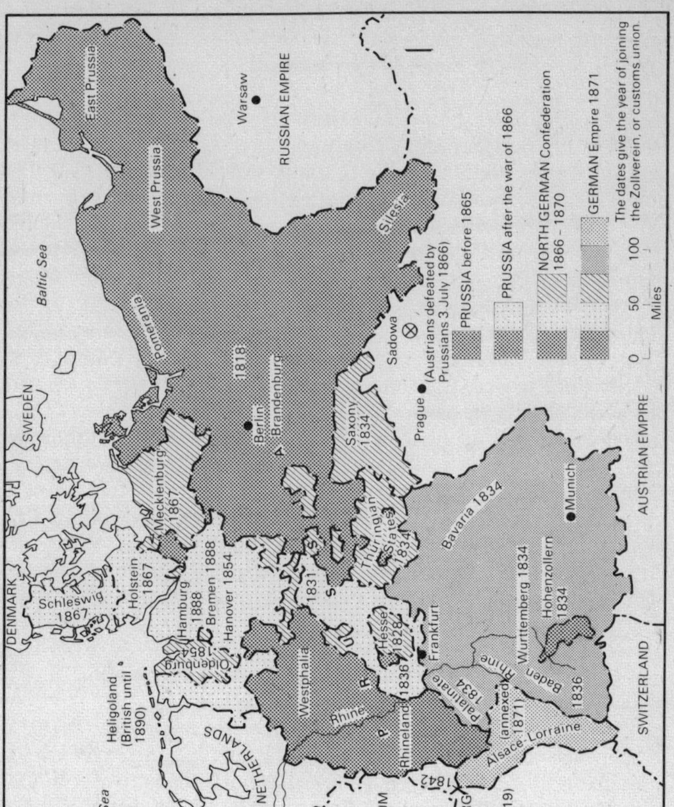

Figure 3. The Unification of Germany 1818–71

members of a **new North German Confederation under Prussian leadership**. **Austria was excluded from participation in German** affairs and **Venetia** was surrendered through France to **Italy**. The **southern German states** were left **seemingly independent** but were rapidly tied to **Prussia** through a series of **secret military alliances**.

By 1866, Bismarck had managed to achieve 'by iron and blood' what the liberals had failed to achieve in 1848. He had, in effect, **captured German nationalism and separated it from liberalism**. German nationalism became identified with Hohenzollern authoritarianism and Prussian militarism, and the moderate liberals now gave their support and allegiance to Bismarck and his plans for the extension of Prussian control.

The Franco–Prussian War

The coupling of Prussian expansion with German nationalism meant that Prussia's next move must lead to the **union of the Northern Confederation with the South**. The problem with this, however, was that it was likely, at the least, to **antagonize France** and would most probably lead to confrontation and intervention. Exactly whether Bismarck worked towards war with France or not remains a matter of dispute, for, even though war appeared likely, Bismarck always **favoured diplomatic success over military action**. What the wrangles with France would show was the extent of **Bismarck's diplomatic superiority**, but in the end it would be **Prussia's military power** that would make the victory final.

For **Napoleon III** the outcome of the 'Seven Weeks' War', as it became known, was a disaster. Unable to play the role of mediator he tried, through Benedetti, the Ambassador to Prussia, to suggest that France would recognize Prussian gains in return for land in the Rhine provinces. Though Bismarck had no intention of allowing this, he induced Benedetti to make a formal statement of French claims and then decisively rejected them, making the southern German states aware of Napoleon III's real intentions. Added to French failures in Mexico and the abortive attempt to purchase the Grand Duchy of Luxembourg, this made relations between France and Prussia hostile. Although France saw in the growth of Prussia a threat to its own security, it remained dangerously **isolated**, and Napoleon III's ill-health and a series of continuing diplomatic blunders did little to improve this situation.

However, for Bismarck, too, not everything ran smoothly. The southern German states were **fearful of being swallowed up by Prussia** and were united to an extent in their **Catholicism**. They presented a considerable obstacle to Bismarck's plans for unification. The way out of this impasse was provided by the issue of the **Hohenzollern candidature**. Spain had been ruled by a military junta since the enforced abdication of Queen Isabella in 1868. It agreed, however, in the following year, to establish a liberal government under a constitutional monarchy and scoured Europe to find a suitable candidate. Their eventual choice was Prince Leopold of Hohenzollern-Sigmaringen. Bismarck appears to have played only a minor part in these affairs at this early stage, but, actually, he was both **lobbying William I to support the candidature** and **attempting to bribe the Spanish Cortes**.

The French reaction was predictably one of **alarm at the prospect of a Hohenzollern on the Spanish throne**, and, before the candidature was ratified by the Spanish Cortes, the French protested. Napoleon III decided to deal directly with William I, who was at the summer resort of Ems, and after pressure from Benedetti, William I agreed to withdraw the candidature on his son's behalf. The French had scored a major diplomatic victory by forcing Prussia to retreat, but their success was short-lived. The next day, 13 July, they pressed their claim further, **demanding that the Hohenzollern candidature should never be renewed** but William I emphatically refused and sent a telegram to Bismarck informing him of this event. To Bismarck, who claimed to have been on the point of resigning, the **Ems telegram** provided the answer to the crisis. An edited version highlighting the differences of opinion was published, and with it war became almost inevitable.

Unable to climb down, the French declared war on 19 July and found themselves without allies and unable to match Prussia's military preparedness. Bismarck, able to fight the war as a **patriotic defence of Germany**, saw the French rapidly outmanoeuvred. **Metz** was quickly encircled, and on 1 August the French were decisively beaten at **Sedan**, with Napoleon III among the prisoners. Metz finally capitulated in October and, although the revolutionaries held out in Paris until January, its eventual fate never seemed in doubt.

Under the terms of the peace treaty, France was forced to pay an **indemnity** of five billion francs and to cede **Alsace and Lorraine** to the German Empire that was proclaimed under William I. For Bismarck, the war victory **completed German unification**, and in the constitution, William, as **German Kaiser**, had the control over

Germany that Prussia had always sought. The two other direct results of the war were the **incorporation of the papal states into Italy** and the **transfer of the capital to Rome**, and the **decision by Russia not to be bound by the Black Sea clauses of the Treaty of Paris** (1855).

Summary

German unification had been achieved through careful policies rather than through liberal sentiment. Bismarck had above all realized the **need for Prussia to be seen as the instrument of German nationalism** and for the **isolation** of those who would oppose it. Bismarck's actions were not without good fortune, but his success was almost wholly due to **careful planning** and a **talent for diplomacy**, which none of his contemporaries approached and few politicians, if any, have had since.

Chapter 7
Russia 1855–1917

Introduction

For Russia the Crimean War had not only been a humiliating defeat – it had also called into question the very nature of Russian society. The new Tsar, **Alexander II**, had been able to obtain a peace settlement upon his accession in 1855, but it became obvious that, as after the defeats by Napoleon, reforms of some kind were required. The nature of these **reforms** and Russia's **backwardness in almost every field** presented twin problems for the Tsar and his government, for it would be **difficult to advance the cause of progress without weakening tsarist authority**. Yet this is exactly the contradiction that successive tsars had to grapple with for the next sixty years.

Attempts at reform

Although Russia was a major power, it had suffered military defeat twice in the space of fifty years and had, on numerous occasions, been limited by the actions of the other powers. Yet, both in terms of population and resources, Russia was potentially mightier than any other European power – its problem lay in how to realize this potential. By the mid-nineteenth century, Russian society was still **pre-industrial** and, in practice, almost medieval. Of the almost seventy million inhabitants, the vast majority were either **landless serfs** or **'state peasants'**. This illiterate and discontented mass had **no recourse to law**, only to the benevolence of their owners, who openly resisted the forces of change. Such conditions bred rebellion, and in the 1840s and 1850s there were numerous **serf revolts**. If Russia was to move into the modern age, change was obviously required. The reforms should **not be permitted to weaken tsarist control**, however – rather, they should enhance it by **propelling Russia into the modern age, renewing its prosperity**, and **re-establishing its status as a great power**. The humiliation in the Crimean War gave Alexander II the justification for implementing changes, among which the **abolition of serfdom** was the most pressing. Alexander reasoned that the emancipation of the serfs was a development that was in the best interests of the state, and, after due investigation, the **Statute of Emancipation** was proclaimed in March 1861. Over 40 million serfs and peasants were **set free from servitude** and given **ownership of portions of land**. The extent of the change was considerable, but beneath the obvious humanitarian advance lay the continuing bonds of restriction. The serfs, it was true, had been given land, but it was often of **poor**

fertility and had to be **paid for** over a 49-year period. These payments were to finance the state treasury bonds given to the original owners. Worse still, however, there was no individual title to the land, only **communal ownership by the village** (*mir*), and the **new administrative system**, the *Volost* courts, still remained in the **hands of the landed nobility**. The emancipation was an important step forward, but, as in many other instances, its effects were negated by the **short-sighted desire for maintenance of the status quo.**

The limited success and acceptability of emancipation to the nobility, who still retained control, led to the introduction of other reforms of which the most notable was the **Zemstvo Law**. This established a system of **locally-elected assemblies** or *Zemstvos*. These assemblies were again **dominated by the nobility**, but they were a development towards more representative government and made advances in improving **public health** and **education** facilities. Later in 1864, the **judicial system** was revised along the lines of the French system, in which the principle of **equality before the law**, the **rule of the law** and **trial by jury**, replaced the existing corruption-riddled system. The ***Volost* courts were excluded** and the **Tsar retained the right of special interference**, but now redress in the courts was at least plausible. Other reforms included the **liberalization of education**, within the bounds of acceptability, the **modernization of the army**, and the **stimulation** of **industrial activity** through the relaxation of tariffs. Considerable moves forward had thus been made in almost all areas of society, but the measures introduced, in almost all the instances, had been **half-measures**.

Alexander II's failure lay in the very nature of his **'revolution from above'**. Reform must encompass all parts of society and be directed by necessity rather than expediency. Alexander sought not only the maintenance of tsarist autocracy but its **extension**. All the developments or reforms he introduced were Western developments that were usually linked with the creation of at least parliamentary assemblies and, in many instances, constitutional monarchies. The reforms had briefly entertained the support of liberals but, as it became clear that these were only half-measures, **liberal support diminished** and **political terrorism** increased. Urged on by revolutionaries, writers and philosophers such as **Nikolai Chernyshevsky**, disaffection grew to the extent that in 1866 an **assassination attempt** was made on the Tsar. The era of reform ended, but populist groups such as **'Land and Freedom'**, and **'The Will of the People'** continued to thrive, even though they were unable to foment peasant revolt. Revolutionaries like

Nechaiev and **Tkachoev** inspired frequent terrorist outbursts, and in **1881 Alexander II was assassinated**–ironically, while in the process of implementing greater political concessions. With his demise, the era of reform came firmly to an end.

Reaction

The assassination of Alexander II, together with the poor results of the reforms, undermined any hopes of success that liberalism had. Instead, the new regime of **Alexander III** heralded a **conservative reaction**. Alexander III did not hold his father's belief in the need for reform; rather, he sought to **bolster the autocratic system** and to rule with **paternalistic concern** for his subjects. Western liberalism was rejected as something alien to the Russian experience and, instead, in order to safeguard the composite nature of autocratic rule under the Tsar, Alexander III encouraged a **spiritual revival** through the Orthodox Church and embarked upon a blatant policy of **repression** and **Russification**.

His aide in all these endeavours was his former tutor **Konstantin Pobedonostsev**, who became Alexander's most important counsellor and procurator of the Holy Synod, which controlled the Russian Church. Pobedonostsev, through his influence on Alexander III, effectively halted the trend towards Westernization in Russia. In tightening autocratic control, he instituted an era of severe repression in every sphere. The need for greater control led to **centralization** being the avowed aim of the bureaucracy, with the resultant **reversal** of many of Alexander II's reforms. The ***Zemstvos*** were obvious targets for this policy, and by 1889 even the limited say the peasants had was withdrawn; their representation was now to be made through a **Land Captain**, who was to be at least a minor noble. **General censorship** was imposed and the **universities** were once again brought under the control of inspectors. In Alexander III's search for national unity, all **other nationalities** within the tsarist empire were to be subject to **Russification**. The **Jews** were the most susceptible group and the first **pogrom** was in 1881. Finally, to safeguard the regime, **all political parties in opposition were banned**.

For Russia to advance, **industrial expansion** was necessary, and in this the government was forced to the limits of its paternalistic role. Two base requirements were the **stabilization of finances** and the active **encouragement of industrialization**. Here, if anywhere, liberal sentiment survived in the guise of **Sergei Witte** who masterminded the Ministry of Finance from 1892 to 1903. Witte believed in the need for **state intervention** to protect and encourage the growth of Russia's industry. **Protective tariffs** gave industry a **guaranteed home market**, and a **state railway boom** led to much **greater industrial mobility**. These measures also presented the government with revenue that was used to **put the rouble on the Gold Standard** which, in turn, attracted **foreign capital**. Although expansion was achieved, it was **too dependent on the state** and, more importantly, on **obtaining revenue from those who could least afford it** – the peasants. Witte's programme for recovery floundered, not on economic failure, but on the **reluctance of the ruling classes to relinquish any of their power or control**. State capitalism could not succeed in a vacuum. For Russia to advance, **political and social reform** would also be required.

The Revolution of 1905

The revolutionary movements which had pressured and eventually brought about the demise of Alexander II had been repressed under the subsequent tsars, but had nevertheless been continually active in their attempts to overthrow the tsarist regime. During the reign of Alexander II, the leaders had been nihilists or anarchists, but by the 1890s the influence of **Karl Marx** was beginning to be most influential. Marx himself had initially discounted the possibility of revolution in a country as backward as Russia, but towards the end of his life he had admitted that, theoretically at least, a proletarian revolution in Russia was a possibility. The 'Land and Freedom' movement of the 1870s had collapsed, and from its remains came the **Social Revolutionaries** or SRs who sought **peasant socialism**, and others, like **Georgi Plekhanov**, who sought to **apply Marxist ideology** to Russia's problems.

These Marxist ideas flourished particularly in the wake of the populist failure, and because of the attractiveness of intellectual ideology, the movement appealed to the **radical young intellectuals**. Thus, while they were not as numerous as the SRs, the **Marxists were potentially more dangerous**. The final moulding of Russian Marxism into a potent movement took place under the leadership of one Vladimir Ilyich Ulyanov who took the pseudonym of **Lenin**. Lenin came from a middle-class background, but both his university education and the execution of his brother convinced him of the need for revolution along Marxist lines. He had the twin skills of **intellectual ability** and **organizational flair**, and, armed with these, he gained control of the Marxist Social Democratic Party. At its 1903 Congress in exile in Brussels, his demand for revolutionary activity through the party leadership split the party into **Bolsheviks** (Russian for majority) and **Mensheviks** (minority). The **Bolsheviks** under Lenin, saw **revolution as an absolute necessity**, while the **Mensheviks** were willing to accept a **progression to parliamentary democracy**. Together they were still far smaller than the SRs but their organization and discipline would, in the end, prove the more effective.

While the revolutionary groups sought to overthrow the tsarist regime, there always remained a significant group of **liberals** who simply sought a **constitutional monarchy**. Their objective required **development** rather than **revolution**, yet even minimal advances in this direction were **rejected** both by the **Tsar** and his **advisers**, who saw in any delegation of authority the seeds of their own destruction. Thus, by 1904, a whole series of groups found themselves directly opposed to the obstinacy of the government: the **urban workers**, because of low wages and poor working conditions, the **peasants**, because of continuing malpractice by the nobles, and almost all **politically active groups** because of their inability to influence government decisions. A series of **strikes** in 1903 gave ample warning of the discontent, but instead of constructive action the government response was renewed **repression**. The answer, it was decided, would be a **stirring national victory** similar to that over the Turks in 1877, the occasion this time being provided by Japan, which was in dispute over Manchuria, an area threatened by Russian expansion.

Japan was a developing power, but it was not expected to be able to stand up to the might of imperial Russia. However, when hostilities broke out in February 1904, it became clear that, far from being defeated, Japan had become a major power herself. **Port Arthur** fell with alarming ease to the Japanese forces, and **Russian forces** on both land and at sea were **heavily defeated** at **Mukden** and **Tsushima** respectively. A war that had been unpopular from the beginning now focussed attention on the failings of the Tsar and his government, and the strength of this feeling was highlighted in July with the **assassination of the Minister of the Interior, Plehve**.

Even though Plehve's successor responded to the mounting pressure to call a *Zemstvo* congress, the Tsar chose to **ignore calls for more representative government**, and the momentum for action built up. Finally, in January 1905, the revolution was precipitated when **troops fired on a workers' protest group** trying to present their demands to the Tsar in his winter palace in St Petersburg. Several hundred demonstrators were killed in what became known as Bloody Sunday, and its effect was to plunge Russia into months of **strikes**, **provincial riots** and **general disorder**. In February the Tsar's uncle, the Grand Duke Sergei, was **assassinated** and, with the Japanese war obviously lost, June saw the **mutiny** of the battleship *Potemkin*. In July a **peasant union** was formed and October saw the formation of **workers' councils** or *Soviets* and a **general strike**.

The government was now powerless to deal with the revolution by force, so, through the wise council of Witte, who had returned from concluding peace with Japan, the Tsar agreed to **legislative government** through a decree known as the **October Manifesto.** The promise of full civil liberties and the election of a Russian Parliament, the Duma, was enough to satisfy the liberals, and the **revolutionary cohesion disappeared**. The initial promise of the October Manifesto led the St Petersburg Soviet to call an end to the general strike, but when Poland was not granted the same autonomy as Finland, a sympathy strike gave Witte the opportunity to **reimpose the Soviet's control**. The government declared **martial law in St Petersburg** in December, and most of the leaders of the Soviet were arrested. Elsewhere, peasant risings were put down, and by the time the first Duma met in May 1906, **government control was complete**.

The failure to reform 1906–17

Witte's reward for saving the Tsar from his own inabilities was his dismissal as a result of conservative pressure in May 1906. At the same time the true power of the **Duma** was made apparent with the issuing of the **Fundamental Laws**. Through these the Tsar retained **complete control** over the **executive** and **armed forces**; **legislative power** was to be shared between the **Duma** and the **Imperial Council**; and the government was to be able to **rule by decree** when the Duma was not in session. In April, therefore, when the first **Duma** met, it was thought too radical, dominated as it was by Constitutional Democrats or Cadets, and this led to its early dissolution in July. By the time of the second Duma in February 1907, the number of liberals had been reduced, but again it proved too radical and lasted only until June. Now the government, certain of its strength, **changed the electoral laws** to increase greatly the representation of the propertied classes, with the result that the third Duma–called in November 1907–had a conservative majority, as did the final Duma which was called in 1912. The Duma was not there simply to **rubber-stamp the tsarist policy**; on occasions it voiced united criticism, but its powers were limited and its influence regulated.

The key figure to emerge during this period of semi-constitutional rule was **Peter Stolypin** who, as Prime Minister, set about rebuilding the power of the Tsar. He was **authoritarian** but also a **nationalist** who believed that the key to Russia's problems was the **removal of discontent**. The **rounding-up** and **exile** of the **Soviet leaders** and hundreds of field **court-martials** made Stolypin hated, but he also attempted to **create opportunity for both the peasants and the urban workers**. Peasants were given the opportunity to leave the communes and to consolidate their holdings. It was also hoped that the urban workers would benefit from the industrial growth brought about by further foreign investment and the need for Russia to be in a state of much better military preparedness. However, Stolypin's success made him a **target** for both the **revolutionaries** and other **tsarist ministers** jealous of his power, and it was not surprising that his **assassination** in 1911 was linked both to the 'SRs' and the tsarist secret police.

In 1914 Russia's internal problems again took second place to **war**, which once more offered the opportunity for **diversionary glory**. Yet again, however, while the Tsar could bask in the glory of a possible victory, he would also have to shoulder the blame for defeat. His government, now without a capable Prime Minister and increasingly open to the influence of the reckless Rasputin, was almost universally reviled, and at the same time the economic boom appeared to be coming to an end. **Success in the war** would possibly **alleviate the discontent** and **unite** the people, but **failure** could once again **spark off the revolt** as it had done in 1905.

Summary

Russia's problem throughout the late nineteenth and early twentieth century was that of **bringing itself into line with the economic advances of the other Western nations**, while at the same time **maintaining tsarist rule**. However, this was at best difficult and at worst impossible. To bring about **industrial development without political or social reform** was to attempt to achieve what **no other Western nation had been able to do**, and, in the final analysis, the tsarist regime made a noose for its own neck.

Chapter 8
The Origins of the First World War

Introduction

The outbreak of war in 1914 plunged Europe into four years of armed conflict in which over 10 million lost their lives. The war was largely a European affair but also involved the colonial possessions of the powers, and, in the final stages, also the United States. It was, in many ways, the war that nobody wanted but which everybody expected, and, as with most other wars, long-term causes created the atmosphere in which it could take place and short-term causes precipitated the actual conflict. The question of who was responsible and how important the individual causes were remain matters of considerable debate amongst historians.

Nationalism and militarism

Although World War I can be looked at as a progression of disputes and friction between the major powers, their actions can also be seen as a response to, and as a result of, the dominant spirits of the age. Of these the most potent and influential were **nationalism** and **militarism**, both of which provided conditions conducive to the development of conflict. **Nationalism** had been a major force in the nineteenth century, either allied with liberalism or by itself. **Italy's and Germany's success** in achieving their national self-determination acted as a **guiding beacon to others who had yet to achieve national unity**. However, at the same time, the **established nations** sought to enhance their position by **acquiring colonial possessions**.

By the twentieth century the power of **nationalism**, fuelled by **urbanization** and **increased literacy**, was **challenging the autocratic regimes within Europe.** Political and social developments in the rest of mainland Europe were combined with the ideas of a **racial legacy**. The Germans could stress the importance of the Germanic race and the English the superiority of the Anglo-Saxon, but equally the Slavs and Serbs could see their common racial background as a uniting factor.

For the Germans, nationalistic feeling under Bismarck's careful handling had been strong enough to achieve unification, and now its aim was to **make Germany pre-eminent**. Organizations like the Pan-German League sought the union of all Germanic peoples, and similarly nationalistic forces, though of less persuasive nature, could be found in Italy. In **Southern Europe**, and in particular the **Balkans**, smaller national groups saw in the triumph of Germany and Italy the path to their own salvation. The volatile state of the **Turkish Empire**, **Austria-Hungary** and **Russia** made nationalism seem an attainable goal, but **alliances** amongst the powers made such moves not only more difficult, but also highly **dangerous** in terms of maintaining peace in Europe.

Closely linked to nationalism was **militarism**, for how was a country to display its nationalistic prowess except through its military might? Where once standing armies had been feared as the instruments of autocratic or dictatorial powers, they were now accepted as a **nationalistic necessity**. France, Russia, Germany, Austria-Hungary and Italy all had standing armies, and in the period leading up to World War 1, **military expenditure increased** alarmingly. With the military build-up came threats to neighbouring countries, who responded if they could. Britain did not share the same concern for having a conscripted army, but it saw as dangerous the expansion of German sea power. Thus, during the pre-war period, a **naval race** developed which was based on the building of the new super battleships of the Dreadnought class. Not only was the cost very high, but when war eventually came, they were to play a very minor role.

The significance of the military build-up, however, was that with it came not only an implicit threat, but also a publicized threat. Books such as *Germany and the Next War*, published by General von Bernhard in 1908, did much to heighten tension and to create an aura of inevitability about conflict. As each country secured its own interests to the best of its ability, a web was woven that implicated all the major European powers in an incident that twenty years earlier would have been of isolated interest.

Diplomacy

Having achieved German unification, after the Congress of Berlin **Bismarck** followed a policy of **creating alliances to safeguard Germany's position**. In particular, he wished to ensure that **France remained isolated** and that Germany remained allied with the other powers to create balance. For Bismarck the worst possible scenario was that of France and Russia in alliance. To prevent this he obtained

Russian neutrality through, firstly, the **Dreikaiserbund** and then the **Reinsurance Treaty**.

When Bismarck fell from power in 1890, however, this careful balance was ignored, and instead Kaiser William II announced a **new course for German foreign policy**. This new era was to be one of *Weltpolitik* or World Policy in which the stress was to be on **German imperialism**. No longer was Germany to continue the 'Continental' policy of Bismarck – it now reserved the **right to become involved in any sphere in the interests of Germany and the German Emperor**. The effects of this change on Germany's relations with the other powers were both immediate and dramatic. For **Austria-Hungary**, **alliance with Germany** was both logical and necessary in view of its otherwise isolated position but any additional alliance was fraught with complications. **Russia**, with which Bismarck had fostered friendship, was ignored when it attempted to renew the Reinsurance Treaty in 1890. Russia, now without an ally, looked towards France, which was in a similar predicament, and in August 1891 **republican France and tsarist Russia** signed the **Franco – Russian Entente**. This was followed in January 1893 by a formal alliance. The so-called 'nightmare coalition' feared by Bismarck became a reality.

Of the remaining powers, **Italy had joined Germany and Austria-Hungary** to create the Triple Alliance in 1882, but this was a **defensive** agreement and it was hard to imagine that the Italians would fight on the side of their long-time oppressors. They had only agreed to be included because they were afraid of French expansion in North Africa. The Treaty, although it was not made known until after the war, contained the proviso that in no circumstances would action be taken against Great Britain. **Britain** itself remained at this stage in **'splendid isolation'**, but it was becoming clear that this was at best foolish and quite possibly dangerous. If Britain was to maintain its position, it also had to seek allies.

Until the turn of the century alliance with Germany against France would have been both the most logical, natural and popular action to take, but the growth of German **industrial and naval power** was seen as a **threat to Britain**. Further, with Bismarck gone, Germany's change of course seemed to **threaten Britain's colonial possessions**. The German desire for territorial acquisitions led it to encourage the Boers actively in their defiance of Britain. Instead of gaining Britain's friendship, the Germans made Britain's alignment with France more likely. Thus in 1904,

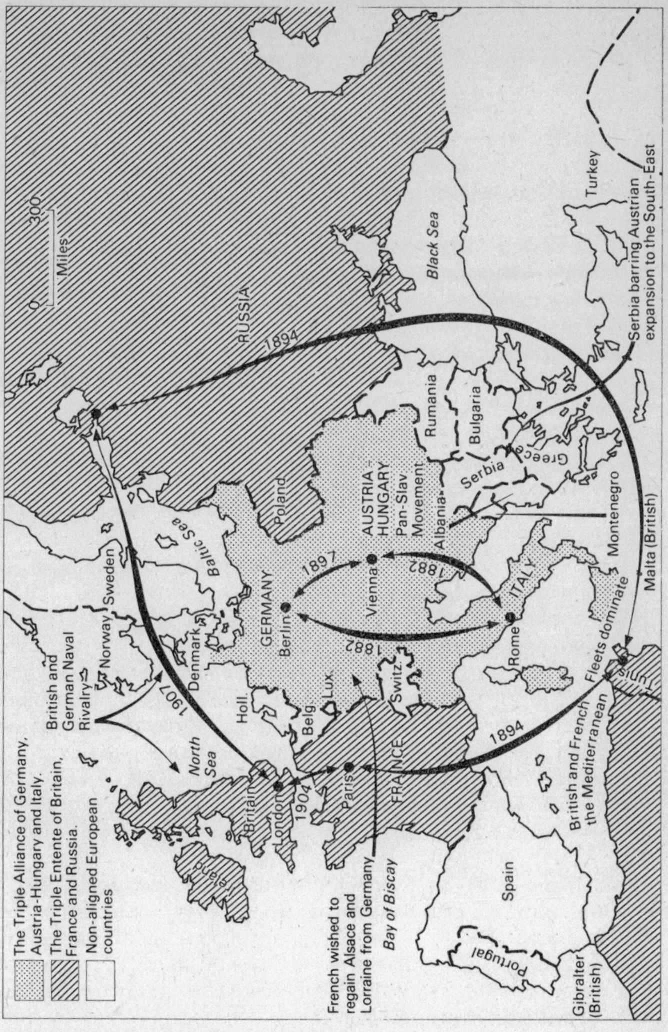

Figure 4. The origins of the First World War and the emergence of two rival armed camps

following a thawing of relations, **France** and **Britain** signed the **Entente Cordiale**. It related only to **colonial affairs** and the recognition of **spheres of influence**, but quite obviously it marked a change in policy that the Germans viewed with some concern.

To test the strength of this new entente, the Kaiser visited Tangiers in March 1905. This was a region under French influence. Here he indicated his desire for an independent **Morocco** and managed to bully France into dismissing Delcassé, the architect of the Entente Cordiale, and calling an international conference which met at **Algeciras** in 1906. At this conference however, far from scoring a great diplomatic victory, the Kaiser found Austria-Hungary his only ally – not only **Britain** and **Russia** backed **France**, but also **Italy**. The following year the worst German fears were realized when **Britain** entered talks with **Russia** and came to **agreement over spheres of influence** in relation to **Afghanistan**, **Persia** and **Tibet**. The **triple entente** which people now began to talk about may not have been a concrete reality, but France, Britain and Russia were allies in all but name.

The Balkans

Though economic and military rivalry, together with the powers' jockeying for position made open conflict ever more likely, disputes over colonial possessions were unlikely to prove important enough to provoke full-scale conflict. The German attempt to make capital out of the **Moroccan situation** in 1911, when it sent in the gunboat ***Panther***, was ample proof of this. Germany was able to pressurize France into granting it some territory in the **Congo**, but apart from causing a public outcry, this quite obviously was not a legitimate cause for action within Europe. For the powers to react, the issue had to be one which directly affected them, and such an issue was provided by the **tension in the Balkans**.

The Balkans had been a developing problem since the Turkish Empire had proved **unable to contain the nationalist aspirations** of the Balkan peoples. As Turkish control lessened, however, both **Austria-Hungary** and **Russia** sought to add these territories to their existing empires, but the clash of interests made the area the most volatile in Europe. For **Austria**, the recognition of Slav demands would, it was felt, **endanger the Empire** itself, as would **Russia's expansion** through to the Mediterranean. For **Russia** the **expansion of Austria-Hungary was detrimental to its interests**, and at the same time Russia saw itself as the **champion of the Pan-Slav Movement**. Finally, the Balkan states, of which the most important was undoubtedly Serbia, were induced by this situation to **seek the support of the appropriate power** to safeguard or enhance their position.

The first major incident which could have led to conflict came in **1908** when **Austria annexed Bosnia and Herzegovina**. This annexation had been decided as a result of negotiation between the Austrian Foreign Minister Aehrenthal and the Russian Foreign Minister Izvolsky, but the Austrians decided to act **independently** and Russia, which had been hoping to use this opportunity to end its exclusion from the Straits, was left with nothing. Russia understandably felt cheated, yet it was a matter on which it could not expect international support. **Serbia**, horrified at Austrian control of Bosnia, urged Russian action, and through the winter months of 1908 war did seem possible. In March 1909, however, the **German government demanded that Russia recognize the annexation or accept the consequences**. Russia was in no position to fight and bowed to the pressure, but a number of points became much clearer as a result of this incident: **Austria-Hungary** was now seen to be set upon the **subjugation of Serbia**, the **extent of German support** was seen as possibly leading to **joint conflict**, and **Russian enmity** towards both **Austria-Hungary** and **Germany** was confirmed.

The annexation of 1908 showed the **susceptibility of the Balkans to power intrigue**, and the seizure in 1911 of **Tripoli** by Italian forces indicated the extent to which **Turkish strength had diminished**. It was no surprise therefore when in 1912 Serbia, Greece, Montenegro and Bulgaria, urged on by Russia, joined together in a **Balkan League** to attack **Turkey**. Following a brief but highly successful campaign, the **Turks were convincingly defeated**. However, before territorial changes were made, Austria intervened and, as a result, an international conference was called in London. As a result of this, an independent Albania was created, with Serbia's reward being expansion inland. However, no sooner had peace been arranged than **Bulgaria**, disputing her territorial allocation, **declared war on her former allies**. **Romania** and **Turkey** also took the opportunity to declare war on Bulgaria, with the result that Bulgaria suffered heavy and rapid losses. By the **Treaty of Bucharest** signed in August 1913, Serbia and Greece acquired most of Macedonia, Romania made small gains, along with Turkey, while Bulgaria was limited in expansion to small areas in Thrace and Macedonia. More significantly, however, not only did **Serbia** make gains but **Romania**, **Greece** and **Serbia**, the influential countries of this Balkan rearrangement, were **confirmed in their anti-Austrian stance**.

Sarajevo

The result of the Balkan wars was, as Austria-Hungary had feared, a **strong Serbia**. It was believed Serbia could act, as Piedmont and Prussia had, to form a **nucleus for unification**. Such a Slav state would mean the **virtual collapse of the Empire**, and consequently Austria now looked for a way to **neutralize** the problem. **Germany** too was worried by Serbia's renewed threat, for it also **interfered with Pan-German designs to extend Germanic influence from Berlin to Constantinople** along the Berlin – Baghdad railway. A strong Serbia upset this linkage and allowed interference by the Entente powers. Austria could not act by itself but, as Serbian actions were restricting German plans, Germany was prepared to back its ally.

The incident which precipitated the crisis was the **assassination** of the Austro-Hungarian heir-apparent, **Franz Ferdinand**, together with his wife, in the Bosnian capital Sarajevo. Even though this was outside Serbia, the assassin, a Serbian terrorist named Gavrilo Princip gave the **Austrians** the opportunity to **pressurize Serbia**. Having first obtained **German support** for their action, an ultimatum was sent to Serbia, couched in such terms that its rejection was almost certain. A reply was required in 48 hours, and when it came, it surprisingly acceded to all the demands except those concerning the hunting-down of the perpetrators in Serbia itself. Even the Kaiser, who returned home unexpectedly from holiday, thought the reply acceptable, but Austria, determined to deal with the Serbian problem, rejected it and on 28 July **declared war**.

Both Russia and Britain had attempted to mediate, but the Austrian Foreign Minister, Berchtold, and his Chief of Staff, Conrad, were set on dealing with the Serbian problem by force. Belatedly the Kaiser, together with his foreign Minister, Bethmann-Hollweg, tried to float the idea of Austria taking Belgrade as security for Serbian compliance with the ultimatum (the so-called 'Halt in Belgrade'), but by now the military staff had become involved. It now emerged, however, that the military mobilization plans of the great powers were based on the belief that **mobilization would be general** rather than in answer to a specific problem. Thus, when in answer to Serbian requests, **Russia** mobilized on 30 July, it provoked Germany to declare war on 1 August. Since German plans laid down by von Schlieffen envisaged a two pronged attack against both Russia and France, war was subsequently declared on **France** on 3 August. Finally, with Belgium's rejection of Germany's ultimatum and the subsequent invasion, **Britain declared war** on 4 August.

Summary

World War I as it has become known, was the war which no country really wanted but for which they had all planned. No single country was responsible, although Article 231 of the Treaty of Versailles would blame Germany and its allies alone. The blame lay with them all for **creating a situation in which war could occur**. The **thoughtless military action of Austria-Hungary**, **the opportunism of Serbia, the militarism, diplomatic bungling and secrecy** of the other powers, all created an atmosphere of tension. War came not because it was inevitable, but because nobody had the power or foresight to be able to stop it.

Chapter 9
The Peace Treaties and International Restraint

Introduction

When World War I ended in November 1918, an opportunity was created similar to that which had existed when the Congress of Vienna was convened in 1815. The powers of Europe were in disarray, yet through a conference such as the one that opened in Paris in January 1919 it should have been possible to have produced a fair and just settlement, and one which would have laid the foundations for the future prosperity of Europe. Unfortunately, however, the lessons of Vienna were not heeded, and the resultant settlement proved to be a **recipe for discontent** which would do much to make **further conflict** more likely.

Background to the treaties

Before the end of the war, US President Woodrow Wilson had issued his **Fourteen Points**, which it was believed would form the basis of the peace settlement. These expressed a belief in **political liberty** and **national self-determination**, and the need for an **international organization to be created to help preserve peace**. Wilson was, however, an idealist and, while his attempts to 'make the world safe for democracy' were influential, the **more pragmatic requirements of nationalism** and of the two other major victorious powers, **Britain** and **France**, led to the creation of a settlement based on harsher principles. The peace-makers were all genuinely trying to work towards a **lasting peace**, but at the same time they also wanted to **punish the guilty**. While Wilson could afford to be idealistic, the victorious European powers were more pragmatic. Democracy meant they had to take heed of **public opinion** that urged harsh action against Germany and its allies.

The conference, when it met in Paris, was the largest of its type since the congress of Vienna but, unlike the latter, it was made up only of **representatives of the victorious powers**. Thus, missing from negotiation were Germany, Austria, Hungary, Bulgaria, Turkey and Soviet Russia, which the allies as yet refused to recognize. Also to be taken into account was the fact that during the course of the war, **secret treaties** had been agreed as to the division of central Europe in the event of victory. Among those promised territory were Italy, Serbia and the Poles, while the Czechs too had believed themselves likely to benefit. Such provisions did not seem incompatible with national self-determination, but they limited the scope for manoeuvre. Actions ceding such territory would quite obviously **signal the end of the Hapsburg Empire**, but would the end of this, together with the **decline of the Russian and Turkish Empires** and their replacement with a series of **small independent states**, make for **lasting stability**?

The real decision-making at the conference could not realistically be carried out by the unwieldy assembly and, therefore, the heads of the more important countries formed themselves into a **Council of Ten**. Even this, however, was ignored, and it became a question of the three major powers: the **United States, Britain and France**, together with **Italy** and, where appropriate, **Japan**. The bulk of the negotiations were therefore concluded as a result of discussions between **Wilson**, representing the United States, **Lloyd George** of Britain and **Clémenceau** of France. **Vittorio Orlando**, Italian Prime Minister, had some influence, but Italy was obviously a lesser power. Wilson's decision to appeal over the head of Orlando to the Italian people concerning the question of Italian claims which led to the walk-out of the Italian delegation in May, is a clear indication of this.

Each of the three major leaders had a great say in the nature of the settlement and each took a different standpoint. **Wilson's idealism** had been revealed before the settlement with the issue of the Fourteen Points and he undoubtedly thought himself able to mediate justly in the settlement. The **complexities of European diplomacy**, however, could not be ignored, and Wilson became frustrated with the wranglings of Clémenceau and Lloyd George. Furthermore, his need to return to the United States midway through negotiations and the loss to the Republican Party of the United States Congress, made his position weaker than he had anticipated. The latter of these occurrences caused Wilson to include the Monroe Doctrine in a clause of the League Charter and to drop the provision for an international army, even though in the end he still failed either to get the Treaties ratified or to obtain the entry of the United States in to the League.

Clémenceau was concerned not with **justice**, but with **defence**. He was 78 years old, bore the nickname 'The Tiger' and had vivid memories of 1871. He also wanted to **make Germany pay for World War I**. Clémenceau was the most uncompromising of the three and his objective was to **end Germany's status as a great power**. Germany had held out for four years against the combined might of France, Britain and Russia – only the entry of the United States in 1917 had tipped the balance in the allies' favour, Clémenceau consequently sought **maximum security** for France and **compensation for French war losses**, and when it was suggested that his demands were too harsh he pointed to the humiliating settlement that Germany had forced on Russia at Brest-Litovsk.

Lloyd George held a position somewhere between Wilson and Clémenceau, and is often portrayed as a **counter-balance**. He had been re-elected in 1918 with the promise that he would 'hang the Kaiser', but at the peace conference he followed a **moderate line** which proved unpopular at home. Lloyd George believed that Germany should be **punished**, but in his view it was to be done **justly** and **not vindictively**. However, once punishment had been decided as a principle, the force of **Clémenceau's resolve** and **public opinion** led to Lloyd George's view becoming unrealistic. The answer to Clémenceau's intransigence should have been a united moderate front from Britain and the United States, but none was forthcoming.

The treaties

Paris had been chosen as the location for the peace conference because of its central position and facilities. The major negotiations concerned the settlement with Germany, which took place at **Versailles**, but the treaties with the other defeated central powers were signed in other places near Paris and took their names from them. Austria was dealt with at St Germain, Hungary at Trianon, Bulgaria at Neuilly and Turkey at Sèvres, although a second treaty at Lausanne was needed to deal with Turkey.

These defeated nations, and in particular Germany, had initially believed that they would have a chance to negotiate their peace settlement or, failing this, that it would be based on Wilson's Fourteen Points. When they were summoned to Paris at the end of June 1919, however, they found themselves presented with, as they saw it, a **diktat**. There was little that they could do, however – under the terms of the armistice, the German armed forces had been required to surrender their weapons and leave the west bank of the Rhine. The allied blockade was still in effect and the German people were in no mood to continue what they saw as a lost cause. The German Chancellor, Scheidmann, resigned, but the new Weimar Republic had little option but to vote to accept the treaty.

The fact that Germany had been unable to negotiate terms, together with the requirements of these terms, were to prove **seeds of future discontent**, but not all of the treaty came as a surprise. The land gains Germany had made as a result of the even harsher **Treaty of Brest-Litovsk** in March 1918 had been removed at the time of the armistice, and **Alsace-Lorraine** was returned to France. Also, much in the spirit of self-determination, **Eupen** and **Malmédy** were ceded to Belgium and a plebiscite was held to determine the fate of **Schleswig** on the Danish – German border. Many of the remaining provisions, however, seemed to Germany to be overly harsh.

France, in addition to the return of Alsace-Lorraine, obtained the use for fifteen years of the **coal mines** of the adjoining **Saar Basin**. To the German people, the creation of the new states of **Czechoslovakia** and **Poland** seemed bad enough, but in addition Poland was given an **outlet to the sea**, the Polish corridor, which **cut off East Prussia** from the rest of Germany, and included within the new Czechoslovakia was German-speaking **Sudetenland**. The port of Danzig was made a 'free city' under League supervision, and the final insult, as far as Germany was concerned, was the **fifteen-year military occupation of the Rhineland** and the **demilitarization** of a zone thirty miles wide on the east bank of the Rhine. German nationalism found such territorial impositions difficult to accept.

The **military limitations** imposed in Germany also seemed unpalatable but were more easily understood. The German **army** was to be limited to a force of **100 000**, with very limited armament; the **navy** was to have **no submarines** and only **six 10 000-tonne battleships**, and the **air force was to be disbanded**. Critics in Germany noted dismally that Germany was less able to defend itself than Belgium. The need for a large naval fleet, however, had been removed due to the dissolution of the German Empire. This dissolution did not lead to the annexation of these colonies by the other powers but to a system of **Mandates** arranged by the **League of Nations**. Germany, nevertheless, **lost developing overseas markets** and valuable **trading rights**, particularly in China.

The final provision of the Treaty, however, was for Germany the most abhorent of all. This was Article 231, the famous **war guilt** clause. The wording of this clause, as it appeared in the Treaty, **laid the blame for starting the war on Germany and its allies alone**, and as such Germany was to be **held financially responsible**. An allied Reparation Commission was set up. It finally announced its deliberations in April 1921, but by this time Germany's movable properties had been seized, as had German private property abroad. The amount finally fixed for reparations was £6600 million plus interest, a ridiculous figure which was made even worse by the fact that initial payments were to be in the form of **raw materials and manufactured products**. Not only did Germany lose lands and resources, but its ailing and restricted industries were to share what they did manage to produce. The clause was to prove not only **unfair** and an **incitement to revenge**, but also **unworkable**.

The other central powers were dealt with after Germany, and suffered in varying degrees. The **Austro-Hungarian Empire had virtually collapsed** as the war drew to a close, as the Czechoslovak presence at the Paris Peace Conference illustrated. The treaties of **St Germain** and **Trianon** signalled the end of the once-mighty Hapsburg Empire. Under the provisions of the St Germain Treaty, **Austria** was reduced to the **German-speaking western provinces of the former Empire**, now little more than a small independent republic. **Trieste**, **Istria** and the **Southern Tyrol** had gone to Italy. Austria was **severed from Hungary**, the **Sudetenland** went to Czechoslovakia and its **Slav provinces** went to form what was to become Yugoslavia. **Union with Germany**, which was actually sought in March 1919, was **forbidden**, and so poor was the new republic, so starved of resources, that no reparation payments were ever made by Austria.

Hungary too suffered as her territories were taken to **bolster Romania** and **create Czechoslovakia**. Plebiscites, though used elsewhere, were not employed in Hungary and the result left 3 million Magyars subject to foreign governments. As a consequence, the new Hungary was a **quarter of its original size** with only **half the population**. **Bulgaria** suffered far less than either Austria or Hungary, for while under the **Treaty of Neuilly** it did lose a few border regions and access to the Aegean Sea, it remained **relatively unchanged** and even gained a small area of land from Turkey.

The final Treaty, or Treaties, as they became, was with Turkey. The first was concluded at **Sévres** in 1920. It led to the overthrow of the Sultan and the rise to power of the nationalist leader Mustapha Kemal. He rejected the terms of the first Treaty, which would have ended all Turkish influence in Europe and North Africa, and found the powers not unwilling to renegotiate. A brief and successful war with Greece strengthened the Turkish position, and in 1923 the **Treaty of Lausanne** was concluded. Under its terms the **Arab** and **Mediterranean parts of the Ottoman Empire** became

Figure 5. European frontier changes as a result of the peace settlements at the end of the First World War

Mandates of the League of Nations – an arrangement that was almost the same as had been agreed at Sèvres. However, Turkey **regained East Thrace** from Greece, was **freed from occupation by foreign troops** and **regained control of the Straits**, although these were to remain **demilitarized**.

The settlements worked out in Paris had involved the redistribution of territory within Europe, motivated by a desire to punish the 'transgressors'. The settlements arrived at were seen by some as harsh, but when measured against Germany's treatment of Russia at Brest-Litovsk, they seemed mild, **Germany's power had been restricted** and it had lost **thirteen per cent of its territories** but, as its economic growth in the 1930s was to reveal, this was hardly crippling. **Austria and Hungary** had far more reason to be upset by the results, because their countries emerged as mere **shadows of their former glory**. The spirit of national self-determination had led to the creation of **new or enlarged states in central Europe**. A **desire for peace** now pervaded war-torn Europe.

However, as well as these successes there were some important failings, foremost of which was the meaningless **'war guilt' clause**. It weighed heavily on the **Weimar Republic**, provoking German nationalists to **seek just retribution**. In addition, the victors, for example **Britain**, began to **doubt the wisdom of the reparations**. **France**, too, began to worry about the **victors' failure to disable Germany completely**. **Italy felt cheated** by the other powers with what it considered to be a **paltry reward**, and the **United States receded into its isolationist shell**. The promised era of international co-operation was transformed into an era of suspicion and distrust, and the **new central European states** which had been created along broadly **ethnic, not economic, lines**, found themselves struggling with little assistance. The Paris Peace Conference had undoubtedly had a difficult task, but its failure to achieve a widely accepted and just peace and its inability to prolong the momentum of co-operation made the future peace of Europe at best uncertain.

The League of Nations

Included in all the peace treaties was the covenant of the League of Nations, the last of Wilson's Fourteen Points, which had referred to 'a general association of Nations'. The idea was not new – in fact, its origin was the Congress System created after the Napoleonic Wars. However, that sort of limited association was rejected in this instance in favour of a much broader body, a concert of the governments of the whole world – whole that is, apart from the **defeated powers** that were **excluded**, **Russia**, which was not yet recognized, and the **United States** which, much to Wilson's annoyance, chose to return to their isolationist stance. The true ideals of the League were thus **compromised** before it even came into being.

The League was intended to present a **united front against aggression** by means of **economic** and, if necessary, **military sanctions**. There was to be a **permanent Assembly** of the member states in Geneva to respond to any crisis, and an **International Court of Justice** at The Hague to make the necessary judgements. Beyond this, the League also had **supervisory functions** such as the Commission to administer the **Mandates**, and agencies like the **International Labour Organization** to co-ordinate international co-operation. The League marked an **important developmnent** in the field of international relations simply by coming into existence but its success **depended on the support of the major powers**.

The **omission** for various reasons of some **key nations** was a **serious handicap** to begin with, and it soon became clear that those who had joined were **unwilling to relinquish national sovereignty**. The League began to resemble a European club, with the members uncertain about the extent of its powers. **Economic sanctions** could prove effective but tended to harm the interests of those applying the sanctions as well; and **military action** required a commitment and a resolve which in post-war Europe it was difficult, if not impossible, to achieve. Over small disputes the League enjoyed a limited success, but major issues were to prove that **appeasement was a more powerful concept than a commitment to international justice**.

The search for stability

The war over and its settlement complete; the nations of Europe were now faced with the problem of rebuilding their economies. Four years of struggle had caused considerable economic disruption on a global scale, and the war economies now had to revert to their normal format as quickly as possible. Before the war, Germany had been Europe's greatest industrial power; now it not only had to revitalize its industries but had to work in the knowledge that the majority of what it produced would, if the allies and, in particular, France had their way, go towards meeting the huge **reparation demands** made on Germany. The announcement of the £6600 million sum in April 1921 had brought about a change of government, and German nationalists felt embittered by the nature and extent of the demands. When, in January 1923,

Germany defaulted on her payments and **French and Belgian troops occupied the Ruhr**, the strain became more acute and conflict seemed likely. Fortunately, however, mainly passive resistance, non-co-operation and strikes made the action of the French worthless. At the same time the Weimar government actively **accelerated the decline in the German currency**, until the mark from a pre-war level of twenty to the British pound, dropped to 20 million to the pound.

The action had clearly failed and had created doubts as to whether the other measures and provisions of the Treaty of Versailles could be enforced, but, ironically, from this situation emerged a **true German statesman – Gustav Stresemann**. Stresemann took office in August 1923 as Chancellor over a wide-based coalition. He managed to **restore confidence**, agree to a **resumption of reparation payments** and to obtain for Germany **growing international respectability**.

For **France**, the resumption of payments and the projection of an internationally-responsible Germany was attractive, but it still **harboured fears about the rebirth of Germany as a power**. As a result of this and of failure to renew its alliance with Britain, and the United States' absence from the League of Nations, France entered into **military or friendly agreements with the smaller powers**. Military agreements were concluded with Belgium (1920) and Czechoslovakia (1924), and a friendship treaty was signed with Poland (1921), to be followed by later agreements with Romania (1926) and Yugoslavia (1927).

By 1924, however, French fears about renewed German aggression were temporarily submerged beneath a **new spirit of international optimism**. Even the French government at the time sought to solve the problems constructively, and the result was the formation of a committee under an American, Charles Dawes, to examine ways of restoring German finances. The Committee's recommendations known as the **Dawes Plan**, were to **reduce the size of Germany's annual payment** and, at the same time, to provide Germany with **foreign loans** to assist investment and thus repayment. It was again ironical that Germany would in fact receive more in foreign aid than it would ever pay in reparations, but the stigma proved more important than the facts.

The spirit of optimism, however, was still pervasive and in October 1925 the representatives of Britain, France, Germany,

Italy and Belgium met at the Swiss town of **Locarno**, where they signed a series of agreements. The results of these were a **guarantee of the existing Franco–German and German–Belgian borders** and an agreement to **take future disputes to arbitration**. Locarno, at least, seemed to settle the question of Alsace-Lorraine, which Germany now appeared to accept as French territory, but the 'Spirit of Locarno', although persuasive, did not offer any solution to the more contentious problem of the '**Polish corridor**'. Even moderate German politicians saw the retrieval of this territory as important, although not as an immediate problem. It was hoped that Germany would seek a peaceful and diplomatic solution to its disputes, and, as a sign of its restored international legitimacy, **Germany was admitted to the League of Nations**.

Continuing in the vein of reducing international tension, the French Foreign Minister, Briand, together with his American counterpart, Kellogg, concluded the final major diplomatic agreement of this initiative in Paris in 1928. Their Paris Pact was better known as the **Kellogg–Briand Pact**. Under this Pact, sixty-five states agreed to **renounce war 'as an instrument of national policy'**. The sentiments were laudable, but, as time was to tell, sentiment had little effect in international politics when it could not be enforced. The final diplomatic measure of this search for peace and stability came in June 1929, when the allies once again looked into the question of **German reparations**. The resultant **Young Plan** (named after its American Chairman) **lowered the total bill, rescheduled payments** over a 59-year period and agreed to **remove the foreign occupation troops five years early**. The Germans were grateful for the rescheduling, but the resentment still remained and would be easily revived in the next few years as Germany suffered in the economic slump.

Summary

The settlement of World War I was no easy task, but it was an opportunity to lay the foundations of Europe's future. The peacemakers at Paris had the choice of destroying Germany or showing it the leniency shown France in 1815. In the end they did neither and concluded a **harsh settlement**, but one which **did not disable Germany** and, worse **could not be enforced**. The politicians in the 1920s did their best to create a spirit of international co-operation and stability, but the failings of the peace settlement threw a shadow over their achievements and the events of the 1930s would prove to be its true fruits.

Chapter 10
Russia 1917–19

Introduction

Tsarist rule in Russia had only briefly seemed enlightened enough to propel Russia into the modern age. Ancient loyalties and people's passive submission to the Tsar made revolution difficult, but war, with its hardships and polarization of interests, had twice brought about change: after Russia's defeat in the Crimea and later in the Russo–Japanese war. World War I was to prove an even greater disaster for Russia, and as the war progressed, Russian patriotic feeling turned to **discontent**. The Tsar, as leader of his army, was responsible for its failure as well as its success. After World War I, the enormous failure, the weight of political suppression and economic stagnation all combined to signal the end of Tsarist rule.

The March Revolution and the provisional government

The **ineffectiveness and corruption of Tsarism** had been clearly illustrated in the **heavy military defeats, appalling casualties** and **mismanagement of the war effort**. Even the assassination of the ultra-reactionary Rasputin and calling of the Duma in November failed to dampen discontent, and the Tsar, guided by the hopelessly inaccurate assessments and advice of the Tsarina, did nothing to palliate his subjects' growing disaffection. The revolution, when it came in March 1917 (February in the old Tsarist calendar) was not planned, even though revolutionary activity had continued to thrive.

On 8 March **bread riots** broke out and a **general strike** followed in which the loyalty of the troops and police could not be relied upon. It was clear that this dissension was more serious than a simple riot, and political groups now moved to take advantage of the situation. The Duma which had just been dismissed by the Tsar, was in the position of being the most workable body to form a **provisional government** and this they accordingly did, under Prince Lvov. Having received the abdication of Nicholas II, they had initially hoped to set up a **democratic monarchy** under his brother Grand Duke Michael, but his refusal forced them to form a **Republic**.

Other bodies, however, also sought power. Foremost amongst

these was the **Petrograd Soviet**, a council of workers, peasants and soldiers. The Soviets simply sprang up as they had in 1905 and, not unnaturally, they sought to make certain that the **interests of the ordinary people** would be represented in any new government. If any particular group was powerful within the Soviets, it was the **Mensheviks**. In line with their belief in the necessity of creating a parliamentary system, the Soviets **co-operated with the provisional government**. The co-operation was rather uneasy and laced with suspicion, but it was also helped by the fact that a few men belonged to both groups, notable amongst whom was **Kerensky**.

However, the **Bolsheviks** too sought to exploit the situation, though their belief in the necessity of the proletarian revolution prevented them from collaborating with the provisional government. Under the careful guidance of **Lenin**, who rapidly returned from exile through Finland, they built up their organization and waited patiently for the appropriate moment to make their move.

Lenin had been surprised by the collapse of the monarchy and dismayed at the formation of the **Provisional Government**, yet he knew his followers to be the most proficient of the Russian revolutionaries. The power of the Bolsheviks within the Soviets grew as Lenin's programme (the *April Theses*) calling for an **end to the war**, an end to the **large landowners**, and **all power to the Soviets** became widely known. With the slogan 'Peace, Bread and Land' the Bolsheviks **appealed to the peasants**, and, to undermine the continuing war effort, Lenin **called upon Russian soldiers to desert**. Against this growing menace the provisional government found itself unable to settle the land problem quickly or to make headway with the corrupt Tsarist administration, and it was **committed to a continuation of the war** with little sign of victory or an end in sight.

The provisional government was, as its title suggests, only a stop-gap measure until elections could be held and, as such, its **power-base was limited** and its **popularity dependent on its ability to achieve results quickly**. The crippled state of the Russian economy and the inbuilt administrative failings of the Tsarist bureaucracy made such **rapid results not only unlikely but virtually impossible**. In respect of this, therefore, it is admirable and noteworthy that the provisional government achieved anything at all. As it was, the **eight-hour working day was established, political prisoners freed and Poland given its independence**. The continuation of the war may well have been a mistake, but if Russia wished to maintain its international respectability, then fulfilment of its alliance commitments seemed important. With hindsight, the provisional government might have acted differently, but, equally, if military success had been forthcoming, this would have given a considerable boost to its prestige and standing.

The Bolsheviks, however, were agitating to considerable effect and they rapidly out-manoeuvred their rivals, the Mensheviks and SRs, through calls for a **proletarian revolution** and by the attractiveness of their **land provision programme** to the peasants. The continuing military failures increased discontent, but a revolt in July, the so-called **July Rising**, was not Bolshevik-led, only Bolshevik-inspired. The **soldiers** and **workers** led a **premature revolt** against the government but Lenin had gauged that the time was not yet right. The rising was put down quickly and, although they were not directly responsible, the **Bolsheviks were held responsible** and were virtually proscribed. Lenin fled to Finland, Trotsky was arrested and the other leading figures went into hiding. However, the Provisional government also underwent changes and Kerensky, a leading figure already, became its head.

Kerensky was well aware of the danger the Bolsheviks presented, but the damage was too serious and the Provisional Government had failed to win the necessary support it needed to stay in control of the situation. This was clearly illustrated when, following the fall of Riga, **General Kornilov attempted to march on St Petersburg** in September. Kerensky was forced to **call on the Bolsheviks** and their militia, the **Red Guards**, to defeat Kornilov, which they achieved mainly through agitation. For Kerensky the situation was becoming hopeless. He was under pressure from both right and left, and his power was based on little more than respect. With the Bolsheviks building on continued success, only the **timing** of their action seemed uncertain, but here again Lenin's preparation proved brilliant.

It was clear that, for however much longer the Bolsheviks built up their support, they would **not obtain majority popularity**. Lenin, therefore, had decided to **seize power in a *coup***. This was successfully engineered in the early hours of **7th November** when Bolshevik forces seized the key installations in Petrograd and captured or drove out the members of the Provisional Government. The other groups were stunned by the effectiveness of the Bolshevik move and were out-manoeuvred by the stance which Lenin took at the Congress of Soviets that afternoon when he **nominally transferred power from the Provisional Government to the Congress**. In reality, however, the **Congress was forced to accept a Council of Commissars composed of the top Bolshevik leaders**. It was not 'power to the Soviets' but power to the Bolsheviks, a point made clear by the walk-out from the Congress of the Mensheviks and the Social Revolutionaries. This was reinforced when the constituent assembly, comprising a Bolshevik minority, was allowed to sit for only one session.

In effect, the Bolsheviks had **replaced one dictatorship with another**, yet Lenin believed that the people would **need to be dictated to until their political education was complete**. Regardless of this, it was a government which kept its word. **Land was siezed from private landowners, food was distributed and peace negotiations were begun with Germany**. The fact that events would sour all of these achievements mattered little in these early days. The Russian people, used to Tsarist inefficiency, could not help but be impressed by Bolshevik resolve. They could, however, object to the **oppression**, particularly as administered by the State Security Police, the so-called **Cheka**. Slowly, as the shock of the Bolshevik takeover passed, **opposition** to their rule began to emerge and organize, and the relatively bloodless revolution was transformed into a bloody **civil war**.

The civil war

Once in power, the Bolsheviks had taken very little time to **dismantle the workings of capitalism** in Russia, and were convinced that the logic of communism would lead to **similar Bolshevik revolutions in adjoining territories**. Tight Russian control over Finland and the Ukraine was therefore relaxed. However, this resulted in the rise of **nationalist** rather than communist movements, the former being assisted in their rise by Germany.

The Germans had been amazed at the success of the Bolsheviks and reaped the benefits of their assistance to Lenin through the peace negotiations which began in late 1917 at **Brest-Litovsk**. The Bolsheviks, committed to ending the war, and responsible for the mutinous state of the Russian army, were in no position to negotiate and the Germans enforced on them by March 1918 a diktat that would make Versailles look generous. Under its provisions, the Russians were to **demobilize entirely** and to **cede large sections of land to Germany and the surrounding states**. The combined measures resulted in a loss of almost 20 per cent of Russia's territory and nearly 25 per cent of its population, with the further burden of a 3000 million-rouble indemnity.

The results of Brest-Litovsk were to bring peace, but at a price that even some Bolsheviks thought was too high, among them Bukharin. Lenin, however, was convinced that **peace was a necessity**, and amid growing **internal disaffection**, his judgement may well have saved the revolution from collapse. The conservatives and middle-classes now began to organize opposition, and, led by Tsarist officers, so-called **White Armies** began to develop. **National minorities** saw the chance to free themselves from the Russian yoke and the allied forces saw the opportunity of toppling the Bolsheviks and bringing Russia back into the war. A series of counter-governments sprang up and forces with Tsarist sympathies, foreign troops, nationalist groups and allied troops put the Bolsheviks under **considerable pressure**. At one point they held little more than the central region containing Petrograd and Moscow and the industrial areas west of the Urals, and had been moved to execute the Tsar and his family at **Ekaterinburg**. But by the end of 1920 the Bolshevik forces had triumphed and the White forces had been repulsed on all fronts.

The **reasons for the Bolshevik success** were a combination of factors which centred on the question of **acceptable rule**. The Bolsheviks may well have polarized the opposition, but they had also fulfilled their promises of **providing food and land and ending the war**. The peasants, having obtained the land, were **suspicious of the White forces**, especially since they appeared to be **supported by the Old Order**, and experience in regions under White control did not promise any certainty for the future. The creation of the **Red Army** gave the Bolsheviks a **unity** which the anti-Bolshevik forces never obtained and, in **Trotsky**, a leader who **galvanized** and **co-ordinated** them. Denikin and Kolchak seemed to stand for the Russia the people had already rejected, and, worse, their use of allied assistance **gave the Bolsheviks the appearance of being defenders of Russia**. The **centralized position** of the Bolshevik forces was a further key factor in the victory, but in the final analysis the Bolsheviks were successful because their **resolve** and **organization** were stronger than that of their opponents.

Lenin's rule

The period of civil war had forced Lenin and the Bolsheviks to adopt a **militarized policy** which became known as **war communism**. Under this, **military conscription** was introduced and **forced labour battalions** had been created to extend control over the urban workers. The peasants proved more intransigent, however, and the Red Army was forced to **requisition much food**. As the battle against external forces came to an end, Lenin was given a clear indication of consequences of the harsh conflict when, in March 1921, a **naval mutiny** took place at **Kronstadt**. These previously loyal Bolsheviks calling for 'Soviets without communists' were quickly **defeated**, but the warning of discontent did not go unheeded.

As a response to the growing **criticisms**, especially from the vast peasant population, Lenin introduced a **New Economic Policy**, or NEP as it became known. It was, in effect, a dilution of Marxist philosophy and a **partial restoration of capitalism**, the overall aim being to **give inducements to get the economy moving again**. Under the directive of the NEP, **peasants** were allowed, after paying minimal taxes, **to sell surplus crops**, to **sell or lease their land** and to **hire workers**. **Private enterprise in small industrial units was allowed** and, by 1922, **treaties** had been signed with fifteen countries including Finland, Britain and Germany. Some Bolsheviks, among them Trotsky, resented this return to bourgeois habits and kulaks, but the concessions were **cosmetic rather than fundamental**. The important sectors of the economy, heavy industry, foreign trade, finance and transportation remained fully in control of the state.

In 1922 Lenin suffered a stroke and, from then until his death in January 1924, he suffered poor health. The NEP which Lenin had created had been a transitional plan and awaited change. With Lenin's demise the **question of his successor** began to trouble the communists. Lenin had made no specific provision for a leader to follow him and no single person matched his unquestioned pre-eminence. Among the likely candidates were Leon **Trotsky**, Grigory **Zinoviev** and Nikolai **Bukharin**, with the Secretary General Josef **Stalin** as an outside candidate. However, both Zinoviev and Bukharin were shown to have no practical political qualities and popular support, and the contest was narrowed to Trotsky and Stalin. Trotsky had been the charismatic leader of the Red Army, a man of action, while Stalin had risen to the top through the Party system. Trotsky was an intellectual and a believer in the 'permanent revolution'. Stalin was a politician and the supporter of 'socialism in one country'.

Stalin overcame Trotsky for various reasons, but mainly because he put in the necessary **political groundwork**, building a base for his followers and **cultivating alliances**, and because at the time of the struggle for power he appeared the neutral, **moderate choice** whom the other Politburo members believed they could control. While Stalin involved himself with the Party organization, Zinoviev and

Bukharin set out to stop Trotsky. Trotsky found himself under increasing pressure and at the same time unable to attack the Party structure. He resigned as Commissar for War and was forced into first internal and then foreign exile. Stalin now played off Bukharin against Zinoviev, effecting the latter's demotion from the Politburo along with Kamenev's. Bukharin himself was now isolated and by 1929 Stalin was in full dictatorial control of the Party.

Stalin industrializes Russia

Stalin was clearly neither an intellectual nor a fundamental Marxist. His ability was to **face a problem with a clear-cut pragmatic solution**, unmoved by sentiment. Stalin **held no particular approach or view sacrosanct**, and this was nowhere more evident than in his approach to the **industrialization of Russia**. Until 1927 Stalin had supported the NEP, but in early 1928, as a logical extension of 'socialism in one country', he announced plans for the industrialization of the whole Soviet economy. This was to involve both **industrial and agricultural reorganization and investment**, and was extremely ambitious, particularly with its projected aim of raising agricultural production by some 150 per cent.

The **peasants** represented the greatest problem to Stalin. They comprised some 80 per cent of the population yet were the **social group least under government control**. The degree of economic control Stalin was promulgating **could not allow such independence**, nor could industrial expansion occur without an **increased and guaranteed food supply** and a **diversion of some of the labour force**. Stalin's answer to this problem was **collectivization**, which would allow mechanization and thus greater efficiency. In 1928, over 25 million peasant holdings existed and on some holdings the kulaks made profits they were unwilling to give up easily. Stalin tried reason, inducements and penalties to force collectivization through, but if this failed he was quite prepared to send in **OEPU squads** and even the **Red Army**.

Destruction of stock by the kulaks, forced labour camps and famine made the transition a costly one, with over 5 million deaths. By World War II, however, Russia had a **stable, expanding and increasingly productive state-controlled agricultural system** which sold 90 per cent of its produce to the State. Over 25 million peasants had been freed to work in **industry**, and it was now **relatively easy for the State to control the peasantry**. Stalin also made slight concessions to the new collective farms, the *kolkhozes* by allowing them to be run as **joint collectives**, receiving a share of the profit, but the

machinery stayed in the hands of the State and this relaxation was a mere shadow of what had existed under the NEP.

In terms of **industrial expansion** the abandonment of the NEP in 1928 coincided with the creation of a **Five Year Plan** which laid down **production targets** and **penalties for failure**. The targets were often set ridiculously high, but the idea captured the imagination of the people who were also driven on by fear of failures and the lure of rewards for success. The problems of inexperienced managerial staff, a lack of skilled workers, supply of raw materials, transport delays and world-wide economic depression, all worked against the Plans but, by the outbreak of World War II, **production in all the key areas of the economy had made startling progress**–for example, electricity, coal and steel production had all more than quadrupled since 1928.

For the ordinary people the rewards were slight in terms of wages, but the **rebirth of pride** and the **cohesion of the Soviet Union's force** had begun. As always, individual people benefited the least–the welfare of the State was more important–but the quality of life did improve. The **health education service** grew, **trade unions supervised labour codes**, and **care for the aged and sick** was made statutory by the 1936 Constitution. The Soviet economy after 1928 bore little resemblance to that which had existed prior to the war, and while it was easy to question Stalin's **methods** and the **human cost**, the achievement in economic terms was colossal.

Stalin: political rule

Stalin had risen to power by exploiting the weaknesses of his opponents, isolating them and disposing of them. His position by 1929 was supremely **secure**, yet he still insisted on unquestioned obedience and became **obsessed with rooting out those disloyal to himself and the State**. This obsession had been instrumental in causing his wife's suicide in 1932, but it reached its peak following the assassination of one of Stalin's chief deputies, Sergei Kirov, in December 1934. The immediate response was an NKVD crackdown or **purge** in which thousands were deported from Russia, but the following year a massive **purge of party members at all levels** began to take place. At risk, in particular, were those who had been **members of the Bolshevik party in Lenin's day**, the figures who were the **natural heirs in the event of Stalin's death**.

The extent of the purge increased as Stalin began to allow his paranoia to subvert his reason. The old Bolsheviks, steeled to support the revolution, proved unable or unwilling to oppose Stalin and appeared only too willing to confess their guilt. They were even paraded in show trials to publicize their guilt.

In this way fell, among others, **Zinoviev and Bukharin**. The **fear and paranoia thus created permeated the whole of Soviet society** and in 1937 the **army** came under scrutiny, with the subsequent removal of over three-quarters of the high-ranking officers. Towards the end of 1938, the pace began to ease and the removal of the NKVD Chief, Yezhov, marked the end of the great purge, though other purges would occur after the war.

Whatever the rationale behind Stalin's moves, the purges confirmed his position as **absolute ruler** but did little to further the Soviet cause. Ironically, in the middle of the purges, Stalin installed a **new Soviet Constitution** which included written guarantees of human liberties. It specified the **nomination of candidates, universal suffrage and a bicameral legislative body**, which made it seem like a liberalization of the regime, but in fact the Constitution merely **defined the existing power structure**, with Stalin firmly in control, surrounded by carefully selected officials who were ever fearful of failing to satisfy him.

Stalin: foreign policy

The failure of 'permanent revolution' both as an occurrence and as an acceptable policy, had been a contributory factor in Stalin's rise to power. His adoption of 'socialism in one country' had satisfied many that the USSR, at the moment at least, did not pose a real threat and by 1924 almost all the major powers had recognized its Soviet regime. Stalin's foreign policy, however, was confusing. The **Comintern**, created to co-ordinate international communist activity in 1919, was, even in its subdued state, **pledged to international revolution**, and pronouncements about the inevitability of world revolution did little to instil faith in the regime. The 1922 **Treaty of Rapallo** and assistance to China were weighed against Soviet entry to the **League of Nations** in 1934 and action in the **Spanish Civil War**.

The purges seemed intent on neutralizing opposition to Stalin, but, at the same time, Stalin was forced to **seek unity** and preparation for **possible action against the growing Nazi menace**. The actions of Hitler and particularly the Spanish Civil War had illustrated not only the danger but also the **lack of resolve amongst the other Western powers**. If Czechoslovakia could be sacrificed with little concern for international justice, what chance had Communist Russia? Stalin attempted to co-operate and co-ordinate his efforts with the West, but his **demand for access through Poland** was one to which the Western powers found impossible to acquiesce. As a result, Stalin countered by concluding the unlikeliest of alliances in August 1939 – the **Nazi – Soviet Non-Aggression Pact**. For Stalin, the deal bought both **time and some Polish territory**, but it was obvious that the two states were uneasy partners. In June 1941 Hitler fulfilled his plan of invading the USSR, but **Operation Barbarossa** was to prove his downfall, not Stalin's. For Stalin, the patriotic call would **revive his popularity, confirm the strength of the communist structure** and provide, in the post-war years, the **opportunity for expansion**.

Summary

Between them, Lenin and Stalin created, moulded and established the communist state in Russia. Without Lenin's charismatic figure, organizational flair and unswerving belief, Bolshevism might well have failed. His **perception** and **leadership** provided the base, and it was left to Stalin to **add permanency to the structure** and to force the Soviet Union through an **industrialization** programme that would ensure its survival. Another less dictatorial, more humane approach might have achieved the same ends, but it may equally be true that without Stalin's efforts, communism might have floundered, or alternatively internal dissension might have ensued. Such internal unrest could well have enabled Hitler to bring about the downfall of the Soviet Union.

Chapter 11
Mussolini and Italian Fascism

Introduction

The latter half of the nineteenth century had seen the divorce of liberalism and nationalism, with the military aspects of the latter being exploited to gain independence, most notably in the case of Germany. The continued **failure of liberalism** in the early twentieth century to satisfy **middle-class fears** about **economic stability** and **political control** allowed **nationalism to develop** further into its most extreme form, **Fascism**. This was to prove the only new ideological and political movement of the post-war decade, even though its component elements were not new. It made its first appearance in Italy.

Problems of the Italian state

Fascism developed out of a rejection of liberal ideas which, in Italy, began even before Italy's entry into the war. The dominant political figure, **Giovanni Giolitti**, had enraged the nationalists firstly by his collusions with the Socialist Party and then by leading the lobby in favour of Italy's **neutrality** in the war. Following a concerted press campaign in favour of Italy's intervention and after several street demonstrations in support of this, the Italian Parliament finally committed itself to entry on the side of Britain, France and Russia. That Giolitti had been right to advise against intervention was shown in 1919 when Italy considered the resulting gains and losses. The nation had **lost half a million people, industrial production was down 25 per cent**, the **war debt** was enormous and the only territorial gains were **Istria** and **the Tyrol**.

In the new post-war Italy, the ghost of **Italian failure in the war clouded the future**. Military failure at **Caporetto** might have been balanced by the success of **Vittorio Veneto**, but public opinion was totally unimpressed by the gains made by Italy in the peace settlement. Italy appeared to have been snubbed by its allies, and, in particular, the failure to obtain the Italian-speaking town of **Fiume**, which went to Yugoslavia, outraged Italians. **Orlando** proved a casualty of this outrage and, worse, in an era of political uncertainty, the government allowed the nationalist poet **Gabriele D'Annunzio to seize Fiume with his volunteer force**. Not only did the government fail to stop him from organizing the venture, but they proved unwilling or unable to dislodge him, thus **giving encouragement to other nationalist groups through their inaction**.

The lack of government control stemmed, in part, from a **failure to solve the economic problems** which had been exacerbated by the demands of a **war economy**. In its wake came **unemployment**, high **inflation** and clear indication of the basic faults of a **backward economy**. The war acted as a catalyst for **discontent, strikes** and **street demonstrations**. Socialist agitation ran largely within the confines of democratic convention, but, to the nationalists, the threat of revolution appeared real and popular support began to swell for measures that would bring a **return to order**.

Mussolini and the growth of Fascism

The failure of the **socialists** to gain power or successfully to influence the nature of government action led to **nationwide frustration and disillusionment** among supporters of socialism. The time appeared ripe for a new approach, and in early 1919 a former socialist, **Benito Mussolini**, created a new group called the *Fascio Italiano di Combattimento* which evolved into the **Italian National Fascist Party**. They did not come into being with a distinct ideology; rather, they developed an ideology as a **pragmatic response** to the problems they felt Italy was facing. At first this appeared to be an attempt to combine nationalism and socialism, but initial failure to capture popularity amongst the masses led it to evolve along more **nationalistic** lines.

The Fascists had no clear ideology or programme of measures; instead, they wove pronouncements and policies around a number of central ideas or themes. Of paramount importance was **national unity**, for, if Italy was to be great again, there must be **no class conflict**. Allied to this was **reverence for Italian culture and national institutions** which confirmed the individuality and greatness of Italy. To be recognized internationally, Italy also had to **expand** and **spread her influence through the Mediterranean**, therefore the **state had to be strong**. Belief in the **supremacy of the state over the individual** had to be accepted as the only true form of patriotism. Finally, all this could not be achieved without recourse to **violence**, and Fascism held that not only could violence be **creative** but, further, that in its proper context it was **morally desirable**.

In the period of public disorder, confusion and disillusionment after the war, the **order** suggested by Fascism was an attractive proposition, especially to the **middle and landowning classes**, who saw in socialism the seeds of revolution. Mussolini's ***fascisti* squads** began a campaign of **strong-arm tactics against the socialists**, and because of their tight organization and mobility, they were seen to be very effective. Socialist syndicates, newspapers and leading spokesmen all became targets for Fascist action, and with their success came support from the landowners and middle classes. Even Mussolini was surprised at the **growth of Fascist support**, especially in the agrarian areas, but through the numerous financial donations, his public appearances and oratory, and through his editorship of *Il Popolo d'Italia*, Mussolini both preserved his position as mentor of the Fascist movement and established himself as a national figure.

Fascism in power

The return of **Giolitti** to power in the summer of 1920 marked an attempt to bring some return to order, but gifted politician though he was, Giolitti could not manage to find a **workable compromise** to satisfy all the parties. Some socialists, in fact, alarmed by the failure of the government and of the growth of Fascism, formed the **Italian Communist Party** in early 1921. Giolitti's response was a last attempt, following the general election of May 1921, to restore the authority of the state through a **coalition** of Liberals, Nationalists and Fascists. The Fascists gained a respectable 35 seats, but the coalition failed and Giolitti resigned. He was replaced by **Bonomi**, who, in turn was replaced by **Facta**. The governments were becoming increasingly unable to deal with the situation, and at the same time it was becoming clear that the **Fascists represented a danger to the constitution**. Bonomi had attempted to curb their actions, but failed, and Facta proved ineffectual. Strikes by the socialists allowed Fascist influence to grow through threats to, and action against, the Socialists, because the Fascists seemed to restore order.

In October 1922 came the opportunity for the Fascists to assume power when, in a show of strength and solidarity, **Mussolini challenged the government** either to solve Italy's problems or to allow the Fascists to do so. Facta's feeble government resigned and Mussolini's followers launched a '**March on Rome**'. Unwilling to grant special powers to Facta to deal with the Fascists, the King, **Victor Emmanuel III**, decided to try to avert civil war by **appointing Mussolini Prime Minister**. Mussolini was summoned from Milan and what could well have been his political suicide was his greatest triumph. The mere threat of the 'March on Rome' and doubts about the loyalty of the army had allowed Mussolini to be successful. The inability of any other politician to present a credible alternative had ensured a large degree of **popularity**, and undoubtedly many people welcomed the prospect of a **return to order**.

At first sight, Mussolini appeared to have taken heed of calls for national conciliation, for his first Cabinet contained only four Fascist ministers and he had made the wise decision of appointing General Diaz, the hero of Vittorio Veneto, head of the War Office, thus gaining the support of the army. However, the seeds of **dictatorship** were already being sown: Mussolini forced the parliament to give him power to **rule by decree** for one year and **converted his Fascist Blackshirts into a national militia**. In 1923 the electoral system was changed by the **Acerbo Law** which laid down that the party which obtained the largest number of votes above 25 per cent of the total would obtain two-thirds of the parliamentary seats. In the 1924 elections, the Fascists, through various overt means, obtained such a majority and the foundations of the Fascist state were laid.

In June 1924, however, Mussolini was severely shaken when his leading Socialist opponent, **Giacomo Matteotti**, was murdered. While the murder could not be directly linked to Mussolini and the Fascists, they were obviously the only ones who could benefit from such action, and a **public outcry** occurred. Mussolini was forced to admit a moral responsibility for the Matteotti murder, but his opponents failed to make the necessary political capital out of it and their brief unity quickly disappeared. The **Aventine Secession**, as the opponents' walk-out from parliament was known, was to prove their last major move against the Fascists, for in the latter half of 1925 Fascists were appointed to all major positions, and at the end of 1926 all **political opposition was outlawed**. After 1928 the Fascist Grand Council presented the electors with a **list of approved candidates** (all Fascists) and all the electors could do was accept or reject the list.

Fascist government

Fascism was, by its very definition, a movement of **unswerving belief in a nationalist goal**. **Order** and **obedience** dictated success, efficiency might be a by-product but was, more often than not, a casualty of Fascism. Mussolini's dictatorship was necessary for a strong Fascist Party, but its danger is exemplified by the slogan 'Mussolini is always right'. **Censorship, repression and persecution** led to a waste of talent in the economy, and the **propaganda** which espoused a belief in the efficiency and vitality of the Italian economy served only to mask reality. Worse, the Fascists, in particular Mussolini, began to believe their own propaganda!

Many of Mussolini's achievements were either isolated or prestigious feats. Making the trains run on time was laudable but not the key to economic stability. What was required was an overall plan; what occurred was a **piecemeal development, unco-ordinated and laced with corruption**. The idea of the **corporate state** with separate economic corporations appeared to be an answer to industrial unrest, since it replaced conflict with partnership, but the restrictions it imposed, particularly on the trade unions, were in fact aimed at **controlling possible opposition**.

Mussolini desired, in his search for national greatness, to make Italy **self-sufficient**, but again this clashed too often with a **desire for greater prestige**. Thus, when the lira was in difficulties during the mid-1920s, the response was to **revalue** it at far too high a rate. The effect was to **make Italian exports even less competitive** than they had been before. The building of **motorways** (autostradas) and the **electrification of Italian railways** were two of the most impressive achievements, but their aims were as much **military** as **economic**.

Mussolini's way of dealing with specific problems was to use the propaganda machine to the full. Thus, in an attempt to make Italy self-sufficient, a **'battle for grain'** was launched. Little heed was taken of the effect on the economy as a whole, or of the suitability of grain production in specific fruit-growing areas. The same method, when applied to the problem of Italy's population, the so-called **'battle for births'**, was less successful. To foreign governments, the Fascists appeared to have achieved much to admire. The corporations gave the **appearance of industrial democracy** and the prestige developments the outward signs of a thriving and affluent state. The reality was a **facade of prosperity held together by repression and geared towards militarism**.

One of Mussolini's greatest successes, if not *the* greatest, was his success in resolving the long-held **dispute between the Italian government and the Pope** which dated back to the *Risorgimento*. This success, which seems amazing when the Fascists' extreme anti-clericalism is taken into account, was based on a policy of **mutual benefit**. The Pope had allowed the formation of the Catholic Popular Party after World War I and it had become a powerful group within the parliamentary opposition. Through careful diplomacy, the Pope agreed to its disbanding in 1924, and in 1926 there followed secret negotiations over the dispute between the Church and the state, the so-called Roman Question. As a consequence, in February 1929 the **Lateran Treaty** was signed.

By this Treaty the Papacy was granted **formal independence** and received **full sovereignty** over a small region around the Vatican, to be known as the **Vatican City**. The Catholic Church was also given special influence over **education**, and the regulations of common law were to govern marriage. For Mussolini the **prestige** he gained, both in Italy and abroad, far outweighed the minor dissension within the Party, for here was a clear endorsement of the Fascist regime. In the 1929 'list' elections, the **Church** gave directives to its members to **vote for the single Fascist list**, but as Mussolini's policies began to move closer to Hitler's their racialist overtones created **friction**. By the outbreak of World War II, the new Pope, Pius XII, was engaged in dissociating the Catholic Church from Fascism.

Fascist foreign policy

The strong nationalistic elements of Fascism dictated an **aggressive foreign policy**. Mussolini talked of 'seven million bayonets', and thoughts of reviving the Roman Empire moved him to over-extend the limited resources at Italy's disposal. The years after World War I were a period in which British and French domination gave **little scope for Italian action**. Italy put pressure on Greece over **Corfu** in 1923 and on Yugoslavia in 1924 over **Fiume**, but Mussolini was initially either too concerned with internal affairs, or unwilling to take a risk in foreign policy.

The major opportunity for expansion came as a **by-product of Hitler's rise to power**, for, as Britain and France concerned themselves with the resurgent Germany, Mussolini sought to extend Italian colonial interests in Africa by attacking **Ethiopia**. The Ethiopians put up a brave fight but were no match for the better equipped Italian troops, who rapidly overran the country. The resultant gain was popular with the Italian people, but the sanctions the League of Nations attempted to enforce moved public opinion against Britain and France, and Italy began to **realign itself with Nazi Germany**. Mussolini believed he could handle Hitler, but, as Hitler urged Mussolini to greater involvement in the **Spanish Civil War**, it was clear that any gain would be Germany's. Unable to prevent the *Anschluss* with Austria, Mussolini cemented links with Hitler in 1939 with the **Rome–Berlin Axis**. The invasion of Albania on March 1939 was to prove Mussolini's last individual act, and when war broke out he waited until Germany appeared on the brink of victory and threw Italy into a war in which it remained ill at ease. Italian forces generally fared badly, and Mussolini, having been forced to resign in July 1945, was re-appointed by the Germans, only to be executed by anti-Fascist forces at the end of the war.

Summary

Fascism was a European phenomenon born of the **disillusionment** of the post-war period. Its **unifying nationalistic call** seemed to offer **order** and promised the **restoration of national pride**. In Italy Mussolini showed what Fascism could achieve in a lesser power when applied with moderate force. In Germany, Hitler would show what could be achieved when Fascism was applied rigidly to a major industrial power.

Chapter 12
The Weimar Republic and the Rise of Hitler

Introduction

Following Germany's capitulation at the end of World War I, power passed from the Kaiser (who had abdicated) to a presidential democracy, which had evolved rapidly in the ancient town of Weimar. Its task was an extremely difficult one: the initial aim was to **survive the extremes**, both left and right, which had been released by Germany's collapse, and, following that, to **apply the terms of the Versailles settlement** with which the Weimar government was constantly linked. The government's term of office was certain to be far from smooth and its future laced with uncertainty.

The Weimar government established

The end of World War I brought **chaos and confusion** to Germany. The Kaiser fled and was followed in his flight by twenty-two reigning princes. Communists and extreme socialists attempted to seize power, and then the coalition government of social democrats and the Centre Party, newly elected that year, resigned in protest at the terms of the **Versailles Diktat**. A new ministry did, however, sign the settlement some five days later, and the next month, in Weimar, Germany's Constitution was worked out to be known henceforth as the **Weimar Republic**. The Constitution was, at face value, one of the more progressive of its time. There was a **bicameral legislative**: the **Reichstag**, elected by **universal suffrage**, and the **Landrat**, which represented the interests of the **federal states**. The **Chancellor** and his **Cabinet** were **responsible to the Reichstag**, and the **President**, who, except in times of national crisis was a mere figurehead, was also **voted in by an electoral system based on proportional representation**.

The Constitution appeared very attractive, but within it were a number of **flaws** which would contribute to its downfall. **Proportional representation** was an undoubtedly fair way of distributing votes, but it had the effect of creating governments based on **coalitions**. Small parties and interests had a say in policy-making, and this often led to **compromise rather than constructive legislation**. Similarly, **groupings of parties within the government** produced ministers with **conflicting party interests**, which made the Chancellor's task of

co-ordinating very difficult. However, the **most dangerous flaw**, as time was to reveal, was the **power wielded by the President**. His election by popular vote carried with it the threat that he could **subordinate the Reichstag** and by Article 48 of the Constitution, the President was granted the **right to rule by decree in time of national emergency**. This measure was designed to **protect the Republic**, especially in its infancy, but it could be, and later would be, used to **undermine the Constitution itself**.

Regardless of its inherent faults, the Weimar Republic suffered not only from being associated with **defeat**, but also from the **conditions** in which it was forced to achieve success. Germany, after World War I, had experienced a **social upheaval** in which the **forces of the left and right vied to take control**. The creation of the Republic did not end this struggle. The **Free Corps**, **Spartacists** and **communists** threatened its early existence, and it was largely through **Ebert's agreement** with the army to **avoid major socialist reforms** that the government survived. The seizure of Berlin by the Free Corps in the **'Kapp Putsch'** showed the extent of the danger from the right, and even when order was restored political parties such as the Communists and National Socialists remained openly hostile to the Republic.

Economically, Germany had suffered the same disruption and wastage of resources and capital through the war effort as other European countries. **Higher internal taxation** would have been necessary to rebuild the economy quite apart from the **reparations**, but these added a further and seemingly enormous burden. The Versailles settlement and its war guilt clause had been greeted with open hostility at the time. The reparation payments and their **strangulation of German economic recovery** stood as a constant reminder of this humiliation, and failure to meet these repayments in January 1923 led to an **invasion of the Ruhr** by French and Belgian troops. The aim was to force Germany to pay, but the plan backfired both in Germany and internationally. Britain, among others, condemned the move as illegal, and passive resistance by the Ruhr workers resulted in minimal production. On top of this, the Weimar government actively encouraged rampant inflation and the French recognized they had been out-manoeuvred. The troops were withdrawn and a new currency established, the ***Rentenmark***, which was equivalent to a billion old marks. The Republic had survived, but its standing and future remained uncertain.

Stresemann and recovery

Out of the problems of the Ruhr occupation emerged the Weimar Republic's only politician of note, **Gustav Stresemann**. In September 1923, as leader of the National Liberal Party (the People's Party), he formed a government of **moderates**. They had engineered an end to the **Ruhr problem**, and at the same time the army, under **General Seeckt**, was used either to **disperse or prevent action by would-be extremist groups or areas such as Bavaria**. By the beginning of 1924 this policy had brought **order**. It coincided both with a period of **economic recovery** and a rescheduling of the reparation payments under the **Dawes Plan**. This Plan set the repayments at a more realistic level and gave the German economy a boost through an initial loan from the United States.

Stresemann was a nationalist, but he believed in building up Germany's greatness by peaceful means – **international recognition** and **diplomacy**. As German Foreign Minister he gained that international recognition firstly through German involvement in the **Locarno Treaty** and then in 1926 when Germany was **admitted to the League of Nations**. The spirit of Locarno, exemplified in 1928 by the Kellogg – Briand Pact, owed much to Stresemann's desire for Germany to win back its place in the international community, and in this general spirit of optimism Germany and the Weimar Republic thrived. There were, however, danger signs underneath this smooth exterior.

In 1925 Ebert, the Weimar Republic's first President, had died and was replaced by the old war-hero, **Hindenburg**. Where Ebert had been one of the architects of the Republic, Hindenburg was at best lukewarm to the cause. More importantly, however, during this period the **problems of Versailles** were far from solved – they were **pushed to one side**. Only one leader of a major power, Ramsay MacDonald of Britain, was prepared to consider re-evaluating the Treaty, and even Stresemann, while prepared to give absolute guarantees about Germany's western frontiers, saw the eastern frontiers as negotiable. The **seeds of discontent** were thus still to be found under the surface, and in 1929 the **Wall Street Crash** and the **death of Stresemann** allowed these seeds to ripen and destroy the insecure foundations of the Republic.

Hitler and the Nazis

At the same time as the Weimar Republic was struggling to assert itself in the immediate post-war period, a seemingly insignificant

Austrian, **Adolf Hitler**, was becoming influential in the National Socialist German Workers' Party, or Nazi Party, as it was more commonly known. Prior to the war, Hitler had been an unsuccessful artist drifting in the low levels of Viennese society. Here, his hatred of Jews and sense of German nationalism were developed, and in 1914 he proudly fought for Germany in a Bavarian regiment. After the war he remained in Munich, becoming a political spy for the army, and it was in this way that he first came across the Nazi Party. Soon afterwards he became a member and began to mould it into a party capable of achieving his dream of a new Germany. The initial Nazi programme was a mixture of **nationalism** and **socialism**, and, although by the early 1920s the Party had several thousand members, its influence in German politics as a whole was negligible.

In 1923, however, Hitler decided to take a gamble and imitate Mussolini's 'March on Rome'. The centre for this attempted coup was Munich in semi-independent Bavaria. Hitler hoped that, by corporate action including the assistance of some army elements, among them General Ludendorff, the Government would crumble. The move, however, had been delayed too long, and this **Munich Putsch or Beer-hall Putsch**, as it is sometimes known, led only to the shooting of some Nazis in the attempt, and the arrest of Hitler. However, such was the government's nature and sympathy with the ideals of the revived Germany that Hitler, having been sentenced to five years imprisonment, was in fact released on parole after six months.

The significance of this failure was threefold. Firstly, it confirmed Hitler's belief that to obtain power he **must work alongside, not against, the major forces in power** – the key was exploitation of their weaknesses, not confrontation. Secondly, it **gave Hitler** a **national platform** through which, by long speeches, he was able to **press his claim for national recognition and leadership**, and, finally, it gave him time to **crystallize his policies in his autobiographical manifesto, *Mein Kampf***. In the book, Hitler clearly set out both the ideology of the Nazi movement and his blueprint for future action.

As Hitler rose to power, his opponents and observers could reflect that in *Mein Kampf* was open and clear indication of the path Hitler took. It stressed the **inherent greatness of Germany**, its **need to be united** and the **racial superiority of the Nordic race**, the Aryan breed. The **Jews** were blamed as the root cause of Germany's problems and **communism** was identified as the next greatest threat. The

shackles of Versailles and also of the **Republic were to be thrown off** and Germany was to achieve the goal of **Pan-Germanism**: *Anschluss* with Austria and *Lebensraum* in the east.

To the German people such ideas were very **persuasive**, particularly to the **lower middle classes** who had fared so badly in the war and the subsequent inflationary period. In times of prosperity the Weimar Republic sufficed, but in times of instability Nazism appeared a **potent and effective front to communism**. The Party was projected as a **people's party** and, under the guidance of **Joseph Goebbels**, Nazi propaganda worked during the 1920s to build up a firm foundation of support. The Nazi militia, the **Sturmabteilung**, the **SA**, endowed the Party with a sense of menace and power, but, equally, Hitler played down the socialist aspects, and through **Hermann Goering** forged **links with German big business**. Hitler's own suspicions about the accountability and loyalties of the SA led him to form his own bodyguard, the *Schutzstaffel*, the **SS**, and this was put under the command of **Heinrich Himmler**. He completed the initial inner ring of the Nazi leadership.

Hitler's rise to power

The mid-1920s gave little comfort to Hitler and the Nazis. Prosperity bred contentment and an acceptance of the existing political situation, and was thus anathema to the extremist views of the Nazis. In 1929, however, the **Wall Street Crash** and the **depression** that followed created perfect conditions for the growth of the Nazi Party. The retraction of foreign loans led to a **banking crisis**, the banking crisis to a **starvation of economic capital** and **mass unemployment**. By 1930 unemployment topped three million, and in the autumn election of 1930 the number of Nazi seats in the Reichstag rose from 12 to 107. The then Chancellor, **Bruning**, welcomed the Nazi increase as a counterbalance to the Socialists, but from July 1930 Germany was ruled not by Parliamentary majority but by presidential decree.

This air of **crisis**, coupled with **concern about possible socialist and communist collusion**, was exploited by the Nazi propaganda machine to full effect. Converts flocked to join the Nazis, and Hitler's oratory and Goebbels' organization created an image which compared very favourably to the Bruning government. Bruning, aware of this declining influence, attempted to arrange a tariff union with Austria in 1931, but unfortunately, far from achieving a nationalist success, he was forced to climb down after pressure from France. The resentment over the humiliating restrictions of the Versailles settlement was thus fuelled and the Nazis further enhanced their position.

In 1932 Hitler took a gamble, based on the growing mass support for the Nazis, and **opposed Hindenburg in the presidential election**. Hitler lost, polling only 13 million votes against Hindenburg's 19 million, but the Nazi vote was double that of 1930, and against the aged war-hero the result was a moral victory. Bruning, unable to command continued support, resigned two months later in May. His successor was a figure with views very similar to Hindenburg's, **Franz von Papen**. Papen's directive was to form a ministry responsible solely to the executive, but he had little support in the Reichstag and relied solely on the President and the army, which was under the control of the Minister of Defence, General Kurt von Schleicher. In the July 1932 elections the Nazis became the largest party in the Reichstag, taking 230 of the 608 seats, but the Communists took 89, and it was impossible to organize a working majority. **Hitler was offered the vice-chancellorship** under Papen, but he was unwilling to sacrifice the possibility of total victory; he similarly rejected **a conditional offer of the chancellorship** made by Hindenburg following Papen's resignation in November 1932.

Papen's downfall had been partly caused by his moves to restructure the Constitution and partly by the loss of the support given by **Schleicher**, who now became the new Chancellor. Schleicher believed he could put forward policies attractive to both left and right, but he proved unable to reconcile the two sides. The November elections, meanwhile, had surprisingly reduced the Nazi vote and parliamentary standing, but while some felt the opportunity had passed, Hitler remained confident. In January this confidence proved well-founded, as Schleicher, unable to gain any degree of political support, resigned. Papen, still smarting from Schleicher's actions, now attempted to turn the tables on him by convincing **Hindenburg** that he should **install Hitler as Chancellor**, with himself as Vice-Chancellor. Hindenburg was swayed by conservative pressure and complied. Papen believed he could control Hitler, but, as events were quickly to prove, this was an illusion that cost him dearly.

Hitler's rise from failed revolutionary in 1923 to Chancellor in 1933 was, at least, impressive. He had **exploited the failings of the system**, learnt from his errors and believed resolutely in his ability to succeed. His **political astuteness**, in particular his awareness of the need for **popular support** and the need to **sell his policies**, were qualities his opposition never displayed. The parliamentary politicians proved unable to present coherent and constructive policies, and the conservative ruling class could find only an eighty-year-old war veteran as their representative. Thus Hitler's rise was a combination of **political opportunism** and the **failure of the system to present a credible alternative**.

Hitler in power

Hitler had come to power through conservative collusion. They believed they could control the Nazis, but Hitler was a far shrewder politician than they, and he had simply required their support to gain his legitimate rise to power. Once there, however, Hitler intended to make sure that his **Third Reich** survived. Elections were called with the objective of gaining a Nazi majority, but even with the special powers granted as a result of the convenient **Reichstag fire**, the Nazis still polled only 44 per cent of the vote. The fire was used by Hitler as evidence of a supposed insurrection threatened by communists, and the Nazis were given powers that **suspended civil liberties**. The Communist Party lasted only until May, and in March the **Enabling Act** was passed which gave Hitler the right to **rule by decree for four years**. The basis of the dictatorship had been laid. It was cemented firstly by the **appointment of Reich governors to override state law** and confirmed in July when **all political parties except the Nazi Party were declared illegal**.

The outlawing of the Catholic Centre Party was compensated by the Concordat agreed with the **Vatican** in July 1933, but the agreement was of little value. The Protestant churches, however, were treated with even less respect, being forced to combine under a Reich Bishop, Müller, who was, not surprisingly, Hitler's choice. The **Jews**, earmarked for persecution in *Mein Kampf*, now began to realize the horror of a Nazi Germany as first their culture and then their businesses came under attack. Through the **Nuremberg Laws** the persecution was continued: Jews were reduced to second-class citizens, unable to enter the professions and forbidden to marry Aryans. The concentration camps, the 'final solution', as yet remained a figment of Hitler's imagination. They came into being in the war years and testified to the dictatorial madness of the Nazi ideology.

In 1934, however, Hitler had more pressing considerations concerning the **SA**. Obtaining power was only a step in Hitler's plan; once there, he wished to **harness all the aspects of German**

society, firstly to **guarantee his position** and secondly to **fulfil his dream**. It was particularly important to gain the support of the **army**, but this was difficult in view of the vast numbers of SA who had developed as an ill-assorted politically active rabble under **Ernst Roehm**. Unable to defuse this state of affairs, Hitler decided upon a **purge**, the so-called **Night of the Long Knives**. On 30 June, Roehm, other SA leaders, Nazi radicals, and other thorns in Hitler's flesh, amongst them Schleicher, were duly assassinated. The army was relieved and took an **oath of loyalty to Hitler personally**. And when Hindenburg died in August, Hitler **combined the positions of Chancellor and President**. In a plebiscite the move was affirmed by a voting ratio of nearly 8:1.

Hitler's other major area of concern, apart from the army, was the **economy**. The Nazis had risen to power because of the recession; now Germany had to **develop a strong economy**, firstly to **maintain faith in the Nazis** and secondly to **allow Hitler to embark on his aggressive foreign policy**. Fortunately for Hitler, the German economy was basically sound, and the **'big business'** interests which had supported him developed a **confidence** which permeated almost every section of the economy. **Cartelization** and **monopoly** were openly encouraged and, in particular, **heavy industry** was expanded under the **Four-Year Plan** introduced in October 1936. Trade unions had been destroyed in the initial Nazi takeover and had been replaced by the **Nazi Labour Front**. This provided a corporate hold over the workers, but **incentives** and the **rapid movement to almost full employment** negated the possibility of any great labour unrest. **Industrial production rose appreciably**, and by the time that war broke out Hitler had managed to move some considerable way towards his goal of economic independence. Thus, with the German economy bursting with confidence, the populace supportive of the regime, and the army compliant, Hitler was ready to seek the achievement of his foreign policy aims.

Summary

Hitler's rise to power and the failure of the Weimar Republic were firmly linked to the **inability of the Versailles settlement to solve the German problem**. The war guilt clause and the reparation payments consistently dogged the infant republic, and at the time when it required international assistance it was **starved of support in an isolationist Europe**. Germany cannot be uniquely blamed for allowing Hitler and the Nazis to come to power – the allies were also at fault for creating the conditions that allowed this to occur.

Chapter 13
The Path to War: the Failure of Appeasement

Introduction

During the 1930s the foundations of the peace settlement made at Versailles were shown to be not only unsound but, worse, **conducive to aggressive action**. Germany could not accept the impositions and humiliations heaped upon it, and the Nazis were likely to respond with military action if negotiation should fail. The major allied powers, Britain and France, through their **inaction** failed to provide backing that might have made the League of Nations a success, and through their policy of **appeasement** allowed German expansion to take place. Nobody wanted a war, quite possibly not even Hitler at this time, but finally a point was reached where firm action became necessary and appeasement melted into conflict.

The failure of the League of Nations

The attempts at international collaboration and co-operation in the 1920s, the so-called **Spirit of Locarno**, were shattered by the **world economic crisis** which began in 1928. As the national economies teetered on the brink of bankruptcy, governments were forced to concentrate on **domestic issues**; thus **concern for collective international government declined**. At the same time, countries with a short history of democratic rule found themselves **threatened by political extremism. Communism** started to make considerable gains, and this in turn encouraged the development of opposition **Fascist** parties along the lines laid down by Mussolini in Italy.

At Versailles it had been envisaged that the **League of Nations** would be able to guarantee the Versailles settlement and the maintenance of peace. But what the authors of the settlement failed to take into account were the **different responses** that the threat of war could produce. In 1919 the optimists believed that the threat of war would **bring the member countries of the League together** to impose sanctions or to intervene. The conflicts, it was believed, would either be **stopped before they began** or **prevented from becoming too serious**. In practice, however, the **fear of war** actually **prevented nations from taking firm, concerted action** and led to the development of a policy which became known as **appeasement**. The League, far from heralding a new era of international government, developed as a monument to its very failure.

The first ten years of the League's existence coincided with the spirit of optimism and general economic wellbeing, and the League enjoyed relative success. This success, however, was due not to the strength of the League of Nations but to the **relative weaknesses of would-be aggressors**. Warning of this state of affairs had been given when Italy was able to use gunboat diplomacy to force an outrageous compensation over the **Corfu** incident. The illusion was only fully realized however, when in 1931 **Japan invaded China** to gain control of **Manchuria**. Japanese reasons for the invasion included concern about Russian growth and a desire for mineral resources. Their well-marshalled forces quickly overran the province and set up a new puppet state called Manchukino. The Chinese, not unnaturally, appealed to the League of Nations, which sent a Commission under Lord Lytton. The report by the Commission **recognized Japanese interests in the area** and even **recommended a large degree of self-government**, but Japan was not prepared to give up its conquests and showed its **contempt for the League** by leaving it in March 1933.

The League's **inability to prevent the action** in Manchuria and its **total failure to provide any effective counter-action**, military or economic, **damaged its reputation and standing** considerably. Worse, however, it clearly demonstrated not only the deficiencies of the League, but also the **unwillingness of its senior members to take any effective action**. This observation was not lost on certain European countries wishing to improve their post-war standing: most obviously **Germany**, which left the League and the Geneva disarmament talks in October 1933, and also **Italy**. Mussolini had not undertaken any prolonged military action during his first decade in power, but the onset of depression and the rise of Hitler drove him to look for glory abroad.

The European mainland provided little opportunity for empire-building, and Mussolini's actions were aimed more at maintaining than extending Italy's power-base there. The meeting at **Stresa** with the British and French Prime Ministers to voice disapproval of Hitler's actions was clear evidence of this. Mussolini, therefore, turned his attention to **Ethiopia**, which bordered on Somaliland. This was both convenient and a popular choice, because Italians still remembered the humiliating defeat they had suffered at Adowa in 1896. The invasion duly took place in October 1935, and the **Council of the League reacted quickly to declare Italy an aggressor and to impose economic sanctions**. The reality of the situation, however, was that **neither Britain nor France was prepared to countenance**

any effective action. Italian troops continued to use the Suez Canal, and the sanctions excluded oil, coal and steel. Even worse, in the eyes of the general public in France and Britain, was the so-called **Hoare–Laval Plan** which attempted to legitimize Italian action and conclude a territorial settlement.

Germany rearms

The League's failure was a severe **blow to the belief in international collective security**, but it had also shown the **unwillingness of Britain and France to resist aggression**. The Stresa agreement was, of course, destroyed by the action in Ethiopia, and Mussolini was pushed closer to a possible alliance with Germany. **Hitler** had spent the first few months of his time in power securing his position and safeguarding the future, but with the Ethiopia crisis he saw the **chance to begin realizing his dream of German expansion**, laid out so clearly in *Mein Kampf*. The unwillingness of France and Britain to take firm action had made it seem that the settlement of Versailles was becoming negotiable. Hitler had taken Germany out of the League in 1933 and had repudiated the reparation payments in 1934, with little reaction from the powers.

More alarmingly for France, its new alliance system was threatened by the **Non-aggression Pact between Poland and Germany** concluded in January 1934. This agreement appeared to contradict Hitler's other major policy aim ***Lebensraum***, but he was initially concerned with **restoring Germany's military strength through territorial integrity**. Hitler's first moves to achieve this came at the beginning of 1935 when the plebiscite in the Saar Basin promised by the Treaty of Versailles produced an overwhelming majority for reincorporation into Germany. This was followed in June 1935 by the **Anglo–German Naval Agreement** which allowed Germany to build up a navy to 35 per cent of the tonnage of Britain's fleet.

The final move in this sequence came in March 1936 when Hitler decided to take a gamble and send German troops into the **Rhineland**, which had been demilitarized under the terms of the Versailles Treaty. The action took place at the same time as the Italian invasion of Ethiopia, but required only concerted opposition from the French and British to stop Hitler's move. Instead the **French were uncertain** about their response and the **British openly unwilling to take action**. The League condemned Hitler's invasion of the Rhineland, but words had little effect. Though German control of its own defences was credible in British eyes, the action **breached** both the **Versailles** and **Locarno Agreements** and had important **implications for** the future. From now on **France would need to guard its border more securely** than before, and would find it far **more difficult to give assistance to its separate eastern allies**. Germany, however, was now free to ignore the other military stipulations of Versailles and turn its attention to **consolidating its position** and seeking ***Lebensraum*** in the East.

The Spanish Civil War

The **rise of fascist influence** was not limited only to Italy and Germany but permeated almost the whole of Europe. Countries such as Britain and France, with a legacy of democratic development, were able to resist this influence but the **majority of new nations** succumbed to it or to similar forms of dictatorship. In Spain the depression had originally brought down the dictatorship of **Primo de Rivera** in 1931, replacing it with a republican constitution. By 1936, however, the **failure** of successive governments and the **polarization of Spanish politics** into two entrenched 'right' and 'left' groups had created an impasse. In an attempt to overcome this, the right, led by the army commander **General Franco**, attempted to take power in a **coup d'état**. This began in Spanish Morocco but spread quickly to the mainland, where, after Franco won control of roughly half the country, a stalemate was reached. The nationalists held most of the western half of Spain, while the republicans who ranged from liberals through socialists to communists, held the eastern side, including Madrid.

Spain's position in Europe dictated that **all the major powers should show interest and concern**. The nature of their response was, however, predictable from their reactions to other crises of the 1930s. Both **Italy** and **Germany** wished to **assist the development of another fascist state**, although their aid at first was limited to military equipment. France, with its Popular Front Government, initially considered some form of direct intervention. However, it was **afraid of being embroiled in a war against Germany over Spain** and heavily **influenced by British reluctance for any involvement**; this led France to agree to a **non-intervention guarantee** in August 1936. This agreement was signed by Britain, Germany, Italy and Russia, but it was clear that the **two fascist states were flagrantly violating the guarantee** even as it was signed. As a consequence, **Stalin** felt he could not allow a new fascist state to come into existence and began supplying equipment in October, while at the same time helping to organize a volunteer force known as the **International Brigade**.

The involvement of the major powers led to over 60 000 Italian troops and a whole German Air Corps being sent; by 1938 these managed to tip the balance in favour of the nationalist forces. Communist assistance from Stalin had not been as great and had deterred aid from France. In 1939 Franco's forces saw **Barcelona** fall in January, and Madrid in March. By April, Franco was able to announce the end of hostilities and the creation of another fascist dictatorship. The war had once again revealed the **complete lack of resolve** in Britain and France to take effective action and **shattered the Franco-Russian alliance**. Stalin could hardly expect assistance from France if France was prepared to allow the overthrow of a neighbour state, and Russia was forced to consider other means of safeguarding its own security. The war had also **confirmed the growing friendship between Italy and Germany** which Hitler had fostered after the Ethiopian invasion. In November 1936 this had shown itself clearly in the formation of the **Rome–Berlin Axis**, and, as the conflict progressed, Mussolini's Italy became increasingly tied to the fate of Germany.

Anschluss **with Austria**

In Hitler's early months of power, his success with the beginnings of rearmament and the repossession of the Rhineland by the German army had been spoilt only by the **premature assassination** of the Austrian Chancellor, **Dollfuss**. This act had come at a time when the Nazis were in no position to exploit it and served only to allow Mussolini to show his current strength by massing Italian troops on the other side of the Brenner Pass.

By 1938, however, the progress of the Reich allowed Hitler the opportunity to realize the *Anschluss* with Austria (the *Gross-deutsch* dream of German nationalists since the time of Bismarck), clearly stated on the first page of *Mein Kampf*. As with his rise to power, Hitler wished to achieve the *Anschluss* through **legitimate means** if at all possible, and throughout 1936 and 1937 he had tried to bring about an ever increasing **co-ordination** between the countries. This had begun in 1936 with a friendship treaty, but, while not wishing to antagonize Hitler, the new Austrian Chancellor **Schuschnigg** was aware of the dangers posed by the Austrian Nazi Party and had sought actively to **undermine its operations**, though with limited success.

In January 1938, despite concerted attempts to come to closer agreement with the states of the 'little entente' (Czechoslovakia, Romania and Yugoslavia), the Nazi threat had grown to the point where signs of a coup d'état were emerging. Schuschnigg decided to try to **come to terms with Hitler**, but in his meetings in February in the presence of the German military, he saw a series of **outrageous demands** placed upon him. The **Austrian Nazi Party was to be freed from government interference**, **Seyss-Inquart** was to become Minister of the Interior, and Austria was to develop **closer economic and military ties with Germany**. Schuschnigg acquiesced at the time, but when he was back in Austria he spoke out against increasing German demands and called a **plebiscite** for 13 March. Hitler, aware of the problems a popular vote might cause, mobilized German forces, obtained assurance from Mussolini that he would not oppose them, and **demanded that the plebiscite be called off**. In view of the threats, this was duly done, but on the same day, 11 March, Seyss-Inquart sent a telegram to Berlin asking for military assistance to put down disorder in Austria. On 12 March German troops crossed the border and took control, the union was announced the next day, and on 14 March Hitler entered Vienna in triumph.

In a single move Hitler had added the manpower and resources of Austria to the Reich and achieved it without loss of life. The Nazi machine soon turned Austria into **little more than a province**, and the **Nazification** process swiftly **removed any possible opposition**. However, more significant than Austria's loss of independence was the **opening up of the Balkans to German influence** and the ease with which the whole operation had taken place. With his power-base now not only secure but extended and Britain and France seemingly unwilling to commit themselves whatever the provocation, Hitler felt free to press on with his demands for *Lebensraum*.

The fall of Czechoslovakia

The accomplishment of the Austrian *Anschluss* might not have caused great consternation in Britain or France, but it brought to the forefront the much more contentious question of **Czechoslovakia**. A product of the hated Versailles 'Diktat', Czechoslovakia was both the **strongest and richest of the newly created or expanded states**. It was **able to defend itself** as a result of its mountain fortification, efficient army and important Skoda armaments works. The Czechs also felt they could **call upon French support** and, through the French, possibly on **Russian support**. However, with Hitler, who was aware of the lack of resolve shown by the liberal powers so far, **such promises held little sway**.

Hitler's first move was to stir up **resentment** among the 3 million **Sudetenland Germans** and to **encourage nationalist feelings amongst the**

other racial minorities in the area. The Sudeten leader, Konrad Henlein, was briefed by the Nazi leaders and spelt out an eight-point plan in April 1938 for the autonomy of the Sudetenland. Hitler expected little response from the Western powers, but when German troops began to mass near the Czech border, the **Czechs mobilized** part of their forces and drew with them **British and French diplomatic support**. Hitler held back for the time being, but issued **secret orders** to the effect that a **military invasion** would take place on 1 October.

A concerted **propaganda campaign** by Germany against the Czech state followed, and the summer months of 1938 were full of tension. The key figures in the negotiations that followed were the British Prime Minister, Neville Chamberlain, the French Premier, Daladier, and the Czech President, Beneš. **Chamberlain**, however, was to prove the key figure and his policy of **appeasement** the basis of the eventual settlement. Chamberlain's policy was based on the belief that **Czechoslovakia was not defendable and that the Czechs should be urged to make the necessary concessions to the Sudeten Germans**. The motivation for this policy and its logic appear ludicrous now, but Chamberlain was not alone in wanting to believe them. The **fear of war**, the **distrust of communism**, the widely-held belief in the **unfair nature of the Versailles settlement** and the worries of the **material cost of any conflict** made appeasement an attractive solution.

Chamberlain met with Hitler at **Berchtesgaden on 15 September** and urged Beneš to give way to the German demands. Beneš responded by asking the Sudeten leaders what they wanted. Their wishes amounted simply to **autonomy**, and Beneš granted it immediately. Hitler, however, wanted the **destruction of Czechoslovakia** and demanded that all the areas in the Sudetenland with over 50 per cent German-speaking population should be ceded to Germany. This meant the **destruction of the Czech defences**, but, faced with pressure from **Britain** and **France**, the Czechs agreed. Hitler, however, by the time Chamberlain took this amazing concession to him at Godesberg (22 September), had changed his mind and demanded **immediate transfer of the land** instead of the **gradual transfer** that had been agreed. The outburst brought another **show of solidarity from Czechoslovakia**, backed by **France** and even **Britain**. As a consequence, a last-minute meeting was arranged in Munich on 29 September. Here, worried by how close war had come, Chamberlain and Daladier **gave Hitler the Sudetenland without even consulting the Czechs** themselves. The occupation would after all be gradual. However, territory had also been taken opportunistically by **Poland** around Teschen and by **Hungary** on the Czech southern border. Thus, even without Hitler's action the destruction of Czechoslovakia had begun. Chamberlain returned from Munich, bringing 'peace in our time', but Hitler's claim that he had 'no more territorial claims in Europe' would last only another year.

Prelude to war: Poland

The reality of the Munich agreement became apparent in March 1939 when Hitler **took advantage of a domestic dispute in Czechoslovakia** to seize full control. The new Czech President, Hacha, had sought to restore his authority by dismissing the Slovak and Ruthenian premiers. They were instructed to revolt, Hacha was forced into abdicating and the **Czech lands became a German protectorate**, with **Slovakia** a **German satellite state**. These developments caused dismay in the West, and even Chamberlain, the ever-hopeful pursuer of peace, undertook a programme of **re-armament** in Britain. **Public opinion** in Britain and France began to swing in favour of **action rather than appeasement**. In April, this mood was confirmed when **Mussolini** sought to raise Italian morale by invading **Albania** and **Hitler renounced the Anglo–German Naval Agreement** and the **German–Polish Pact signed in 1934**. The Anglo–French response was to make guarantees to **Greece** and **Romania** and to confirm a commitment to **Poland**.

Poland was now quite obviously the target of Hitler's next territorial move, following the rapid cession of the Lithuanian port of Memel which was populated almost entirely by Germans. Poland, and more specifically the **Polish corridor**, remained the **only aspects of the Versailles diktat that Hitler had failed either to overcome or ignore**. However, even with the German military build-up, Hitler still had one remaining worry – the question of **Russian reaction**. **Stalin** was as concerned as the Western powers about the **rapid expansion of Nazi Germany**. In April Stalin had actually suggested an **Anglo–French–Russian** alliance, but the Western powers' fear of communism and objections from Poland made the plan untenable. Negotiations dragged on, but suspicions remained and Poland was still determined to avoid making any concessions to the Russians. The result was that Stalin **could not gain the security he required** and developed the opinion that the Western powers would not come to Russia's aid readily if it was attacked.

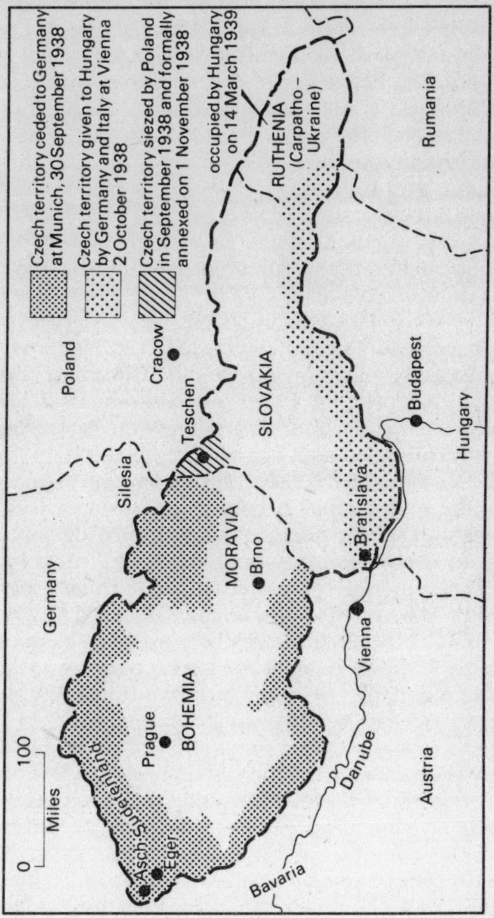

Figure 6. The partition of Czechoslovakia 1938–39

In August 1939, therefore, there began earnest **negotiations** between the two unlikeliest of allies, **Germany and Russia**. For Stalin the aim was to **gain time and a territorial buffer**; for Hitler, the necessity was to **prevent a war on two fronts and to isolate Poland**. After initial trade talks, the Russian Foreign Minister, Molotov, and his German counterpart, Ribbentrop, managed to negotiate a **Non-aggression Pact** between the two countries which was made public on 23 August, and a **secret agreement** concerning the **division of Poland** and **spheres of influence**. Poland was to be partitioned along the so-called Curzon line, with Germany gaining the western portion along with Lithuania and Vilna. Russia in return was to take the eastern provinces and have control over Finland, Estonia and Latvia. The agreement was an amazing **denial of fundamental ideology**, but it suited both parties and left Hitler free to carry out his destruction of Poland.

As a consequence of the Non-aggression Pact, Hitler ordered the **invasion of Poland** at dawn on 1 September. **Mussolini** had tried to stop Hitler by declaring Italy's unpreparedness for war and unwillingness to take action – thus denting the **Pact of Steel** signed in May – but Hitler had not been concerned with Italy's response, only with Russia's. The Polish army fought bravely but were no match for the well-equipped and drilled German forces, and fell back quickly. Despite being unable to provide any effective assistance to Poland, **Britain** honoured her agreement by **declaring war** on 3 September after making the appropriate protestations; **France** followed soon afterwards. Hitler believed that war might still be avoided after Poland's destruction, but the era of Munich had passed and the German desire for *Lebensraum* instituted the start of the bloodiest war in the history of humanity.

Summary

The **legacy of Versailles** had allowed Hitler to come to power, but the **political climate of the 1930s** and the misguided **policy of appeasement** gave him the opportunity to **exploit the political situation** to achieve the wildest dreams of German nationalism. Hitler was never really effectively opposed. Even Stalin was moved by circumstances to allow German expansion, but, ironically, far from destroying communism and imposing Nordic rule, Hitler's eventual failure left a vacuum that communism found all too easy to fill.

Chapter 14
From Co-operation to Conflict: the Cold War

Introduction

The end of World War II marked not only the defeat of Germany and its allies but also the **eclipse of Europe**. The pre-1939 power balance had been destroyed, with all the major west-European powers weakened by defeat, occupation or over-commitment, both as regards manpower and economic resources. Out of this vacuum emerged the two so-called superpowers: the United States and the Soviet Union. Though they had been allies during the war, their ideological differences could not be resolved in peacetime. From co-operation developed conflict: the 'Cold War'.

The conferences

The allied powers necessarily held a number of conferences during the war to plan strategy, and, during the later stages, to consider the problems arising from victory. These meetings concerned themselves with theory and practice, with the practicalities dominating the final meetings. Of the early meetings, the most significant was that between Roosevelt and Churchill off the coast of Newfoundland in August 1941. Here the two leaders devised the **Atlantic Charter**, which was a **liberal statement of fundamental principles for the basis of a post-war settlement**. The Charter was vague enough to avoid any firm commitment but was to prove the **guideline for many nationalist movements** after the war. However, the **Soviet Union's view** was that the Nazi attacks on Eastern Europe made **Soviet control of eastern Poland a necessity**, and vague promises of Polish self-determination would be unlikely to influence this resolve.

In **Tehran** in November 1943 **Roosevelt** and **Churchill** met with **Stalin**. Their primary concern was the **co-ordination of efforts to defeat Hitler**. Churchill, however, was already becoming anxious over the possible **post-war settlements**, especially the question of **Poland**. The Soviet annexation of the Baltic states and some Finnish territory was expected, but Churchill was worried by the possibility of handing over **Poland** to the Soviet Union, given that Britain had declared war in 1939 following Poland's invasion. However, the intransigence of the Polish government in exile in London and the need for unity forced through this **pragmatic solution**: the **Soviets** should keep the **eastern part of Poland** and in compensation **Poland's borders should be pushed west to the river Oder**. The message from Tehran was received with alarm by Eastern European states, but in view of the difficulty which Russia had had in defending her border in the previous thirty years, the Soviet demands for a sphere of influence in Eastern Europe were not unreasonable. When Churchill visited **Moscow** in October 1944, this acceptance of the Soviet sphere of influence was highlighted by his willingness to acknowledge over-riding **Soviet influence** in **Bulgaria** and **Romania** as against British influence in Greece. Churchill's belief at the time of a shared influence in Yugoslavia and Hungary was optimistic.

As the end of the war approached, the problem of **Germany** began to concern the allied powers. The question of **division** and of **reparation** was posed, though the memory of Versailles meant the powers were prepared to be realistic about this. A severe plan for the partition of Germany, the **Morgenthau Plan**, was given consideration in late 1944, but the **danger of a geographically and economically weak state in the centre of Europe** led to its abandonment. At **Yalta** in February 1945 the allies were forced to recognize that the **areas occupied by the Red Army came under Soviet influence** pending the conclusion of peace treaties. The 'Declaration on Liberated Europe', to which all the powers agreed, allowed the allies to consider Soviet occupation as being transitional, but the Soviet Union's actions in occupied territory gave clear warning that removing communist influence would be difficult. The other major results of the meeting were to: **confirm the reorganization of Poland's borders, bring the Soviets into the war against Japan, and temporarily divide Germany into four zones of occupation** (the major powers to have three and the fourth one to be French).

In August 1945 the final meeting in the war series of conferences took place at **Potsdam**, the ancient capital of Prussia, whose militarism was believed to be at the root of the German problem. In the intervening period Roosevelt, who had died, was replaced by Harry S. Truman and Churchill was replaced by Clement Attlee as a result of an overwhelming Labour victory in the 1945 British general election. At Potsdam the ideas and provisions of Yalta were developed. The **new German boundary in the east was confirmed as being the Oder–Niesse line, and the military zones of occupation were also to act as separate economic units**. The other defeated powers were to be dealt with by a council of foreign ministers who devised the peace treaties, but here, as in Paris in

1919, the 'Big Three' largely dictated the nature of the treaties. **Soviet involvement in the Far East** was again discussed, but the dropping of the atom bomb on Hiroshima both **limited the possibility of such involvement** and gave a clear indication (because the bomb had been developed in secret) of the **mistrust rapidly growing between the former allies**.

Figure 7. The post-war division of Europe

Potsdam was the last of the war conferences and, in retrospect, it marked the **watershed between co-operation and mistrust**, since, from this point onwards, relations between the two power blocs steadily deteriorated. However, there still remained, as after World War I, the question of peace treaties. The lessons of Versailles were fortunately heeded, and the **settlements again dictated by the victorious powers were generally moderate and just**. The Soviets had wished to inflict **reparation payments** on the instigators, but the other allies had managed to get this transformed into **payment in kind** rather than in the form of money.

The Council of Ministers deliberated through 1946, and in February 1947 treaties were signed with the lesser enemy powers: Romania, Bulgaria, Hungary and Finland. The changes **took nationalism into account where possible – Italy** lost a large proportion of territory to **Yugoslavia** and **Albania** and **relinquished its African empire**. All these lesser powers faced **heavy but realistic indemnities**, mainly as a result of pressure from the Soviet Union, but the provisions of the treaties were not always to the Soviets' advantage. A clear instance of this was the declaration of the **Danube** and the **Black Sea** as **international waterways**.

The problem of **Austria** and **Germany** was complicated by the fact that these states were joined and that Austria was, in many ways, a **victim of Nazi aggression**. The **occupation of Austria by the Red Army** had been followed by the country's **sub-division into four zones**, as in the case of Germany but, as elsewhere in Central and Eastern Europe, the Soviets were interested in **asset-stripping**. In Austria's case, in particular, they wanted to obtain **oil** from Zistersdorf. This Soviet concern for **economic compensation** delayed negotiations for so long that it was not until 1955 that the **Austrian State Treaty** was finally signed. By this Treaty it was **restored to its 1937 frontiers** and became a **neutral** state but one which, nevertheless, was **free from direct communist influence**.

The German problem

The central problem facing the allies after the war was what to do about **Germany**. As early as January 1943 the allies had jointly agreed to demand Germany's **unconditional surrender**, and when this came about they **divided the Nazi state and the capital into four zones**. The decisions about the **German-Polish border** laid down at Yalta and Potsdam were implemented but, once these **cosmetic alterations and provisional changes** were achieved, the question of the **final settlement** remained unanswered. The Morgenthau Plan, or some other of equal severity, would have been desirable to the Soviets, but by 1945 the other allies were in no mood to repeat the errors of Versailles. However, even Stalin, with his desire for economic reparations, saw a value in **asset-stripping** in the Soviet zone while not achieving a permanent settlement.

The **zonal division** was instituted rapidly, the loss of territory to Poland was taken into account and the problem of control of Berlin was solved by sub-dividing it into four zones. Further agreement was also easy to reach on the **de-Nazification** of the state, while at the same time leading Nazis were tried at **Nuremberg**. This underlined the allied belief that it was the Nazis and not Germany who were responsible for the crimes against humanity over the previous five years. Although unable to influence the development of the new East European states, the West was **not prepared to see the economic and political destruction of Germany**. The Soviet zone may have been beyond their control, but the remaining sectors and their portion of Berlin could be rebuilt and the German economy financed and revived.

Towards the end of 1946 the **merging of the Western Zones** took place against a backdrop of increasing East-West friction. The **Sovietization of Eastern Europe** had been feared and was becoming a reality. In **Poland, Romania, Bulgaria** and **Hungary**, the communists placed in a position of power were quick to **eliminate the opposition**. For Germany the prospects did not look good, but here the Western allies made a resolve to stand firm. The possibility of reintegrating the Soviet zones was ruled out by Soviet intransigence but a revived, if smaller Germany, was considered both necessary and important. The extent of this resolve was shown in June 1948 when, following the introduction of new currency in the Western zones, the Russians **isolated West Berlin**. **The survival of Berlin came to be seen as a clear statement of Western determination**, and when the blockade was lifted 318 days later, the **extent of the post-war split between Russia and its former allies** was clearly revealed. For Germany the division into two parts was traumatic, but a reality that could not be ignored. In 1948, work on a new constitution was begun and in August 1949 the Western sectors became the **German Federal Republic**.

Germany was always likely to prove a problem, but its eventual division came as a result of the **failure of East and West to compromise on their positions**. In Hitler they had found a common enemy, but, with his demise, the old **suspicions** were allowed to destroy the unity achieved during the war years. Stalin's **dictatorial style** and **intransigence over Eastern Europe** was certainly an obstacle to continued co-operation, but equally the allies were unable to see why it was logically necessary for the Soviet Union to be surrounded by friendly or sympathetic states. The **secrecy surrounding the atom bomb** had also undoubtedly soured the atmosphere of trust, and by the time of Potsdam the seeds of the cold war had been sown.

After Potsdam Truman wrote that 'Force is the only thing the Russians understand' and this sentiment was echoed in Churchill's much-publicized statement that 'an **iron curtain**' had descended across Europe. Britain, however, was a declining power and the **United States was now the emergent champion of Western democracy**. The war had **crippled the British economy and put its world-wide commitment at variance with its capabilities**. Thus, in February 1947, Britain gave notice of its intention to withdraw its assistance to Greece and Turkey. The United States, isolationist before the war, were forced to **reorientate their foreign policy commitment**, and from this came the **Truman Doctrine**. Not only did the United States pledge **support to Greece and Turkey**, but also to **all other non-communist parts of the world**. The Truman Doctrine spelt out clearly a policy of **containment**. Soviet expansion following the collapse of Nazi Germany was to be resisted and anti-communist movements encouraged. the doctrine merely confirmed the state of cold war.

Once the division between the two blocs was clearly defined, the next logical move was for military organization to defend the existing position. The **Brussels Treaty** of March 1948 was the first move in such a direction. It pledged Britain, France, Belgium, Holland and Luxembourg in a fifty-year alliance against attack in Europe, but a realistic and binding agreement had to wait until April 1949 when **NATO** (North Atlantic Treaty Organization) came into existence. The position of the United States as 'defender of democracy' and opponent of communism was confirmed by its role as the dominant power in NATO and strengthened further by the inclusion of Canada. The member states (United States, Canada, Britain, Belgium, Denmark, France, Iceland, Italy, Holland, Norway and Portugal) declared that **an armed attack against any one of them in Europe or North America would be regarded as an attack on them all**. But what, to the West, was a **defensive alliance**, was seen by the Soviets as **an offensive pact**, and in 1955 they replied by creating a similarly unified military alliance, the **Warsaw Pact**. The divisions between the two blocs were now not only clear but also organized.

In the **West** the structure and tradition of **democracy along parliamentary lines** survived the ravages of war, and **stability** soon returned. The Communist Parties in France and Italy grew to a strength and position they had not attained before, but socialist forces held power. The war, as in 1918, had challenged the old order but had reshaped it rather than overthrown it. In Britain, the war-time hero, Churchill, was rejected and the Labour Party elected with a working majority for the first time.

In the newly-created states of Central Europe, however, the war brought **radical changes**, as a result of **direct communist intervention** when their territories were occupied, or because of the **fledgling state of Western-style democracy**. In **Poland, Bulgaria, Romania and Hungary** coalition governments ruled at first, but the dominance of the communists was never in doubt, and, together with **Albania**, these states rapidly became subservient to the Soviet Union.

Finland and Austria managed to remain outside communist control by design, since their value was greater to the Soviet Union as **avenues to the West** than as puppet states. The Soviet-occupied zone of Germany became the German Democratic Republic in 1949, when the Western zones formed the Federal Republic. Of the remaining two major states, **Czechoslovakia's** Russian-backed Communist Party carried out a succesful coup in 1948, and **Yugoslavia** managed to set itself up as an independent communist state through the efforts of its leader, Marshal Tito, aided by the fact that it is some distance from Moscow. This independence was confirmed in June 1948 when Yugoslavia was expelled from Comintern for alleged doctrinal reasons. By 1949, Churchill's 'iron curtain' was a seemingly permanent feature of East-West relations.

The post-Stalin situation in Eastern Europe

The **Korean war** which directly or indirectly involved America, the Soviet Union and the fledgling Communist China can be seen, in retrospect, to mark the **climax of the development from co-operation to conflict**. Its end in 1953 saw, for the next few years at least, the spead of communism in Asia halted. The United States had shown its willingness to become directly involved and a position of stasis had been achieved. The confirmation of this development also came in 1953 with the **death of Stalin**. With Stalin gone. Malenkar, Bulganin and Khrushchev sought to **improve relations with the United States**, aided by the knowledge that Russia, too, now had the **hydrogen bomb**. **Khrushchev** emerged as the dominant figure of the original triumvirate and, in 1956, he indicated the extent of the so-called 'thaw' in the Cold War by **attacking aspects of Stalin's policies**. The cult of personality was highlighted and details of the purges revealed but, more importantly for the West, Khrushchev **rejected Stalin's aggressive foreign stance**, and advocated that **'peaceful co-existence' with the West** was not only possible but essential.

Khrushchev's de-Stalinization policies impressed the West but, at the same time, the Warsaw Pact had been formed and the Austrian State Treaty of 1955 should be seen against a background of Russian fears of a possible merger between West Germany and Austria. Even more telling, however, was the Soviet response to the **Hungarian rising** in 1956. In Budapest, the moderate Imre Nagy, encouraged by the relaxation of the Stalinist grip and by Khrushchev's pronouncements, began to implement anti-communist measures. Khrushchev acted swiftly and in October the **Soviet army moved in and Budapest was forced into submission**. Some 20 000 people were killed, another 20 000 left the country and Nagy was executed.

The Hungarian failure showed how finely balanced East-West relations were. The Russians under Khrushchev were bound by the legacy of Stalin. Khrushchev was more tolerant but only within strict parameters. **Hungary** under Nagy had **threatened the military and economic relationships of the satellite states with Russia by indicating a desire for neutrality**. Khrushchev could not allow this, for if Hungary became neutral, **Russia's own protection would be diminished**. More importantly, perhaps, it would be an **invitation for the other satellite states to seek at least some degree of autonomy**.

Khrushchev's handling of the Hungarian rising gave a clear indication to other satellite states of the Russian response to revisionist policies. Even the more independent countries like **Romania** and **Albania** continued to follow the Moscow line. Both of these states are further from Russia than Hungary and have since indicated their **degree of autonomy** – **Romania** through **foreign trade agreements** and **Albania** more drastically through **rejection of Moscow and realignment with China**.

The **independence** of the other Eastern European satellite states has **never been totally irradicated** by the Russians and it remains a **potential problem**. The Moscow authorities watch political developments with suspicion and apply considerable pressure which, although usually in the guise of collective Warsaw Pact action, is quite clearly Russian-orchestrated. In recent times, such pressure has usually been sufficient to obtain the necessary revision of policy but in **Czechoslovakia in 1968** the rise of Alexander Dubček saw the Hungarian situation repeated. The so called 'Dubček Spring' in which **party controls were relaxed and western-style democracy introduced**, horrified the Russians and in August 1968 Czechoslovakia was **invaded by Warsaw Pact forces**. The Czech government offered no resistance and although the Czech people attempted passive resistance the eventual outcome was predictable. Dubček was severely rebuked and the following year he was replaced by a Russian nominee Husak.

East-West relations in the post-Stalin era

The pronouncement of Khrushchev concerning 'peaceful co-existence' came as a welcome relief to the West after the hard-line statements of Stalin. In reality, however, the changes Khrushchev made were more **cosmetic than revolutionary**, as the developments in Hungary in 1956 testified. His period in power did lead to a **greater degree of dialogue between East and West** and this was particularly important in view of the **growing quick-strike nuclear capacity of both America and the Soviet Union.** The sight of ideological disputes at the United Nations became commonplace as the effectiveness of this international body became reduced to that of a debating institution, but again talk was preferable to action.

In 1958, Khrushchev felt confident enough to announce that **Russia no longer recognized the rights of the Western powers in West Berlin**, but, when no response was forthcoming, he did not attempt to press the claim. In 1960, an **American spy plane was shot down over Russia** and feeling that this incident would put public opinion on the side of Russia, Khrushchev raised the subject of West Berlin the following year with the new US President, John F Kennedy. Russian objections to the partition of West Berlin and the rights of the Western powers there werc ignored and, as a result, the **Berlin Wall** was erected.

The most serious incident between Russia and the United States came not as a result of a European confrontation but over the question of **Russian missile deployment in Cuba**. In 1962, American spy planes took photographs of missile sites on Cuba less than 100 miles from the American mainland. Kennedy demanded their withdrawal and, for a short period, it seemed possible that war would break out. Cuba was not considered significant enough, however, and Khrushchev agreed to remove the missiles. The so-called **Hot-Line was installed between Moscow and Washington** the following year to alleviate further tension but the threat was real and the fear remains.

Summary

The end of World War II saw Europe's influence wane. From being a group of powers competing on a world level, it became **a theatre of conflict for the ideologies of the superpowers**. From nationalist struggle developed the potentially more dangerous ideological confrontation of capitalism and communism, which had worked together during the war, but by the late 1940s were separated by suspicion and mistrust. The then leaders failed to continue the wartime co-operation. This either marks a return to reality of their ideological differences or is one of the greatest missed opportunities in the history of mankind. As to which view is more accurate, only time will tell.

Chapter 15
Moves to European Unity

Introduction

In 1939 Europe appeared to be the most powerful of all the continents. Although it was split by nationalistic dissension and objectives, it had influence over vast portions of the world. By the end of the war, Europe lay **ravaged by the physical presence of war**, was in a state of **economic collapse** and had **ceased to exercise the same political authority**. Its empires were now **independent states** and **socialism** had gained the mass appeal it had always threatened. But, far worse, instead of dictating world events, Europe was obliged to play a **passive role**. It was now **reliant on, or victim of, the actions of the two new superpowers: the Soviet Union and the United States**. Slowly but surely, therefore, in the aftermath of war **the idea of European unity** was born. Not only must Europe be **rebuilt**, but it must **unite** to give Europe a realistic voice in world affairs.

The post-war problems

The political changes that affected Europe in the immediate post-war period have been dealt with in the previous chapter. They were, as noted, considerable and far-reaching and were, by their very nature, extra-European in that the European powers themselves – with the possible exception of Britain – had little influence on their outcome. The **political changes**, however, represented only one problem, for Europe had also suffered **physical devastation**, with the resultant **economic and human cost**. The loss of over 30 million people was not only the cause of personal grief; it was also the loss of an important economic resource. The **transport systems** were in a state of considerable disruption, and **industrial output was severely damaged** (especially in Central Europe); in addition, it was linked to the production of goods of very limited value in peace-time. **Agricultural production** was equally **disrupted** and **undermanned**, again especially in Central Europe, and reorganization was both difficult and costly.

The human cost was counted not only in the numbers **killed** and injured and the plight of their surviving dependants, but also in **homeless and displaced persons**, who were either forcibly resettled or stranded because of political views. The **United Nations Relief and Rehabilitation Administration** (UNRRA) did what it could to alleviate the problem, but the scope of the disaster made the task almost impossible. The mass **expulsions of Germans** from **Poland**, **Czechoslovakia** and **Hungary** added to these problems, as did the **repatriation of Slavs from Germany**, and the **refusal** of more than a million **anti-communists to return to their now Soviet-controlled countries**. The real answer to these problems was an **economic recovery** in Europe, but this required **large-scale investment**. The European nations themselves, exhausted by the war, could not command such investment and they looked, therefore, to the **United States**.

The **Truman Doctrine** had been, in essence, a guarantee of political and, if necessary, military assistance, but it became clear that **financial help** would also be required to obtain political and social stability. In June 1948, the United States announced a **long-term economic aid programme** originally known as the European Recovery Programme but more commonly known as the **Marshall Plan** in recognition of its mentor, the American Secretary of State, George Marshall. The aid was available, in principle, to **all European nations** including the Soviet Union, but, wary of Western involvement and partial control of its economy, the **Soviets declined the offer of aid** and also **forebade all their satellite countries to accept it**. The Western European states received, via this aid, some $13 billion, subject to American conditions and restrictions. The Soviets replied by creating their own co-ordinating organization, the **Cominform**, but its effects were paltry compared to the Marshall Plan, which was undoubtedly the **decisive factor in bringing about European recovery**. Through the **Organization for European Economic Co-operation** the money from Marshall aid to the Western European states was **totally successful in reviving the European economies**, but, perhaps more importantly, it **indicated the rewards and value of international co-operation**.

First steps to unity

Immediately following the war, defensive considerations had led to the signing of the **Franco–British Treaty of Dunkirk**, and then the wider **Brussels Treaty**, but beyond this some Europeans wanted a **federalist** Europe. Their dream of **unity**, with a new **central authority born of wartime co-operation and integration**, had **little chance of success**, especially with the upsurge of **nationalist feeling**. More practical and tenable, however, was the **functionalist** approach most ably put forward by Jean Monnet. He proposed the establishment of **specialist agencies** with specific functions and powers, initially in the **economic field**. This he hoped would allay people's fears of the **erosion of their national sovereignty and independence**, and would begin the development towards the **longer-term objective of political integration**.

The OEEC had shown the potential of unified and orchestrated action, and in May 1948 the interested parties met at a **congress in The Hague**. The major result of this meeting was an **agreement that governments should work towards a political and economic union in Europe**, and a year later, following high-level negotiation, a treaty was signed which set up the **Council of Europe**. This took place one month after the creation of NATO. The member countries, Belgium, Denmark, France, Ireland, Italy, Luxembourg, Holland, Norway, Sweden, and Britain, pledged themselves 'to achieve greater unity between members for the purpose of safeguarding and realizing ideals and principles which are their common heritage and facilitating their economic and social progress'. The aims were laudable, but nations' **fears of relinquishing sovereignty stifled the body in its infancy**. It became simply a debating forum, and even then issues such as **defence** were **excluded** from discussions. However, it was the first attempt at political organization of Europe and in its very failure revealed the problems and pitfalls that future plans had to take into account.

The failure of the Council of Europe to become an effective European organization occurred against a backdrop of continuing concern over **the problem of Germany**. A revived Germany was likely to produce certain anxieties within other nations, yet, equally, it was difficult to imagine a European settlement in which it did not play a key part. The problem was already being tackled by way of integrating the four zones into the German Federal Republic, but it was through the **Schuman Plan** that an acceptable solution was achieved. The formulator of this plan, Robert Schuman, was a Frenchman living on the Franco–German border who knew much about the implications of German recovery. He therefore proposed a plan to **unite the French and German coal and steel industries**. The idea was that the pooling of these key resources would **rule out the possibility of unilateral action** and would provide the **basis for even greater economic integration and development**.

The potential of the plan was welcomed by the West German Chancellor, Konrad Adenauer, as 'the first decisive step in the construction of Europe' and his enthusiasm was matched by leaders in Belgium, Luxembourg, Italy and Holland. Together these six nations agreed to accept **voluntary limitations** on their control over one of the most important sectors of their economies.

Britain, as usual reluctant to delegate power, **declined the invitation**. Thus, from the Schuman Plan developed the **European Coal and Steel Community** (ECSC). This was formally set up in April 1951 and was not without its problems, but it was the **first major step towards a united Europe**. At last, countries had been prepared to **devolve power**, and in their doing so the ECSC became the pattern and nucleus for future development.

Another area which seemed ripe for the same sort of co-operative pooling operation was that of **defence**. By 1949, Europe already had **NATO**, but for all its strengths, this organization had two major weaknesses. Firstly, it was a **collective organization: each member did not retain ultimate control and command over its own forces**. Secondly, it left **unsolved the problem of the defence of Germany in the form of the new Federal Republic**. The new state was currently defended by what the German people might still see as an army of occupation and, further, it was felt that the economically revived **Germany** could and should **play a part in Western defence strategy**. While American troops were committed in the Korean War, European opinions were divided over this problem and in October 1950 the French Prime Minister, René Pleven, came up with a plan (the **Pleven Plan**) for a **European army under joint European control**, to be known as the European Defence Community (EDC).

Under the **Pleven Plan** Germany was to be rearmed, but not individually – rather, as part of a European force. The idea was an extension of the Schuman Plan, as its originator had intended, but many people felt it was **premature and unrealistic**. It was thought premature because a European army implied a **political integration** that had, of course, yet to happen, and unrealistic because it left unanswered many of the thorny questions about the **extent to which this international army might be used**. **Britain**, in particular, with its Commonwealth interests, was not prepared to support the idea and, in the end, **France** itself disowned the EDC when the idea was rejected in the National Assembly. As a result of discussions, however, in October 1954 the Brussels Treaty was enlarged to become the **Western European Union** by the **inclusion of Germany and Italy**, who also became members of NATO. The WEU solved the worries of **German rearmament** by controlling it carefully and legitimized the stationing of foreign troops on the European mainland as part of an **overall defence strategy**. Now, freed of the defence problem and its inherent difficulties, the movement for unity could make real progress.

Economic unity achieved

The immediate post-war period had seen **European economies in disarray and near-collapse**. American assistance had facilitated their rebuilding, but it was clear that, in global terms, the individual trading capabilities of the European nations had been seriously undermined by the war. Political reorganization along federalist lines had failed to make any impression upon the member nations of Western Europe, but **functionalist proposals** concerning economic co-operation had become increasingly influential. **Jean Monnet**, the French political economist, had been at the forefront of this movement and had worked closely with Robert Schuman in the ECSC Organization. He became its first president. During the war he had proposed to Churchill the radical idea of a Franco–British union and by 1955 his belief had led him to organize the Action Committee for the United States of Europe.

Monnet's influence was important but he was not in a position to take the necessary initiative. Fortunately though, his ideas influenced some European leaders. Alcide de Gasperi, the Italian Premier, and Konrad Adenauer, the West German Chancellor, both saw in Monnet's work the **basis for European integration**. Both of them, through progressive measures, steered their respective nations into joining the early co-operative organizations. As the support for unity grew, the **economic field** seemed the most likely prospect for success, with the ECSC as an example of what could be achieved. Consequently, in June 1955, the foreign ministers of the ECSC countries met at **Messina** to consider possible ways forward. The Messina Conference under the guidance of another great European unitarian, the Belgian Foreign Minister, **Paul Henri Spaak**, led to the creation of a committee which investigated the setting up of a **common market and customs union** and of ways to **pool Europe's resources for the development of nuclear energy**. This Committee reported back that both developments were **indispensable** if Europe was to maintain its world position, but it was now left to the individual governments to decide what action, if any, to take.

In March 1957, buoyed up by the economic prosperity of the mid-50s, the original six Messina member countries signed the **Treaties of Rome**. The first, minor, treaty set up the **European Atomic Energy Community** (Euratom) which was to run joint research centres and pool information on atomic research. The second treaty established the **European Economic Community** (EEC) and this came into being on 1 January 1958. As with the ECSC, the EEC's immediate aims were **economic**, but its architects hoped that the Community would one day lead to **political unification**. In Spaak's words, 'it symbolizes the triumph of the spirit of co-operation over national selfishness'.

The initial aims of the EEC were to develop **common European policies for industry and technology** whilst at the same time **removing the economic barriers** between the member countries to allow **freedom of movement for goods, labour and capital**. Also a **Common Agricultural Policy** (CAP) was agreed upon, and various **supportive and social institutions** created. The following bodies were created to run the Community: the **Executive Commission**, with members chosen for their impartiality; the **Council of Ministers**, usually the foreign ministers of the member countries with weighted voting rights; the **European Parliament**, which had mainly consultative power; and finally, the **Court of Justice**. **Financial provision** was to be **proportional** to the size and economic capability of the member countries. The organization was more than an inter-governmental body, but obviously it fell far short of a political federation.

Each member country had a **final say**, and the **right of veto** was maintained against suggestions of decision-making by majority voting. Under United States' encouragement and in a favourable economic climate, the EEC overcame its teething problems and showed the **value of economic co-operation**. **Britain**, however, even in the post-Suez climate, **still saw itself as a world power** and **attempted to transform the EEC into a wider free trade area for industrial goods** through negotiations in the **OEEC**. The EEC countries, though, were unwilling to give up the progress that had been achieved and suspected Britain of wishing to destroy the EEC. Undeterred, however, Britain continued to **canvass for a free-trade agreement**, and in May 1959 the **European Free Trade Association** (EFTA) was formed, comprising Austria, Denmark, Norway, Sweden, Switzerland, Portugal and Britain. The Organization consisted mostly of small nations, Britain being the exception. It was very **limited in its scope and ultimately in its success**.

By 1961 it was clear that membership of EFTA was no substitute to Britain for the success of the EEC, and the British Prime Minister, **Harold Macmillan**, began **negotiations for joining it**. The settled EEC, however, and in particular the French President, **General de Gaulle**, were **unconvinced of the value of Britain's membership**. They were worried especially about **Britain's economic state**, its **level**

of commitment and **American connections**. Britain tried again under **Harold Wilson** in 1967, together with Eire and Denmark, but again **de Gaulle** proved the stumbling block. It was not until **January 1973** that all three countries joined the Community. Since then, Greece has obtained membership and Portugal and Spain stand on the threshold. With these admissions, the Community has grown in size and thus represents a larger area of Europe, but the question still remains as to the extent of this unity.

In the early years, prosperity bound the Community together and made progress relatively easy, but its **development** and the extension of **corporate decision-making over national sovereignty** caused problems. The **French**, for instance, displayed their hostility not only in **opposing the entry** of new members but also, in 1965, by **boycotting the Community institutions** for seven months. The 1970s, with their oil crisis and economic slump, arrested the steady progress and revealed faults such as **over-bureaucratization** and the **illogicality of CAP policies**. Further, countries such as **Austria** and **Sweden** have revealed the **possibility of even greater prosperity outside the Community**. The Tindemans report in 1976 showed that the Community had **missed many opportunities**, but it also indicated an **underlying commitment to European unity** by the member countries. Monnet's United States of Europe may still be only a dream, but it was never likely to be easily achieved and remains a goal towards which progress is being made, however slowly.

Summary

European unity grew out of the horrors of World War II as a combination of **idealism** and **pragmatism**. Western Europe, dwarfed by the superpowers and on the frontline of East–West confrontation, has made **considerable steps towards unity**, especially in the **economic field**. That **political integration** has not occurred is hardly surprising, in view of **Europe's past** and the importance of **national sovereignty**. It will not occur rapidly but will develop as necessity dictates. The danger, therefore, lies not with the process but with Europe's ability to achieve the objective. The future of European unity as yet remains unclear, both in terms of the permanancy of the existing institutions and also of the extent to which integration is actually possible.

Part 2
Modern British History

Chapter 16
Britain in 1815

Introduction

To understand the political events in Britain after 1815 it is first necessary to appreciate the **social and economic effects of the war** on large sectors of British society. The Napoleonic Wars witnessed the emergence of a much-changed Britain: population growth, rationalization of farming, the decline of rural-based woollen and cottage industries and large-scale industrialization all played their part in altering the British way of life in the early nineteenth century. These should be looked at in some detail by students wishing to grasp the rationale behind British domestic and foreign policy in this period. At a time when the chief aim of government was to return to the old pre-war order of society, great economic and social changes meant that the long-accepted order of things was in a precarious position. It would be impossible to go into great detail here about such alterations in Britain's social fabric, and students should be prepared for much wider reading. We will, however, look briefly at the major changes and their consequences.

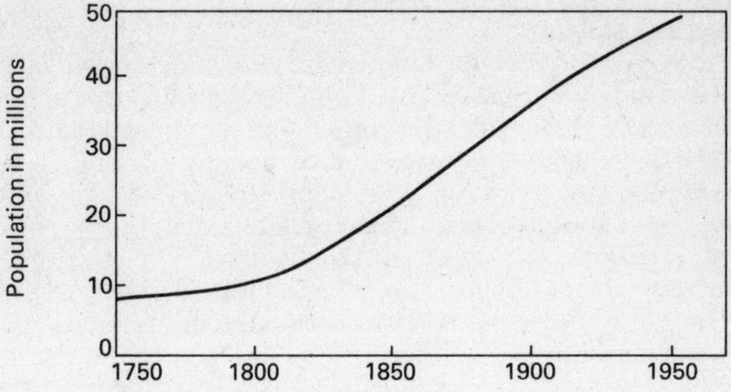

Figure 8. Britain's rapid population growth

Industrialization and the effect of war

The eighteenth century saw a virtual doubling of the population of Britain and, as the move towards enclosure of open fields accelerated, large numbers of the rural workforce were obliged to seek a livelihood in the fast-expanding industrial towns. These had developed with the advent of steam power, while the increase in the coal, iron and cotton industries assisted the demise of traditional cottage-based industrial production. These factors led to the emergence of new classes in British society. Such changes were hastened by the economic requirements of the Napoleonic Wars. The rate of enclosure increased due to large-scale investment in normally unprofitable land. Heavy industry and textiles were stimulated by an increased demand for war supplies, while the European blockade forced exporters to develop new overseas markets.

To counteract the increase of the nation's debt (it had grown by some £620 million) greater indirect taxation and income tax were introduced. This affected both old and new classes. Opposition to the harsh economic measures of the government was seen as Jacobin agitation and dealt with accordingly. With the old order drastically altered, was it only a matter of time before the new classes rejected the hegemony of the old aristocracy over them? How would the backward-looking landed aristrocracy react to powerful new classes trying to assert themselves? In an atmosphere of dissatisfaction and radical ideas, the issues of cash and Catholics were to influence the course of British history in the nineteenth century.

Peace and stability

It had been hoped that the return of peace would bring with it both social stability and prosperity. However, this was not the case. Lower prices led to decreasing profits and subsequent difficulty in repaying the large mortgages taken out on land investments during the war. Bankruptcy amongst the landed and yeoman classes was not uncommon as the sudden influx of foreign corn caused the price of English corn to plummet. The government's response of introducing the Corn Law in 1815 (whereby importation of foreign corn was prohibited until home produce reached 80 shillings a quarter) caused unrest amongst the lower and middle classes in England and also amongst the landlords in Ireland. The danger was that the high price of bread would not only cause unrest amongst the lower orders but would increase the price of labour, making it difficult for new industrialists to compete in foreign markets.

The end of the war also saw a predictable reduction in the demand for industrial output, which led to a scaling-down of production in certain fields. The subsequent rise in unemployment was exacerbated by the demobilization of the large numbers of soldiers. The measures of the Liverpool administration were seen as detrimental to the continued prosperity of the population by industrialists and political economists and also by radicals who saw it as a clear indication of the need for parliamentary reform.

The rise of radicalism

The above factors caused most suffering amongst the working classes (industrial and rural), and it was in this period that radical agitation amongst the lower orders reached a peak. It is difficult to give a clear definition of English radicalism in the early nineteenth century. Radical politics in this period can be regarded largely as a series of popular agitations by which the franchise was extended and which made the possibility of representation in parliament for the working classes a reality. On the other hand it was arguably the closest Britain came to having a mass revolutionary movement.

Nineteenth-century radicals were not always progressive in their aims and many had more in common with seventeenth- and eighteenth-century thinkers than with the radical element in the urban working classes. There has been much debate among historians as to how far city mobs and religious fanatics were radical – in effect, the question to be answered is whether any protest group with popular support was radical. For the most part, however, the ultra-radicals of the lower classes had to play a secondary role to their middle-class parliamentary counterparts.

If you are intending to answer examination questions on the radical movement, you should be aware of the common core of thinking behind the actions of both parliamentary and ultra radicals (e.g. Tom Paine) and should be able to assess to what extent they were a unified movement or two separate ones.

In *The Making of the English Working Class*, E. P. Thompson sees radicalism in these years as having a potential for revolutionary change. It is, however, certain that middle-class parliamentary radicals such as William Cobbett were not attempting to change society but were rather aiming for a return to a non-industrial Golden Age.

Radicalism was, therefore, a multi-faceted movement with both long- and short-term aims, i.e. parliamentary reform and improvement of working conditions. The particular causes and characteristics of radicalism can only be understood in the light of the rapid industrialization and urbanization taking place at the time.

Radical protest 1815–20

Despite the disparate nature of radical protest after the end of the Napoleonic Wars, it was extreme enough for the Liverpool administration to react with force in defence of the law and the old order. The open radicalism of the 1790s had gone underground during the war years but, during that period, it had managed to achieve much support in the local communities. The distress of post-war society and continued industrialization saw, on the one hand, a movement on the part of radicals towards seeing protest in class terms and, on the other hand, an almost pathological fear of revolution on the part of the ruling class: 'England in 1792 had been governed by consent and deference supplemented by the gallows and "church and king" mob. In 1816 the English people were held down by force.' (Thompson, p. 663)

It would be wrong to see the sometimes violent nature of radical opposition to such harsh government as an entirely new phenomenon. Indeed, some historians might argue that the tradition of violent protest, e.g. food rioting in urban areas, and Luddism, were signs of the potentially revolutionary nature of the newly emerging working class. Other historians tend to view such activities merely as spontaneous and isolated protest against the source of working people's economic and social distress. This debate is certain to continue, and it is worth finding out about the various arguments and analysing the effect (if any) that Luddism had upon later radical protest.

It is clear, however, that many of the areas where what has traditionally been termed radical protest broke out had also been at the centre of Luddite activity some four years earlier. Between 1816 and 1819 there were a number of protest marches and riots that have been labelled radical protest. You should know something of these if you have studied the period at O level, and it is important that, apart from knowing about the course that such protest took, you understand the effect it had upon the ruling classes in Britain and how they responded to the challenge. Of the various examples of unrest those best documented are:

1. The **Ely and Littleport riots** by agricultural labourers in 1816–labelled Bread or Blood;

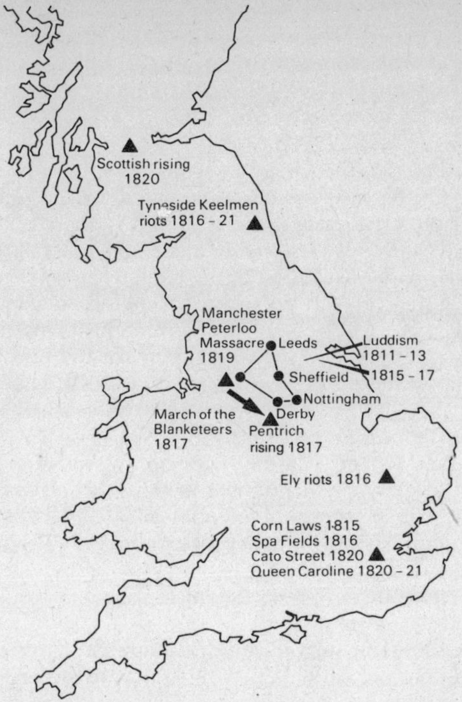

Figure 9. Radical protest and the danger of revolution–social unrest in Britain 1815–21

2. **Spa Fields** in Islington, 1816. Addressed by 'Orator' Hunt, the meeting resolved to demand parliamentary reform in order to assist in the creation of a more just society. Splinter groups armed themselves and marched on the Royal Exchange, this being followed by the government's suspension of Habeas Corpus;
3. The **'Blanketeers' march'** from Manchester to London in 1817;
4. The **Pentrich uprising** in Derbyshire in 1817 which saw an attempt at armed insurrection by framework knitters;
5. **St Peter's Fields**, Manchester, in 1819, more commonly known as Peterloo, where the meeting was broken up by the county yeomanry on the orders of the local magistrates.

In 1818 Lord Liverpool's Tories had been re-elected, largely because the Whigs were unable to offer any realistic alternative to the Tories' rigid maintenance of law and order and because the franchise had not yet been extended to the disaffected classes. The Tories had revived Habeas Corpus in 1818, which enabled many radicals to become active again, the culmination of the disorder being at Peterloo.

It has been said that the Corn Laws and Game Laws were typical legislation of the government dominated by the landowning classes (the old aristocracy), and it is interesting to note that the yeomanry at St Peter's Fields were made up largely of the sons of county farmers, the backbone of the landed classes. Encouraged by the activities of the radicals, the Whigs began to place themselves at the forefront of the movement for parliamentary reform. In an attempt to squash support for the reformers, the government passed the infamous six Acts in 1819. These were to:

1. prohibit the possession of arms;
2. prevent any form of military training by private individuals;
3. prohibit attendance at political meetings to all except those living in the parish where the meeting was to be held;
4. allow magistrates to search property for any literature of a seditious nature;
5. allow magistrates to try cases which previously could only be tried by judge and jury;
6. increase the stamp duty payable on pamphlets and newspapers in the hope that radical papers would become too expensive for the general public to buy.

The radical response was both violent and subversive. The Cato Street conspirators in 1820 plotted the murder of the entire Cabinet, while illegal unstamped journals and pamphlets proliferated.

Revolution averted

Between 1820 and 1822 the economic problems of the immediate post-war period began to disappear. Foreign trade revived and helped to stimulate employment. The radicals continued their agitation and indeed gained much popular support during the sordid divorce case brought in 1820 by George IV against his previously estranged wife, Queen Caroline. The public standing of the monarchy declined after this affair, while the united front of the Whigs and radicals in support of the Queen gave these opposition groups a firm base of public support on which they were able to build. Such popularity was to become important during the reform crisis in the early 1830s.

As we have already pointed out, it is dangerous to look at historical events in isolation during this period. You should not assume that, because there was little violent agitation after 1819, the radical and trade union movements were inactive. The effectiveness of the pressure for parliamentary reform between 1830 and 1832 was as much a result of the **growth in political awareness fostered by the radical press and secret meetings** as it was a result of the radicals' high-profile activities between 1815 and 1820. The unstamped press went from strength to strength after 1820 and radical newspapers proliferated. The aim now was to educate the working classes to a realization of their political and economic strength, as opposed to leading an unorganized working class into violent revolution.

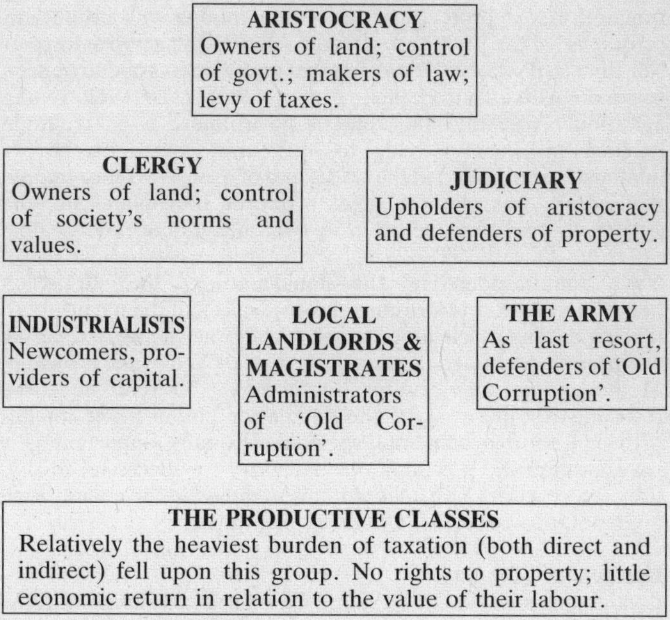

Figure 10. The radical view of the burden of oppression in British society

The radical protest in the 1790s and early 1800s had placed the cause of social distress firmly at the door of the establishment. It was termed Old Corruption and comprised the Church, the law and the aristocracy. **Taxation** levied by this class on the productive classes was seen as the root cause of social distress in Britain. The diagram on page 151 gives some indication of how the radicals saw the burden of the working classes in relation to other groups in society. However, by the late 1820s many radical thinkers were beginning to see **industrial capital** as the new enemy. Their fears were realized with the outcome of the movement for reform in 1832.

Meanwhile the government, remained consistent in its domestic policies, apparently equating reform with revolution. The government's response to the symptoms of unrest remained forceful while the economic causes of social unrest went unchecked. The administration maintained that its primary function was to protect law and order, though with insufficient resources for the job (there was as yet no standing police force or full-time civil service). It was felt that governments had to be seen to govern with a strong hand in order to discourage revolutionary agitation. Arguably, the role of government is to maintain balance in society, and, to this end, Lord Liverpool's administration defended the status quo of aristocratic hegemony. Agriculture was still the chief producer of capital, and the government administered it in its own interests of order.

You should understand the significance of the interaction between middle- and working-class radicals and the means, both ideological and practical, by which revolution was averted during this period. An understanding of the role played by the growth of Methodism is important in this context, both in the social restraints it imposed upon the population and in the training it provided for teachers and speakers. Equally important is a realization of the preconditions necessary for successful revolution to occur. You should also question whether such preconditions existed in Britain at this time.

Liverpool and Canning

Castlereagh's suicide in 1822 and Canning's appointment to the post of Foreign Secretary (which prompted the resignation of several key ministers, supporters of Castlereagh's style of foreign policy and opponents of Canning) gave Liverpool the opportunity to reshuffle his Cabinet. The rising stars of the Party were given key positions – Peel became Home Secretary, William Huskisson was made President of the Board of Trade, Robinson became Chancellor of the Exchequer, whilst Canning combined the posts of Foreign Secretary and Leader of the Commons. All of these men had proved their administrative ability and, being of middle-class origins, were more responsive to the needs of industrialists.

You should be aware that in recent years there has been much debate amongst socialist historians about the failure of revolution during this post-Napoleonic period. They have questioned whether the aristocracy absorbed middle-class thinkers and industrialists with their ideas of political economy in order to maintain the status quo, or whether the economic power of the middle classes enabled them to carry through a 'bloodless' revolution. The main protagonists in this debate have been E. P. Thompson and Perry Anderson, and their work is worth examining for a fuller understanding of this question. Journal articles are also worth reading, as much important historical debate is carried on within their pages. Among journals that are most useful and easily accessible for A-level students are *Past and Present*, *Social History*, *History Workshop* and *History Today*. The essays by Thompson and Anderson which will throw light on the nature of radicalism and social change are 'Origins of the present crisis' by Perry Anderson and 'The Peculiarities of the English' in *The Poverty Theory and Other Essays* by E. P. Thompson.

As has been said already, the economic crisis had all but disappeared by 1822 and, in an attempt to achieve a wider base of popular support, the restructured Liverpool administration felt able to carry through some modest reforms. However, the majority of these were in the economic and legal sectors. It is important to know the main elements of the various **reforms made by the liberal-Tories** – e.g. Peel and the **rationalization of the death penalty**, and **foundation of the Metropolitan Police**, Huskisson's economic reforms at the Board of Trade, such as the **reduction of customs duty** on raw materials, the **Reciprocity of Duties Act** which allowed for mutual reduction of tariffs between Britain and Europe, the **Navigation Acts** which were amended to restrict trade within the British Empire to British ships whilst allowing foreign ships a role in Britain's foreign trade. The Corn Laws, meanwhile, were altered to a sliding-scale system which allowed some flexibility.

The Catholic problem remained, despite the repeal of the Test and Corporation Acts in 1828 which was really only to the advantage of the Nonconformists, who formed a strong parliamentary pressure group. The Catholics had to wait until 1829 for emancipation from a far from enthusiastic government, often seen as liberal where foreign affairs were concerned. Examiners may ask you to compare Canning's support of liberalism and nationalism abroad, and his opposition to the Holy Alliance, with the government's domestic policies.

The reforms of the liberal-Tories and the concessions made on cash, corn and Catholics may appear liberal when compared to the early policies of the Liverpool administration but tend to pale before the Whig reforms of the 1830s. Daniel O'Connell eventually wrested emancipation for the Catholics, but it was more the threat of civil war in Ireland than any reforming zeal that led to the change in the law. The question of how liberal were the liberal-Tories has been popular with the examiners. You should be able to assess, from your knowledge of the repressive Liverpool administration in which all of the so-called reformers served, how innovatory the said reforms were and to what extent there was a continuity in government between 1815 and 1829.

The economic measures of the government had been largely progressive, but there had been little attempt to improve the related social issues and no attempt at all as regards a more representative form of government. It was the division amongst the Tories over such issues that necessitated the King asking Earl Grey to form a Whig administration.

Summary

There are a number of elements to keep in mind after studying the immediate post-Napoleonic period of British history. The first of these is the **importance of Lord Liverpool's role in shaping the nature of British politics** in this period. Accused of mediocrity by Disraeli, he managed, by adept maneouvring, to retain political power against great opposition both within Parliament and from radical and potentially revolutionary movements in the country at large. Compare the view of Asa Briggs, that Liverpool was a skilful manipulator and mediator of men and ideas, with the 'arch-mediocrity' label given him by Disraeli.

A second question worth consideration is one regarding the nature of the administration: how **repressive was it between 1815 and**

1822 and how liberal between 1822 and 1827? You should be able to assess the influence of Castlereagh and Canning on these two periods. It is also important to be aware that the Tories did not divide on strictly ideological grounds dependent upon whether they were reactionary or liberal – see for example the paradox of Castlereagh's support for Catholic emancipation while Peel supported the Protestants. When considering the repressive and liberal nature of the Tory administration, ask yourself whether the Tories were succumbing to Whig and radical pressure in their liberal phases, or whether, in the light of an improvement in the economy and their earlier victories over radical unrest, they felt able to relax their policies. Finally, do not neglect the importance throughout this period of changing fortunes in the economy, which both affected the course of government policy and also fuelled social unrest.

Chapter 17
The Whig Reforms

Introduction

The period 1830–41 contained many active reform movements and saw many alterations in the political framework of Britain. By far the most important changes were brought about by the implementation of the **1832 Reform Act**. This legislation, passed by the Whigs, who had been elected two years earlier on a reforming platform, was **aimed at rectifying the problems of social unrest by granting extended representation**. To a certain extent the Whig administration had been spurred by popular support for radical organizations and pressure groups. You should be aware of the identities of at least some of these groups along with their ideas, for example, the National Union of the Working Class (NUWC) and the Birmingham Political Union (BPU).

Most historians tend to agree that although the 1832 Act was really quite conservative in its nature, it was probably responsible for preventing violent revolution in Britain during the nineteenth century. After 1832 the Whigs introduced a number of further 'liberal' reforms, but few of these went far enough for the radicals, as we shall see. It is important that you understand the impact of the reforms on British society and are able to discuss their relative merits and failures.

In 1830, the general election had been won by the Tories under Wellington. He had quickly discovered his inability to control either the ultra-Tories or the supporters of the late George Canning. Defeated over disagreements about the civil list, the Tory government resigned, whereupon Earl Grey was invited to form a Whig administration. As we have seen from the previous chapter, there was already a background of social, economic and political agitation in Britain when Grey's Whigs came into office. While they were made up largely of members of the aristocracy, the support of the Canningites and the radicals assisted the administration's resolve to deal with the problems of political reform.

Wellington's government had already looked at the possibilities of reforming the political system in 1828, but with growing pressure from below, the government was in a position where its only real option was to decide how far it could go with the reforms without injuring its self-interest.

The need for reform

Before 1832 the unreformed political system was a morass of outdated and confusing legislation and local custom. In effect it was a system that was no system at all, since it was geared to Britain's needs in the seventeenth century, i.e. to a situation that had existed before massive industrialization. The electoral process as it stood was open to great corruption (e.g. the rotten boroughs) and was grossly unrepresentative. England below the line from Bristol to the Wash sent nearly three-quarters of all MPs to the House of Commons. One-quarter was elected from the four counties of south-western England. London was very poorly represented, while Yorkshire had the same representation as tiny Rutland. Such an arrangement had suited Britain in the seventeenth century when the importance of agriculture far outweighed that of industry, and when population density was far greater in the south than in the north. Industrialization and the consequent urbanization saw an increasing percentage of the population settled in industrial towns such as Manchester and Stoke and the industrial belt around Leeds, Rotherham and Sheffield. These towns were subjected to taxes and legislation without fair representation in Parliament to argue their case. The inhabitants of such towns were not alone in their plight, as only 160 000 people were eligible to vote out of a total population of 16 million. In an examination you will need to know what the defects of the electoral system were and be able to give examples.

If you re-examine the diagram on page 151 you will see how the landed aristocracy and the Tory gentry held prominence, with the aid of Church and Army, over British society and its parliament. In defending the existing electoral system the Tories argued that, firstly, the system was now hallowed by tradition, a tradition seen as the mother of parliaments, and this therefore justified its remaining unchanged. Secondly, they claimed that it allowed all classes to be represented (despite the fact that few could afford to stand for Parliament). Thirdly, Parliament was by tradition deliberative. Decisions were taken over time by those best able to govern – in other words, those who could afford to get themselves elected and who could count on the support of their aristocratic colleagues. In fact, rotten boroughs were defended on the grounds that such constituencies had allowed great politicians such as Pitt, Canning and Peel to gain their first seats in parliament.

The reform crisis

The speed of reform, whilst it was affected by the extra-parliamentary movements of the radicals, was also to some extent determined by the **changes within Parliament brought about by splits in the Tory ranks, the consequent repeal of the Test and Corporation Acts, and the emancipation of the Catholics**. It is important to be aware of the effect religious emancipation had upon the nature of British politics in this period of crisis.

As we have seen in the previous chapter, the move for reform began in the 1760s with the activities of Wilkes and the writings of Tom Paine. By the time radicals such as Cartwright and Cobbett reached the peak of their influence, it seemed that, at long last, reforming ideas were making some progress. In an examination you may well be asked to assess how radical the Whig reforms really were: were they something completely new or an example of continuity in traditional British government by the landed aristocracy? In effect, were the reforms introduced out of a spirit of utilitarianism or out of a fear of revolution? Be sure that you know the meaning of such key words as utilitarianism because misinterpretation can lead to a completely wrong answer.

When it became clear that Wellington would oppose reform even if it meant the near-destruction of the Tory Party, Grey was forced into the position of acceding to calls for reform in order to gain power. With cross-party support, Grey was confident that the Whigs could end their long exclusion from government by espousing reform and therefore employing popular support to stay in power. Asa Briggs, in *The Age of Improvement*, hints at the fact that it was self-preservation rather than high liberal or democratic ideals that prompted Whig backing for the Reform Bill.

Grey's cabinet contained only three commoners out of a total of thirteen, the remainder being from the aristocracy. Indeed, Grey gave preference to the aristocrats in his ministry on the grounds that they guaranteed the future security of the state and throne. However, aristocratic and exclusive as they were in their attitude to government, **the Whigs were ready to accept such political innovations as the Reform Bill in order to protect their hegemony**. They were of the belief that, unless the privileged sections of society were prepared to adapt and alter their attitudes to take into account the emerging consciousness of the lower orders, then the existing social order would be swept away by an uncontrollable wave of innovation forced upon them from below.

At this stage, it will be of value to think again about the debate referred to in the previous chapter regarding the way in which revolution was averted in the post-Napoleonic period. In the light of this debate it is interesting to note that the chief aim of the first Reform Bill, introduced by Lord John Russell, was to **gain the support of the middle class for aristocratic hegemony**. For their part, the new industrial middle classes had become both economically and politically influential, and it was they who formed the **Birmingham Political Union**. This aimed at **achieving political representation for those involved in trade and industry**, the source of the nation's wealth. They saw the cause of the country's social problems as being rooted in the maladministration of successive aristocratic governments:

> . . . in the opinion of this meeting, the general distress which now afflicts the country, and which has been so severely felt at different periods during the last 15 years, is entirely to be ascribed to the gross mismanagement and can only be effectually and permanently remedied by an effectual reform in the Commons House of Parliament.
>
> Resolution at a meeting of the Birmingham Political Union, 1830 (pamphlet)

The **class co-operation** found in both the Birmingham Political Union and the National Political Union was a feature of the Reform Bill crisis. The BPU was led by merchants, manufacturers and bankers and contained large numbers of skilled artisans. The social and economic differences between employers and employees were smaller in Birmingham because of the smaller scale of business and industry in that town. The NPU, meanwhile, was made up of middle- and working-class people in the same occupations, i.e. employers and employees. The NPU also included people from the sweated trades, together with some professional people. The main aims of both groups was parliamentary reform along with the creation of a democratic electoral system. The authorities felt that much of the work of the political unions was a danger to the state in that the lowest elements were being unleashed upon society. It is, however, interesting to note that, while there were certainly considerable numbers of unskilled workers in the northern riots, these were not as violent as those in Bristol where the political unions had a good deal of support from craft unions. E. P. Thompson argues that by 1833 the majority of skilled workers in Britain were beginning to see themselves as a united class (hence the title of his book *The Making of the English Working Class*). It was they and their political organizations who were the greatest threats to authority in this period of crisis.

Thompson's claim for class consciousness can be illustrated in two ways. Firstly, there was a consensus of interests between diverse groups of working men expressed in general unionism in the period 1830–34. Secondly, it is clear that there was emerging a consciousness of identity of interests against the interests of other classes. There were also increasing calls for an alternative system of government. The working-class agitators in this crisis can be divided into two main groupings for convenience.

The first group were the **low political unions** in which the control exercised by the middle-class leaders was very precarious. Some of these unions were solely working-class, as in Leeds and Manchester, and were described as having 'men of the lowest description' amongst their membership. It was groups such as these who worried the authorities most, largely because it was felt that they were subversive. It was they who reflected the wide gap between workers and employers in the newer northern industrial towns of Lancashire and Yorkshire.

The second group (the members of the National Union of the Working Classes) were beginning to discuss the problems of society in class terms as they realized they were not going to get the vote. The **NUWC was an independent working-class organization led by artisans** and such well-known activists as Carlisle, Lovett and Hetherington. The *Poor Man's Guardian* gave an impression of fierce class antagonisms, particularly between the NUWC and the major political unions. They were prepared to unite with the NPU, but only on a platform of **universal suffrage, vote by ballot and no property qualification**. In November 1832 Arthur Wade wrote to Thomas Attwood of the BPU in the pages of the *Poor Man's Guardian* on why there was a need for an independent working-class union. His first reason, given below, shows the level of mistrust between the various organizations:

> Because the leaders in other Unions, being men of property living upon the rental of land, the interest of money, or the profits of trade, have separate and distinct interests from the working man; for example he who lives on the rental of the land has an interest opposed to the

abolition of the corn laws, and the abolition of every other monopoly that would diminish his income, he who lives on the interest of money has a great predilection for paper schemes, bubble speculations, cheap productions, and depreciated labour, he who lives on the profits of trade has an interest in obtaining labour, as cheap as possible and selling it at the dearest rate, and, as all of these individual interests are opposed to the best interests of the productive classes, I ask you are those persons so fit and proper to represent them as the working classes themselves?

(Arthur S. Wade, *Poor Man's Guardian* 17 November 1832)

It has been argued by some historians that during this crisis Britain was on the verge of revolution. The public, following the agitation of the political unions, wanted complete reform as promised in the early readings of the Bill. When the Tories managed to defeat various readings of the Bill there was serious street rioting, the most serious being in Bristol in October 1831. Bristol has often been seen as the turning point, as the crowd had gained control for several days. In the light of this and continual warnings of the possibility of revolution from radicals and political unions alike Grey recalled Parliament early and introduced the Reform Bill for the third time. Despite its defeat in the Lords and Grey's subsequent resignation, the Tories under Wellington were unable to form a government. With fears of revolution to back him up, Grey formed another ministry which saw the Reform Bill pass through the House of Lords on 4 June 1832.

The Whigs claimed that the Bill brought moderate reforms yet was essentially a conservative measure – in effect, the least the country would accept without violent protest and the most that the Whigs could expect Parliament to accept without losing the support of the aristocracy. With reference to the debate on hegemony mentioned earlier, it is worth noting here that nearly a quarter of a million members of the educated and propertied classes got the vote under the new legislation. Many Tories were alarmed at the thought of sharing the House of Commons with various radicals and merchants, tradesmen and factory owners. However, it is important to bear in mind the long tradition of violent protest in Britain and to gauge the strength of popular feeling during the crisis in order to see some justification in the Whig concessions. It is also interesting to draw the same parallels that Grey quite possibly did with France in 1789 and more recently in July 1830 when the masses under middle-class leadership disposed of the King and his attendant aristocracy.

There tend to be two main schools of thought regarding the effect the Reform Act had upon British society. The first has argued that the Act only managed to lessen the amount of bribery in political life rather than eradicate it. This school has seen the importance of the Act as minimal. The nightmares of democracy that the Tories imagined in their worst fears did not occur, while the majority of demands made by radicals for democracy and the emancipation of the working classes were not realized. The middle classes, though they gained the vote, did not use it to any great effect. They could have elected financiers and industrialists to represent them but failed to do so, tending on the whole to stand by traditional voting habits. The reformed Parliament looked little different from its unreformed predecessor, and the Act had very little adverse effect upon the influence of the King, the Church or the House of Lords, which all seemed to weather the reform crisis without any apparent curtailment of their powers. The second school of thought, whilst accepting that the Act did not go far enough, felt that it did challenge some of the worst defects of the existing corrupt system. The majority of the rotten boroughs were abolished, but in the end only a further 217 000 were added to the electoral roll, spread over new and existing constituencies, and most of the MPs returned by the newer constituencies, tended to be wealthy industrialists.

Arguably the most important aspect of the Act was the way in which it was passed. **It symbolized the assertion of the Commons' authority over the House of Lords** and, at the same time, showed the influence of public opinion. With the elections that were to follow and with further electoral changes, both Whigs and Tories had to take into account the views of the enlarged electorate and the groundswell of public opinion in favour of democracy. The power rivalry between the two Houses of Parliament did not, however, reach a climax until 1909 and the eventual passing of the Parliament Act in 1911. The Whigs, projecting themselves as the party of reform, hoped for strong middle-class support, and consequently a high percentage of Whig MPs were returned by urban constituencies. Having gained nothing from the Reform Act, the working classes turned to positive action in the form of groups such as the Chartists in order to achieve their aims. The Chartists will be considered in the next chapter. Despite E. P. Thompson's theory that there was a class consciousness present in the working masses by 1833, it seems that:

1. There was a great amount of agitation for reform across all classes, but most notably in the working classes throughout the country. Agitation among the working classes was increasing and

was well organized, but it seems that it was largely spontaneous and not connected with that in other classes.
2. There was a consensus of opinion about the need for reform but little on the finer details. There was also a split amongst middle- and working-class reform leaders.
3. To some extent there was class antagonism, particularly in northern industrial towns, though not in London or Birmingham.
4. Perhaps most important of all was the emergence of a completely new political phenomenon in the form of a government prepared to work with popular agitators (the political unions) over a piece of legislation going through Parliament. The middle-class radical leaders seem to have used popular agitation to achieve a compromise with the Whig government. For his part, Grey had to compromise with the political unions because he was unsure that his government would survive in Parliament. He also had to use the threat of popular unrest in order to gain support in the Commons.

Whose Reform Bill?

E. P. Thompson and Asa Briggs have made much of **middle-class consciousness** during the reform crisis. Thompson sees it as being formed between the Napoleonic Wars and the Reform Bill, and describes it as depending on narrow self-interest. The Reform Bill was a compromise between middle-class radicals who had no desire for universal male suffrage, but who used the threat of working-class rebellion, and Whig leaders desperate to retain political control. Between the middle- and working-class radical leaders there were essential differences over the ideas of political economy. The middle class wanted the abolition of monopolies, incorporated towns, reform of the Church, retrenchment and a planned political economy. It has been said that the banners of Baines and Cobden did not bear *liberté*, *egalité* (and still less *fraternité*), but rather 'free trade' and 'retrenchment'. The dividing line between the classes and class interests had been clearly drawn.

As for the working classes, what did they really expect to receive from the Bill? Most of those active in the political unions would have known, at the very least, not to expect the vote, even though they wanted it. There seems to have been a good deal of working-class support for the Bill, particularly in the NPU. In the NUWC, some members thought the bill should be supported as a 'wedge'. A good many working people seem to have supported it purely because it was an attack upon traditional aristocratic privilege and corruption. There was talk of treachery by the middle-class radicals, but this occurred with greater fervour after the social legislation of the reformed parliament began to take effect.

The reforms 1833–41

Grey and his successor, Melbourne, with their new-found security of office began to come to terms with the social problems caused by Britain's rapid industrialization. On the surface, the reforms tended to exacerbate existing class antagonisms. Many important reforms were enacted during this period, particularly the abolition of slavery in the colonies in 1833. The **Factory Act 1833** set out to remedy the worst conditions in textile manufacture, while local government was reformed in the **Municipal Corporations Act 1835**.

However, by far the most important social legislation of the period was the **Poor Law Amendment Act 1834**. This legislation embodied the strongest elements of Benthamite utilitarianism of any of the Acts, both in its conviction that the vital criterion was the greatest happiness for the greatest number and in its recommendation for workhouse testing. You should be aware of the role of Chadwick in the way this legislation was enacted, his motives and the applications of the Act.

To date, all British social historians have placed the Poor Law Amendment Act within the ideological context of liberal individualism, but there tends to be much **disagreement about how progressive or repressive the legislation was**. The optimists (those seeing the Act as progressive) have been led by Hartwell and Ashton (you should know something of their work). They have fallen into the trap of seeing the evils of the industrial revolution as being no one's fault. The Poor Law was seen as benevolent paternalism, carried out in an amateurish fashion simply because the government was responding to a problem it had not confronted before.

Liberal individualism can be seen as a synthesis of contemporary opinion, containing the political economy of Locke, Smith, Ricardo and John Stuart Mill, along with the political philosophy of Bentham and Chadwick. Smith defined the responsibility of the state as being to ensure that individuals were free to pursue the natural harmony of their interests in competition with others, yet without interfering with individual liberty. Bentham, however, saw that there were certain occasions when the state had to intervene in order to restore harmony by efficient central government. The uncontrollable spiral of the poor rates after 1815 and the apparently bad administration of the Poor Law at a local level prompted government intervention and culminated in the Act of 1834. (Be sure that you know the specific terms of the Act for reference.) Chadwick saw the Act as restoring to the able-bodied pauper an incentive and inducement to work and self-help. He called it a great engine of social improvement. From this point of view, therefore, the Act was progressive. The short-term harshness would produce long-term benefits by helping the individual to be master of his own interests. Such views as 'being cruel to be kind' (Fraser) and 'Heaven helps those who help themselves' (Smiles) were heavily criticized by members of the anti-Poor Law movement who saw the Act as repressive.

Contemporary critics such as Oastler and Fielding and modern ones such as Hobsbawm and Thompson have argued that the Act was **repressive**, on two basic grounds: the first is moral with a strong religious element, the other is political and contains elements of self-interest. For the critics, the Poor Law provided paupers with sustenance but on humiliating and unacceptable terms. It also saw paupers as having a base nature, which it was the duty of government to correct. Thus the tenets of liberal individualism were shelved in order that central government could control the poor. On a political level, the Act was seen as unconstitutional in its usurpation of parliamentary powers. It also withdrew the right of local self-government and was therefore an attack on the middle classes and on the right of ratepayers to decide how the rates were spent.

As important as the repressive nature of the Act are **arguments against the Act being progressive**. Firstly, it was concerned with the deterrence of pauperism rather than with the problem of poverty. Secondly, the Act acknowledged but subsequently dismissed involuntary paupers. It admitted their existence but stated that they would have to suffer in the interests of the majority.

The Whig decline

By 1835, the Whigs were in decline and, although many of their achievements seem to be superficial, they had lasting and in many cases positive future effects upon British society. The Whigs had failed to resolve the Irish Question and move towards a planned political economy, but the seeds of future parliamentary reform had been sown. The superficiality of the reforms was almost certainly due to the continual conflict of interests, tending to political compromises. It is often said that the significance of Grey's time in office has less to do with the achievements of his ministry than with what it failed to do. We have already seen a number of arguments regarding this. However, on a positive note, the Whigs developed a national administrative system to replace its confused local predecessor. In a period when Britain could well have experienced violent revolution, the actual revolution was administrative rather than political or social.

Summary

The overriding issue in this chapter has obviously been one of reform: Tory unwillingness to concede it, radical agitation to influence the government, and Whig determination to tackle the problem with the aid of Canningites and radicals. Be sure to have a grasp of the **contents of the Reform Bill and its reception among the political unions and other radical organizations**. Assess how far the Reform Act and the subsequent reforms firstly **met the aims of their Whig creators** and secondly **fulfilled the expectations of the working classes**. In effect, you should be questioning whom the reforms were designed to help and whether they actually helped those groups.

Benthamite utilitarianism is in itself a significant concept and is of great importance for a fuller understanding of this period of Whig reforms. You should be aware of the **conflict of interests over the question of education** between Anglicans and Dissenters on the one hand and Benthamite reformers on the other.

Further important developments are, of course, **radical working-class and trade union dissatisfaction with continued suppression of trade union activity and lack of further constitutional reforms**, along with **middle-class concern over the continued existence of the Corn Laws**. Such unrest was to be influential in the rise of Chartism and the Anti-Corn Law League.

Chapter 18
Chartism and the Anti-Corn Law League

Introduction

Towards the end of the 1830s the cycle of **economic depression** had returned to Britain. Both lower and middle classes were affected by the decline in the economy. For the working classes, the steep increase in the price of bread while wages remained fairly static had a drastic effect upon their living standards. Where the middle classes were concerned, the effective reduction in the money supply obviously affected them also, particularly in that consumers were unable to spend as much on manufactured goods. In response to economic distress and the unfairness of the existing political system, both working and middle classes developed organizations that reflected their discontent.

Whilst Chartism was, on the one hand, **a product of industrialization**, on the other it was **an integral part of Britain's radical tradition**, taking many of Britain's ideas of manhood suffrage from Cartwright and the Hampden Clubs of 1812. The Anti-Corn Law League was born largely out of a combination of the economic depression after 1836 and dissatisfaction among the middle classes over the continued lack of effective parliamentary representation, even after the Reform Act 1832.

Chartism

It has been argued on various occasions that Chartism evolved directly from the **economic distress of the working classes**, that is, out of what Asa Briggs has termed 'hunger and anger'. However, it is certain that, while this was a driving force, there was also a very real **desire to alter the political and economic conditions of the country by parliamentary means**. By reforming Parliament, the Chartists hoped to bring new vitality to English society and commerce, while at the same time bringing about improved social conditions for the working classes. As we have already seen, Chartism was firmly grounded in the radical tradition, and this is particularly true of the six points of the **People's Charter**. The Charter called for:

1. manhood suffrage for those over 21;
2. secret ballots to protect voters;
3. abolition of the property qualification for MPs, which would enable the election of MPs on merit and not on wealth;

4. payment for MPs, enabling working men to give up work to serve the constituency;
5. equal constituencies whereby enabling representation was to be proportional to the number of electors;
6. annual parliaments which would prevent bribery and intimidation in Parliament.

The Six Points

OF THE

PEOPLE'S

CHARTER.

1. A VOTE for every man twenty-one years of age, of sound mind, and not undergoing punishment for crime.

2. THE BALLOT.—To protect the elector in the exercise of his vote.

3. NO PROPERTY QUALIFICATION for Members of Parliament—thus enabling the constituencies to return the man of their choice, be he rich or poor.

4. PAYMENT OF MEMBERS, thus enabling an honest tradesman, working man, or other person, to serve a constituency, when taken from his business to attend to the interests of the country.

5. EQUAL CONSTITUENCIES, securing the same amount of representation for the same number of electors, instead of allowing small constituencies to swamp the votes of large ones.

6. ANNUAL PARLIAMENTS, thus presenting the most effectual check to bribery and intimidation, since though a constituency might be bought once in seven years (even with the ballot), no purse could buy a constituency (under a system of universal suffrage) in each ensuing twelvemonth; and since members, when elected for a year only, would not be able to defy and betray their constituents as now.

Figure 11. A Chartist handbill outlining the 'six points'

Chartism was therefore echoing many of the ideas which appeared among the Hampden Clubs, but in a new and potentially explosive mixture. At its heart was working-class poverty and from such distress it took strength:

> That Chartism which has fustian jackets, blistered hands and unshorn chins as its emblems, has been denounced by those who would make it a thing of refinement and respectability, while we repeat the fact to our readers that Chartism means poverty – and poverty is a consequence of class legislation, the legitimate deduction from which is, that before poverty ceases, class legislation must be destroyed.
>
> (F. O'Connor, *Northern Star*, 1 August 1846)

Unlike food riots, Luddite activity and anti-Catholic rioting, Chartism was not so much a spontaneous reaction to social deprivation or political inequalities as a conscious and well-organized programme of agitation for political reform and social and economic justice. Chartist leaders had learnt their skills during the post-war agitation and had witnessed the disappointments of the Reform Act 1832, the failures of Robert Owen's general unionism and the reinforcement of the poverty trap with the Poor Law Amendment Act. From this broad spectrum of shared experience, the Chartists succeeded in attracting numerous diverse groups and were able to offer such groups strength by virtue of their shared discontent. **You should know something of the various groups enrolled in Chartism** and should also be aware of **the course of Owenite unionism, the political unions of the reform crisis and the forerunners of Chartism**.

The Chartists gained much of their support through the already well established reform groups such as the London Working Men's Association. Such groups had been set up when radical leaders realized that, far from being a reforming government, the Whigs were tiring of social reform, and were strongly opposed to any further political reform of parliament or the electoral system.

The LWMA was formed in 1836 for the continuation of reform agitation, and in the course of this the People's Charter was developed in 1838 with assistance from a number of radical MPs such as Francis Place. Because of the shared experiences of discontent it was only a short step for a number of other reform groups and political unions to accept the Charter as a common basis for reform agitation. Chartism therefore grew from three starting points:

1. **disillusion with the limitations inherent in the Reform Act 1832** which excluded the working classes from the franchise and saw a hardening of mutual support between the middle and upper classes to the exclusion of the masses;
2. **social distress** as a result of rapid industrialization and urbanization, particularly in periods of economic depression;
3. **unemployment**, which saw a combination of protests amongst articulate artisans and declining handicraft workers.

As we have seen, the original institutionalized Charter groups were largely concerned with **parliamentary reform** and tended to be dominated by the educated elements of the working classes, that is, those who were already politically aware. However, as the economic trough deepened, unemployed workers began joining the Chartist groups in larger numbers. Added to the original political demands which echoed Paine's Rights of Man were new claims for the **economic rights of labour**. These gained strength in the face of the harshness of industrial capitalism.

The most effective way of dispensing with the hardship caused by capitalism, as we have seen in the extract from the *Northern Star*, was to destroy the class legislation that had created the poverty. From originally being a movement solely for political reform in the radical tradition, Chartism, with the influx of the industrial unemployed, became a protest for **universal suffrage on economic as well as political grounds:**

> Universal suffrage means meat and drink and clothing, good hours, and good beds, and good substantial furniture for every man and woman and child who will do a fair day's work. Universal suffrage means a complete mastery by all the people over all the laws and institutions in the country; and with that mastery the power of providing suitable employment for all, as well as of securing to all the full proceeds of their employment.

In support of E. P. Thompson's claims for an established working-class consciousness, we see here, for the first time in an institutionalized form, class conflict between workers and capitalists.

To a great extent Chartism gained strength from its **regional nature**. The movement tended to have the strongest following in areas where traditional industries such as textiles were in a state of decline. Areas where Chartism was powerful included Birmingham, Leeds, London and Nottingham, and in such regions it tended to draw its support from groups such as the handloom weavers and other skilled artisans. The regional nature of the organization had advantages as well as disadvantages. Local grievances did not tend to take a secondary position to national objectives; rather, the nationwide aims of the movement found a vehicle in local issues. The disadvantages were that the image of national unity, far from being a reality, was only a result of the widespread location of Chartist groups. A major difficulty arose out of the localized nature in that it became difficult to take co-ordinated action. Each area had its own leaders and political or economic complaints. In Leeds, under the influence of O'Connor, there was an emphasis amongst the handloom weavers on physical force in protest at being replaced by machinery. (Note the similarities in protest and location between such activity and Luddism 1811–15.)

Chartism was on the whole an **industrial and urban** phenomenon, gaining little support in agricultural regions. From being a political protest in the radical mould it developed into a movement **aware of its role in class conflict**. Chartists began to see the problems of British society not simply as being inherent in the political system or even in the ruling ideology, but as being rooted in the economic rationale underpinning the ruling hegemony.

There was frequent and often fierce debate within the movement over the action to be taken and, more importantly, over the form that action itself should take. The conflict was over **the use of moral or physical force**. The moderates within the movement were prepared to pressurize the government with the aid of Parliament's few radical MPs. However, leaders of the movement such as Attwood and Lovett were not prepared to see the threat of physical violence, which lay under the surface of the movement, spill over into actual physical insurrection. It is certain that the movement was not irrevocably split by this debate, as it was not a clear-cut issue. Underlying all Chartist agitation was the threat of physical violence, and when it became clear that the middle classes were not going to return to the working classes the support they had received during the reform crisis, the calls for direct defiance of the law became stronger.

By 1838, through the pages of the *Northern Star*, Feargus O'Connor emerged as the chief advocate of direct action. Despite continuing to express a desire for the use of moral force for as long as possible, he emphasized that moral force could only remain effective for a certain length of time. In the end it would be better for Chartists to die as free men rather than continue to live under slavery. This element of compromise is of greater significance than any internal strife within the movement. It would appear that **the dilemma was not so much whether violent action was justified but rather how far the movement could be pushed before its moral protest spilled over into violent action**. In a now-famous election speech in 1839 (reported in the *Operative*) Harvey summed up the Chartist position:

> What is it that we want? Not to destroy property and take life, but to preserve our own lives, and to protect our own property – viz, our labour. We are for Peace, Law, Order, but if our oppressors shall violate the law – if our despots shall trample upon order – then we will fall back upon the constitution, and defend the few remaining of the blood-bought rights left us by our fathers. The Whigs shall never violate the constitution of this country as they have done in Canada. They charge us with being Physical Force Men; I fling the charge back in the teeth of these canting liberals. Let them call to mind their own words and deeds during the humbug reform agitation . . . Again I say, we are for peace, but we must have our rights speedily: peaceably if we can, *forcibly if we must*.

This final tenet was eventually adopted by the **People's Convention** of 1839. This had also called for a **national holiday or general strike** among the working classes (an idea that emerges often during the Chartist period and one that has been deemed the forerunner of the 1926 General Strike). When the Convention ended it was in disarray, as the majority of the much-discussed plans had already met with failure – the petition to Parliament, and the national holiday. Many of the leaders had already been imprisoned when the Convention broke up, and this in fact preceded the major outbreak of disorder that year, namely the **Newport uprising**. You should already be aware of the main causes of the rising and the course it took.

The failure of other planned risings in late 1839 and early 1840 saw the Chartists in disarray by the spring of 1840. The number of arrests increased together with the rate of departure of disillusioned moderates. In the face of government determination to arrest Chartist agitators at the first indication of illegal action, the Chartists had to accept the necessity of gradual expansion and consolidation. As a result of this, a legal organization (the public face of Chartism) was formed – the National Charter Association – in July 1840. Within two years there were 48 000 members, by which time the Chartists had recovered enough to present their second petition. As with its predecessor, however, the Charter was rejected by a large majority in the House of Commons.

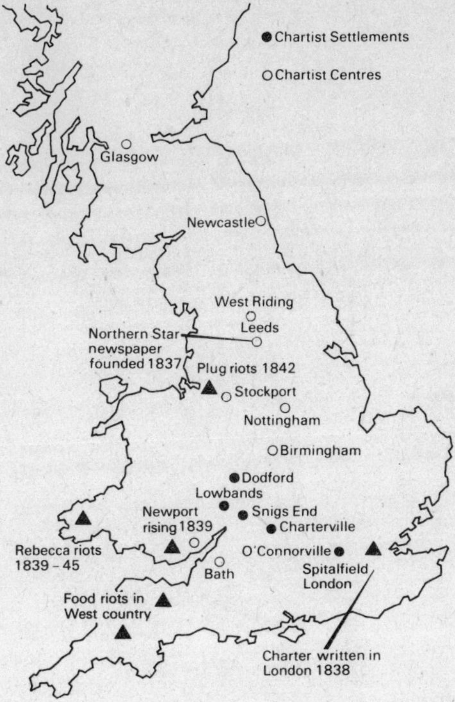

Figure 12. Centres of Chartist activity

Once again the Chartists were faced with the problem of what action to take when legal constitutional methods failed. There was further discussion of violent action, but the organization's leaders were not prepared to take steps which could lead to the arrest of the entire leadership. The economic depression and the increase in inflation took the initiative out of the hands of the Chartist leaders. With a record 10 per cent of the population on poor relief, the atmosphere was charged with the threat of insurrection. Despite the failure of the riots and strikes which spread from

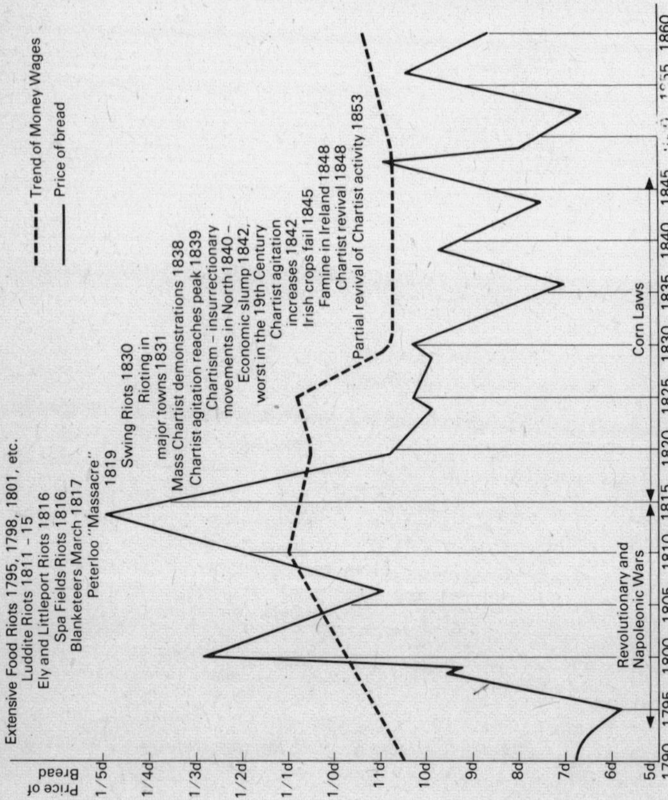

Figure 13. An index of social unrest. The diagram shows the relationship between social tension in Britain between 1790–1860 and the trend of money wages and the price of bread.

Staffordshire through Lancashire to involve fifteen counties and which came to be known as the **'Plug–Plot' riots** (you should know the course that these took), a new political dimension was added to the economic protests of the trades. Although there had been co-ordinated trade union action before, for the first time such action was organized under the banner of Chartism and the ideal of a '**Grand National Holiday**'. The latter it was felt would **sweep away the existing government and make way for the self-government of the people**. It is important to understand the ideas behind William Benbow's 'Grand National Holiday' and to this end there are several very good journal articles available.

With the defeat of the strikes Chartism began to weaken, although O'Connor continued to be active within the working classes. However, by 1851 even O'Connor's Chartist Co-operative Land Society had to be closed down.

With the revolutions of 1848 in Europe to inspire them into a final show of strength, a huge meeting was planned for Kennington Common, to be followed by a march on Parliament. The latter was banned by the government, which at the same time rejected a third petition. This saw the effective destruction of the movement which, however, continued in a small way with Christian and Teetotal Chartism into the 1850s. The mass support was, however, no longer there.

In the light of the aims of the Chartists, is it surprising that they failed? This type of question is common in examinations. **One of the main problems was centred on the desire for revolutionary change by constitutional means, yet without gaining the support of the middle classes**. This and Chartism's **dependence upon economic crisis** saw its downfall. Because of the periodic upturns in the economy there was a gradual draining away of Chartist support. It is thus worth considering the argument that Chartism fell between two stools: wanting revolutionary change without revolution while at the same time alienating any possibility of middle-class support by adopting antagonistic policies towards the landed and manufacturing classes. For their part, the middle classes had already gained the desired influence in Parliament and were quite prepared to use force to defend it from Chartist encroachment.

The Anti-Corn Law League

A large proportion of the middle classes were well pleased with their new-found franchise after 1832. Although a number still opposed the domination of Parliament by the landed aristocracy, they were reasonably content until the trade depression of 1836. When profit margins were hit by inflation and unemployment, the influential industrialists called once again for a return to free trade. If the Corn Laws and other tariffs on foreign goods were lifted, there was the possibility of not only improving the home market, but also expanding foreign trade.

The repeal of the Corn Laws and a return to free trade, it was argued, would improve the standard of living in Britain by **giving British industrialists an expanded market for their manufactured goods, thus reducing unemployment and the cost of bread**. It would also **improve British agriculture through foreign competition**, while at the same time **assisting peace in Europe through mutual trade**. In essence these were the main arguments of **Richard Cobden**; his co-leader of the movement, **John Bright**, was successful in giving the movement for the repeal of the Corn Laws a broader base of support by **attacking the landed aristocracy on moral grounds** (something common in radical activity). The League was shrewd in not aiming for broad reform like the Chartists: they placed the emphasis of their campaign upon one objective, namely the repeal of the Corn Laws. as Asa Briggs has pointed out, 'They saw the advantages of a single formula which everyone could understand and they accurately assessed the particular appeal of that formula in the new industrial areas of England' (*The Age of Improvement,* Longman, 1959).

While the majority of the League's supporters were members of the manufacturing classes, support was also drawn from liberal–humanitarian groups and various dissenting orders (Bright was a Quaker). The League was neither democratic nor always consistent in its arguments, while its methods were in many instances similar to those employed by the major political parties. Pressure was applied to ensure the registration of voters for League supporters, whilst dislodging Tories opposed to the League. Cobden and Bright were frequently accused of being revolutionary agitators, but such accusations were in many ways as unreal as the League's own moral policies.

The importance of the League is twofold: the methods employed and the successes achieved. The League, with its well-organized and masterful campaigning, represented the **first mobilization and manipulation of public opinion on a national scale**. The funds available to the League enabled it to support three newspapers and a host of cheap pamphlets. While the successes were limited (the Corn

Laws were not repealed until after the Irish famine in 1846, and then only at Peel's instigation), the psychological effect of the campaign was of great significance. It was **a struggle for control of government by the middle classes**, an attempt to assert their recently acquired franchise and their economic influence. The struggle was against what was seen as the last remnants of feudalism.

The legacy

Although they had to wait for Peel's repeal of the Corn Laws, the League, and Bright in particular, claimed that the repeal was an indication that the middle classes had asserted their right to govern the country. While maintaining that he had called for repeal of the Corn Laws in response to the famine in Ireland and not as a result of middle-class pressure, it is clear that, since 1841, Peel had been following a policy of free trade aimed at assisting the middle classes and the development of the economy.

While we can see that the repeal of the Corn Laws had neither the drastic economic nor political effect the League claimed it would have, there was certainly a growing awareness by the Tory as well as the Whig aristocracy that the middle classes were a growing political and economic force. Although 1846 cannot be said to be an assertion of middle-class hegemony, it is clear that the 1840s marked a growth of class awareness amongst the middle classes and fuller realization of the implications of 1832.

Summary

Remember that Chartism was as much a part of the radical tradition stretching back to the late eighteenth century as it was a result of industrialization. The cornerstone of Chartist activity was the idea that **political oppression and economic and social deprivation or exploitation could be corrected legitimately through parliamentary action**.

Assess the extent to which Chartism was merely a question of '**hunger and anger**' and ask questions about whether it was more of an **economic movement as opposed to one seeking radical political upheaval**. Important in any study of Chartism is its **growth in the provinces** and the institutional framework of the **LWMA** and political unions such as the **BPU**.

You should be able to suggest reasons for the **local nature** of much Chartist activity and support these with reference to the **decline of staple industries** in these areas, e.g. textiles and more particularly the handloom weavers. Do not forget the **class nature** of much of the movement and the **influence of Irish activists and the unstamped press** on this. Also of importance is the **debate over the adoption of moral or physical force**, i.e. whether the petition or rebellion was the best course of action.

Look at reasons for the **decline of Chartism**. Was there a failure in the strategy adopted or was the decline an inevitable result of the fragmentary nature of the movement?

Regarding the **Anti-Corn Law League**, you should study its **background**, e.g. middle-class dissatisfaction with its minimal gains from the Reform Act 1832 and the **failure of the Whig administration to repeal the Corn Laws**. Another important element is the way in which some League members saw the movement as a means of altering the social structure by **challenging aristocratic hegemony**.

What were the **aims** of the ACLL? Remember that they saw free trade as a means of creating peace through international economic inter-dependence. Compare the **strategy of propaganda and persuasion** employed by the ACLL with the strategies of the Chartists.

Finally, consider the **extent to which ACLL pressure actually influenced the decision to repeal the Corn Laws** and also **how much the aristocracy actually relinquished any power by the repeal**.

Chapter 19
Peel and the Conservative Party

Introduction

Robert Peel came to dominate the political scene in early Victorian England and has often been termed the greatest British Prime Minister of the nineteenth century. Under his ministry, the **Catholics were emancipated**, and after 1832 the **Tory party rebuilt** and the **principles of conservatism redefined**. He was, however, certain that his **loyalty to the nation lay before his loyalty to the Party**. And it was this certainty that led to policy decisions which were eventually to split the Tories and allow his arch-rival in the Party, Disraeli, to gain power.

Peel was the son of a very successful cotton manufacturer and was fortunate enough to be left a substantial inheritance. He also inherited an insight into the lifestyle and economic requirements of the industrial middle classes and the manufacturing élite. His education led to his association with the aristocracy and he began his career as a traditional Tory. However, by the end of his career he had become a liberal–Conservative more in tune with the needs of the middle classes. Peel's success was centred upon his **ability to shift with the changing currents in society**, and the rest of this chapter will attempt to highlight this skill. It is particularly important to note his flexibility on the issues of cash, corn and Catholics.

Peel's apprenticeship

Peel entered Parliament in 1809 and his abilities were soon recognized by Lord Liverpool who appointed him **Chief Secretary for Ireland** in 1812. He retained this post until 1818, having in the meantime become **MP for Oxford University** (1817). In 1819 he was **Chairman of the Committee on the Gold Standard**, while in 1822 he was once again promoted within the Cabinet, this time to **Home Secretary**. Peel's activity in the first of these positions and the subsequent **recommendations of the committee displeased the landed aristocracy** who had invested heavily in agricultural improvements at high mortgage rates, only to find a cut in the money supply forcing consumer demand up and therefore prices down. As Home Secretary, Peel was responsive to calls for **legal and prison reform**, which culminated in the **foundation of the Metropolitan Police Force in London**.

As Home Secretary during the 1820s Peel saw as his main problem **Catholic agitation for emancipation**. Peel had already refused office under Canning on the grounds of his (Peel's) opposition to Catholic emancipation. He had become the defender in Parliament of ultra-Tory and therefore of ultra-Protestant interests. By 1828, however, Peel realized that the strength of feeling in Ireland was such that if emancipation was not forthcoming then full-scale rebellion led by O'Connell and the Catholic Association was a certainty. Peel's acceptance of the need for emancipation led to his being branded a traitor to his Protestant colleagues. You should question whether, in the light of his fall from grace over both cash and Catholics, it is very surprising that Peel opposed the Reform Bill. Was he trying to appease his critics within the Tory Party or did he feel that too many doors had already been opened to the lower orders? Examiners often ask whether **Peel's policy on cash and Catholics** really did amount to a betrayal of his party's principles. **Were these policies early indications of his future liberal–Conservatism, or rather part of a survival plan for the traditional form of government in the face of possible revolution?**

The Conservative Party

Despite losing the 1835 election to a unified front of Whig and Catholic MPs (the Lichfield House Compact), Peel had given the Tories a short term in office late in the previous year. More importantly, he supplied what they needed most urgently: positive leadership and a clear indication of the direction in which the policy of the Party (now to be called the Conservative Party) was to move. The **Tamworth Manifesto** outlined the need for **flexibility and moderation in good government; it recognized the Reform Bill and accepted that moderate future reforms were justifiable if they righted an obvious wrong**.

Peel's main aim within the Tamworth Manifesto and throughout the 1830s was to **persuade Tories that they should change from class self-interest to national interest and to convince the new middle-class electors that the old Tory Party had become the new Conservative Party with the interests of the nation at heart**.

Just as Peel disagreed with reform for reform's sake, so he disapproved of opposition for its own sake. Subsequently he supported the Whig administration whenever he was convinced that their policy was for the good of the nation.

Repeal of the Corn Laws and free trade

Britain had witnessed approximately seventy-five years of industrial development by 1841 when Peel took office for the second time. Most of this expansion had not been planned, and as a result Britain was witnessing a large number of new social problems. The Whig government under Melbourne had also failed to realize the implications of a trade depression, and continued to run an inflated budget which left them with a £2500 000 annual deficit.

Peel's majority of eighty in the 1841 election allowed him much-needed flexibility in policy-making. He decided on the need for renewed confidence by the business community in the economy and therefore embarked on a **programme of economic reform**. He brought to the economy the same standards of national interest he had adopted in everyday political life. Peel first **amended the sliding scale for the price of corn**. Instead of prohibition, Peel envisaged fair protection in the national interest. The backbench protectionists saw this as a measure against landed interests, while Cobden saw it as a pitiful halfway measure.

The most important element of Peel's fiscal policy was the **reduction in tariffs**, particularly in the now famous free trade budgets of 1842 and 1845. The first of these saw a reduction in tariffs to a maximum figure of:

1. 5 per cent on raw materials;
2. 12 per cent on goods which were already partially manufactured;
3. 20 per cent on manufactured goods.

These tariffs were lowered again in 1845 and helped the move towards lower prices, an increase in consumer demand for goods at the cheaper prices and a growth in employment.

The second of Peel's fiscal policies to have lasting effects was the **reintroduction of income tax**, aimed firstly at balancing the deficit inherited from the previous Whig administration and secondly to make up government revenue otherwise reduced by tariff concessions. Despite seemingly crippling deficits inherited from the Whigs and loss of revenue through remission of tariffs, the economy under Peel was running in the black by 1846. This alone is a clear justification for the harsh fiscal policies adopted by this administration. The **Bank Charter** of 1844 helped inspire confidence in the economy, as did the **Companies Act** which followed it. You should be aware of the contents of these Acts and the reasons for their importance. Why was the supremacy of the Bank of England of such importance to the economy?

The **repeal of the Corn Laws** was a logical step within such a free trade policy as Peel's. The Irish famine brought immense pressure on the government to dispense with the importation restrictions on corn. However, it was as much the success of his earlier free-trade policies as the potato blight which saw the repeal of the Corn Laws. Peel felt that improved farming methods rather than protection would bring security to British agriculture. You should not of course neglect the part played by the Anti-Corn Law League (see chapter 18) and should be able to assess to what extent political pressure played a part in Peel's decision.

Summary

It is important to be able to throw light on Peel's political development with reference to his **background**: how he began his career as **a staunch Tory with a sound grasp of the requirements of Britain's growing business community**, and how his **relationship with the aristocracy was always uneasy**.

Peel's **early political career** is essential information for any examination answer on his development; having gained a reputation for honesty and impartiality over Ireland as Chief Secretary in Lord Liverpool's administration, he moved to the important economic post of Chairman of the Bullion Committee in 1819. Here he was to play an important role in the resumption of cash payments and the development of the Bank Act 1844. He was to be instrumental in the creation of an income tax and a more positive move towards free trade.

As **Home Secretary** he was influenced to quite a large extent by Benthamite principles, particularly with regard to prison reforms. During Wellington's administration he resigned his seat in opposition to the ultra-Tory tendency that was growing in the party over the problems of Ireland. Note the **importance of his policies on cash and Catholics**, and **assess the extent to which these were a betrayal of Tory principles** as was argued by Peel's opponents. **Was Peel's opposition to reform an attempt to appease his critics or did he feel that too many concessions had already been made to the lower orders**? His refusal, however, to form an anti-reform administration would seem to indicate that he saw the Reform Act as inevitable.

Peel provided positive leadership and a clear indication of the direction in which the Tories were to move. The **Tamworth Manifesto** of 1834 saw a resurgence in Tory support and the growth of a new Conservative Party. The important policy changes were those which advocated a **move from class self-interest to legislation in the national interest**.

The **political and economic reforms** followed the policy of righting obvious political wrongs and appear to have gone just far enough to prevent any large-scale national opposition to the administration.

The **fiscal policies** of Peel's administration are an important area and you should be able to **assess how radical these were**. Likewise, with the **repeal of the Corn Laws**, it is important to be able to **discuss the extent to which this was a means of preserving the status quo**.

Chapter 20
British Foreign Policy 1815–65

Introduction

Before looking at this chapter, be sure you are aware of the political scene in Europe at the end of the Napoleonic Wars, in order to assess fully the implications of British Foreign policy at this time. After the long period of war there was a desire, amongst all the powers, for stability. Britain particularly urged the peacemakers to **strengthen the new balance of power, hoping to contain French imperialism within Europe and prevent Russian expansion in the east.**

One of the most important things to keep in mind when looking at British foreign affairs between 1815 and 1865 is the **level of continuity** amongst the various British foreign ministers of this period. All were consistently most concerned with protecting and advancing British interests. **Britain's trade and commercial empire was seen by all the British foreign secretaries of this period as the most important British interest**. Not only was British mercantilism aggressive in its search for new markets, but the government was also often seen to be aggressive in its defence of what it saw as British trading interests.

To defend commercial expansion on a worldwide scale, a **strong navy** emerged. With the gain of a number of strategically important bases, the British navy was able, with relative ease, to keep trade routes open and defend British interests from rival powers. This then was the period when Brittania really did 'rule the waves', although it is fair to say that she did so relatively unchallenged.

It would be a reasonably accurate assessment of British foreign policy to say that most of it was concerned with **European affairs** (containing France and restraining Russia), allowing imperial affairs to be run largely for and by British mercantile interests. Be sure that you are aware of how Britain saw the **balance of power in Europe** operating in its own interests, and why this was important. Likewise, you should know something of **Anglo–Russian** relations and the **Near- and Far-Eastern rivalry** between these two immense empires.

Castlereagh

While the other victorious powers at the Congress of Vienna made territorial demands, Britain was content with its acquisition of a number of islands and ports, thereby enhancing its **naval superiority** and strengthening its oceanic empire. Castlereagh was able to detach Britain from costly embroilments in Europe by virtue of this **strengthening of its position in world trade**. Castlereagh's chief aim at Vienna, however, was to **restore the balance of power in Europe and curtail any future expansionist policies harboured by the French**.

While Castlereagh was well aware of the need to protect British Imperial interests, he was also a firm believer in the need for European states to have a **forum for discussion** where mutual problems could be solved. It was thus of little surprise when Castlereagh in conjunction with the other European statesmen **dismissed the newly-emerging spirits of nationalism and liberalism** in favour of policies that were both workable and relevant at that very time. With this in mind, it is worth noting that Castlereagh **deemed the Holy Alliance to be mystical nonsense**, though he agreed with its sentiments. He preferred to **promote the continuation of the Quadruple Alliance** which had already proved itself, without recourse to 'sublime mysticism.'

Castlereagh's contemporary critics preferred to make little distinction between the two alliances, thus allowing them to link him conveniently with the despotic regimes of the European emperors, and to accuse him of ignoring liberalism and nationalism. By working with the continental powers, Castlereagh hoped to achieve Britain's diplomatic and imperial aims without the need for conflict.

The Quadruple Alliance and its associated Congress System would, it was hoped, provide European states with the forum for discussion which could prevent more costly wars. Do not accept the term 'Congress System' at face value or overestimate the extent to which it was a system at all, for there was no permanent discussion body in session. However, what has been termed the Congress System was based upon five major congresses, namely Vienna in 1815, Aix-la-Chapelle in 1818, Troppau in 1820, Laibach in 1821 and Verona in 1822.

At Aix-la-Chapelle it was agreed that the allied armies would withdraw from France, which would then return to full diplomatic status within the framework of post-Napoleonic Europe. Despite seeing the need for Europe's sovereigns and their ministers to take any actions necessary for the peace of Europe, Castlereagh was **only prepared for the Congresses to have limited functions**. The Carlsbad Decrees and the revolutions in Naples and Spain highlighted fundamental differences between the powers over the question of intervention. Whilst supporting the **rights of Europe's rulers to suppress revolutionary activity**, Castlereagh **refused to accept Tsar Alexander I's claim for the right to intervene in the affairs of other countries**.

It is important to **understand the interests of Austria in Naples and later Piedmont and the implications of the Troppau protocol**. Disappointed by Austria's employment of the terms of the Holy Alliance in its dealings with Piedmont, especially after his concessions over Naples, Castlereagh saw his European policy fragmenting. Meanwhile the continued attacks on him in Britain (which associated him with all things oppressive both home and abroad) did little to enhance his position.

In conclusion, Castlereagh's foreign policy has been termed a very personal one which used Britain's strength to **thwart expansionist policies** by its European rivals. As with his aristocratic colleagues in the Home Office, Castlereagh tended to see government and diplomacy as the **domain of the aristocracy**, and like his colleagues in the Home Office ignored (or failed to see the importance of) the growing political currents of **nationalism and liberalism**. You should consider **the extent to which his foreign policies were in the best interests of Britain or simply maintained the status quo**.

Canning

There was a certain amount of continuity in the foreign policies of Castlereagh and Canning. The latter, however, far from being a tool of aristocratic hegemony, was more **in tune with the economic requirements of Britain's capitalist classes**. Under Canning's direction, British foreign policy was positively **hostile towards the so-called Congress System favouring a vigorous endorsement of British nationalist self-interest**. While following in principle the tenets of Castlereagh's State Paper of 1820, i.e. preserving peace by maintaining the balance of power, Canning affirmed that the chief interests of foreign policy were the interests of England.

During his period as Foreign Secretary Castlereagh had been unfortunate in that Britain was experiencing a severe economic depression. Any signs of concession in European affairs had brought hostile responses from the population at home. In contrast, Canning served in the Foreign Office during a period of economic boom. Foreign policy could become more forceful, since Canning knew that opposition at home had relaxed.

There were four major crises during Canning's office, and each one saw a new and positively self-interested attitude to world affairs by the members of the Foreign Office. Unable to respond with arms or men to the first crisis when **France (supported by the Holy Alliance) invaded Spain to suppress a liberal rising**, Canning refused to allow the British government to become associated with the action. Instead, he chose to **exploit the disorder by cultivating trade with former Spanish colonies**. He said, regarding the French action; 'I looked another way; I sought materials for compensation in another hemisphere.'

The second crisis saw **the French threatening to claim former Spanish colonies in the West Indies and South America**. Following President Monroe's declaration that any such action by a European state would be deemed an unfriendly act towards the United States, **Canning threatened to use the British navy to defend the sovereignty of the Latin American states**. Similarly, Canning felt able to **use the British navy to defend the constitutionalists against reactionary forces in Portugal in 1824 and 1826**. In all of these instances we can witness Britain employing a foreign policy radically different from that of its European rivals. British policy was no longer concerned with *territorial* acquisition, but rather with acquiring an *economic* empire.

The fourth and potentially most volatile issue during Canning's term of office was the question of **Greek independence**. By the second decade of the nineteenth century, Turkey was fast losing its ability to contain liberal and nationalist elements within the diverse regions of its Empire. In the face of Russian attempts to gain more influence in the Balkans, Britain had either to see the Turkish Empire disintegrate under Russian pressure or work with the Tsar for Greek independence in order to **restrain Russian expansionism**. Canning chose the latter course, and with France and Russia agreed the **Petersburg Protocol** whereby Greece would become autonomous within the Turkish Empire. In order to persuade the Turks of the determination of the Petersburg signatories to enforce the Protocol, the allies sent a **joint fleet to blockade Turkish ports**. The subsequent battle of Navarino caused an outrage in

Europe, but in spite of this the Greeks were eventually to achieve independence in 1830.

It was argued by Metternich that Canning's ministry brought about the end of an era in European diplomacy. However, rather than being a staunch liberal (as he portrayed himself) Canning tended to **use liberalism to further his policies**. Neither Castlereagh nor Canning were particularly liberal in their outlook and only differed as foreign ministers in the way they applied their foreign policies. It is important to remember that both were Tories in the Liverpool administration and as such their chief interest was the **continuation and continuity of Tory policy**. If there is a major difference between the two men it is that Canning was **more aware of the economic and political needs of the newly-emerged and increasingly influential middle classes**.

Palmerston

Palmerston, it may be argued, drew upon the most successful elements of Castlereagh's and Canning's policies, using them to his own political ends. He was prepared to use congresses for the European states to discuss mutual problems whilst on other occasions his nationalism would harden considerably. Likewise, Britain's allies were chosen to suit current policy requirements ranging from liberal to reactionary. As with earlier British foreign policy, Palmerston's aim was to **arbitrate for the European states on worldwide issues to Britain's best interest and without committing himself to any one cause**. In this respect Palmerston was following the principles of foreign policy established by Castlereagh and Canning.

It is usual for Palmerston's career to be divided into **three periods**, which is both convenient and shows Palmerston and his policies at different stages of development. Whether as Foreign Secretary, Home Secretary or Prime Minister, Palmerston always tended to be greatly concerned with foreign affairs. The most successful of these periods was the earliest, **1830–41**. During this period in office Palmerston was able to **manipulate Belgian independence** to such an extent that the only parties to gain in real terms were Britain and the Belgians. The latter moved from being part of a united Netherlands to an independent state with guaranteed neutrality. French ambitions in the Low Countries had been thwarted, as had attempts at invoking the Troppau Protocol by the other members of the Holy Alliance, while the Low Countries became a buffer between Britain and potential European aggressors.

In Spain and Portugal in 1834, Palmerston had used British forces in an attempt to establish liberalism and even democracy in opposition to autocratic government on the rest of the Continent. In China during the **Opium War** of 1839–42 Britain **forced the Chinese to accept a policy of trade which was far better suited to British merchants than it was to the Chinese economy**. In the Near East, meanwhile, Palmerston was succesful in achieving his four-fold policy:

1. maintaining as strong a Turkish Empire as possible under the political circumstances;
2. preventing the spread of diverse nationalist revolts within the Ottoman Empire by defeating Mehemet Ali;
3. thwarting France's aims to expand its influence in the region through Mehemet Ali;
4. preventing Russian domination of the Balkans and large areas of the Near and Middle East.

Palmerston's **second period** ran from **1846 to 1851** and saw some minor successes in foreign policy, as well as stalemates. In a bid to increase French influence on the Iberian peninsula, Louis Philippe had arranged marriages for Queen Isabella and her sister. Aberdeen (Palmerston's predecessor) had agreed not to oppose the Orleanist candidacy for the Spanish throne openly. Palmerston, however, ended the Anglo-French entente with his **announcement that the French could not justifiably exclude a Coburg candidate**. Despite this setback to British policy, Palmerston **argued successfully against the partition of Switzerland, while remaining strictly neutral during the liberal revolutions of 1848**. Alongside these comparatively neutral or non-positive examples of Palmerston's foreign policy, we can set his **preparedness to use the British navy without parliamentary approval over the Kossuth and Don Pacifico affairs**, although the navy was never directly used in the Kossuth affair–diplomatic pressure and the threat of using force were sufficient. Such unconstitutional action prompted a rebuff from the Queen, and in the following year when Palmerston **unilaterally recognized Louis Napoleon's coup d'état**, he was dismissed from the Foreign Office and was without a post until he was appointed Home Secretary ten months later under Aberdeen.

The **final period** from **1855 to 1865** saw Palmerston as Prime Minister but deeply involved in foreign policy. Europe was much changed, both politically and diplomatically, following the Crimean War. Some of the major powers and newly emerging ones were controlled by fiercely nationalist governments to which the principles of balance of power and aristocratic diplomacy were symbols of the now obsolete dominance of the old order. Errors in European policy followed in the face of such opposition, although the British navy ensured the continued security of British interests outside the European sphere.

Palmerston has been termed a blusterer and a diplomatic bully. His aggressively British policy made him unpopular with allies but caught the imagination of the popular press and its readers at home. But for all of this, he was undoubtedly a very **shrewd manipulator of European affairs**. This enabled Britain to **avoid war with its chief rival (Russia)** for a quarter of a century while at the same time **limiting Russian encroachment upon British spheres of influence**.

Summary

By far the easiest way of analysing foreign policy in this period is to divide it into the terms of office of Castlereagh, Canning and Palmerston, and then to **compare the aims, achievements and failures of their respective policies**. Assess **how international relations had changed after 1815** and be prepared to indicate **how British foreign policy had altered** to meet the changed circumstances. **Was there a consensus in Britain's foreign policy aims** during this period and to what extent were variations in policy merely indications of different approaches to the same goal?

Be aware of **Castlereagh's aims** when working within the Concert of Europe and be able to indicate **how successful** these were in enhancing Britain's **economic and strategic position**. He aimed to maintain the balance of power in Europe, and you should **consider the extent to which this was in the best interests of Britain as well as maintaining the status quo**.

Canning, meanwhile, moved away from collaboration in the Congress System, preferring national self-interest. **Compare Britain's reactions to the major crises in Europe during Canning's office** and come to some conclusions about whether he was **a defender of liberalism or merely an opportunist** when it came to furthering Britain's economic and political interests.

You should question the **extent to which Palmerston was a Canningite**, and look at how he was **prepared to use the most effective measures of his predecessors** in order to achieve British aims. His final period in office saw failures in policy regarding the American Civil War, and the error in encouraging Polish and Danish national and liberal movements in 1863 and 1864.

Chapter 21
Disraeli and Conservatism

Introduction

Born of a relatively wealthy Jewish family in 1804, Disraeli was to emerge as one of the most controversial figures in British politics and the development of conservatism in the nineteenth century. His approach to political life was certainly unconventional: a flamboyant dresser, successful novelist and extreme egotist he managed to get elected to Parliament on the fourth attempt in 1837 as Member for Maidstone. In 1842 he joined the '**Young England**' movement, which had as its aim the forging of a link between the old aristocracy and the working classes in opposition to the new and powerful middle class. This would achieve, or so Disraeli hoped, a return to the ideals and deference of the pre-industrial era.

Party leader

Disraeli was an opponent of Peel's brand of liberal-conservatism and was to challenge Peel over both the Maynooth Grant and later the repeal of the Corn Laws. Siding with Lord George Bentinck and other Protectionists, Disraeli accused Peel of betraying both Conservative principles and the Conservative Party. As you will have seen from Chapter 18, Peel was a firm believer in government on national rather than party grounds. He supported the Whigs when he felt their policies were in the best interests of the country. Disraeli, however, felt that a strict division of principles and interests separated Whigs and Tories.

After Peel's defeat over the Coercion Bill for Ireland and subsequent resignation, the Conservative Party was in a state of disarray. The period 1846–66 was, however, a turning point for both Disraeli and the Conservative Party. Disraeli was soon to **abandon the agrarian principles of his 'Young England' period**. In 1849 he became leader of the Party in the Commons after Bentinck's death, and, as Chancellor of the Exchequer in Lord Derby's first administration, was soon to **discard his protectionist ideals** as well. In 1866 Disraeli convinced the Conservative Party of the need for **franchise reform**. He forced through electoral reforms that were far more radical than Gladstone's Bill of the previous year which he had helped defeat.

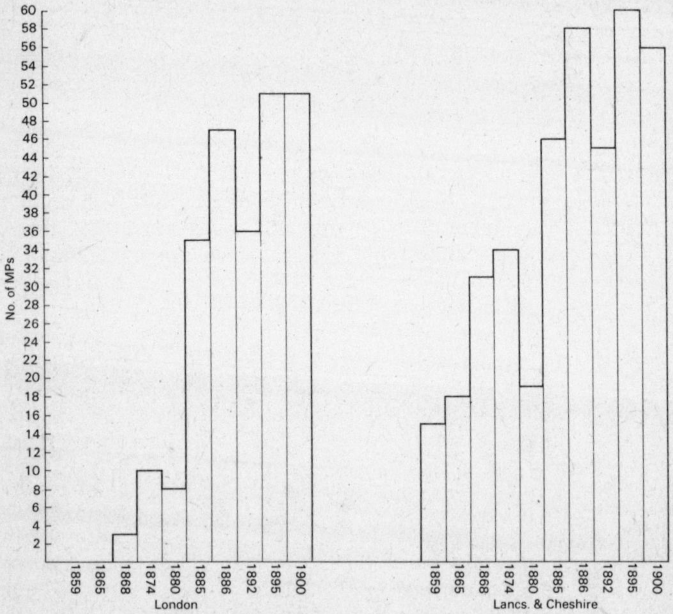

Figure 14. The growth of the 'New Conservative Party'

There are a number of important questions to be raised regarding Disraeli and his contribution to the development of a new and dynamic Conservative Party. **Did the dynamism stem from Disraeli's belief in Tory democracy or from a desperate bid by Disraeli to gain power for the Tories in order to keep his own position as Party leader?** Examiners may well ask candidates to **assess the extent to which Disraeli actually had any real policy on Tory democracy**. They may also ask **to what extent Disraeli's actions were merely reactions to Gladstone's liberalism**.

Conservative reform

From all the evidence it would appear that Disraeli was rather more concerned about using his political skill to keep the Conservatives in power than to assist the socially deprived areas of the community. The Reform Bill of 1867 was passed as much by the pressure on Parliament of public opinion and social unrest as it was by any well-laid plans of either Disraeli or Derby. Thus we must ask how much of the reforming zeal attributed to Disraeli was reality and how much propaganda.

A laudatory mythology tends to grow up around great or popular political leaders, and Disraeli is no exception. He has been attributed with the creation of the principles of 'Tory democracy', yet neither he nor Lord Derby had any belief in the need for increased democracy. We shall look at the myth of Tory democracy more closely in the next section on Disraeli in power. For the moment, however, it would be accurate to affirm Disraeli's **astute judgment in choosing the Tory Party as a vehicle for his ambitions**. The culmination of his success as Party leader came with the passing of the **second Reform Act**.

The Act also marked a new advancement for democracy within the British political system. It is important that you **know the main features of the Act and the course of the many conflicts** between Disraeli and Gladstone which led to its passing. Of particular note is the effect which **household suffrage** was to have upon the political scene, and you should also be aware of the importance of the **Redistribution Act which excluded urban and suburban voters from the county constituencies**. More reforms were to follow in Disraeli's second administration, but the extent to which the importance of these may have been overemphasized by the government is worth remembering.

It is, however, certain that, following the electoral defeat at the hands of Gladstone late in 1868, Disraeli was forced to rethink the Tory approach to politics in general and to the electorate in particular. As we have already noted, much of Disraeli's policy was a reaction to Gladstonian liberalism. He attacked the way in which Gladstone appeared to favour the interests and rights of other European nations over those of Britain. Gladstone's administration was also too narrow according to Disraeli. He argued that it ignored Britain's fundamental social problems in favour of utilitarian reforms which were administrative, rather than ones which could radically improve the deprivations experienced by large sections of the population. Disraeli also claimed that Gladstonian liberalism had a divisive effect upon British society, since it was centred upon middle-class non-conformism, thus excluding a large proportion of the population.

It was in the face of such divisiveness that Disraeli adopted Gorst's plan for a new and **paternalistic brand of Conservatism**, which was outlined in his now famous **speeches at Manchester and Crystal Palace in 1872**. In these addresses Disraeli emphasized the uniting influence the Tory Party would have once it was in power. In much of this philosophy Disraeli echoed his 'Young England' days where the supremacy of true English traditions inherited from some imaginary golden age was stressed. **The Church, the Crown, the fairness of the Anglo-Saxon constitution and the principle of empire were all deemed to be the true foundations of British society**. They had to be protected at all costs. However, with the decline in deference voting after the electoral reforms, it became clear that, if the Tories were going to attract the vote of the newly enlarged electorate, they had to offer something in return. The assurance of the county votes was no longer enough to defeat the liberals, particularly with large urban areas now returning MPs. The Tories could not, however, introduce a series of reforms which would lose them the county vote altogether. They therefore adopted a policy of **moderate social reform at home combined with a strident imperial policy abroad**.

In power 1874–80

Once Disraeli had been returned to power, he did not follow any radical new domestic policy even if we allow for the institution of various social reforms. Rather, he was content to follow the same brand of liberal–conservatism of which he had been so critical when it had been followed by Peel. In his novels and in his speeches Disraeli had criticized the terrible conditions in which much of the British population lived, calling for government action to correct them:

> Pure air, pure water, the inspection of unhealthy habitations, the adulteration of food, these and many kindred matters may be legitimately dealt with by the legislature . . . After all, the first consideration of a minister should be the health of the people . . .
>
> (Extract from Disraeli's speech at Manchester, April 1872)

In office, however, Disraeli tended to leave the initiative for social reform up to his Home Secretary, R. A. Cross, and to the Civil Service. The latter instituted a number of administrative umbrella Acts to incorporate a number of similar pieces of legislation. For example, the **Public Health Act 1875**, brought together a number of individual Health Acts dealing with nuisance, burials and refuse disposal into one comprehensive piece of legislation. You should **know the main elements of this Act and other reforming social legislation of the period, e.g. Artisans Dwelling Act 1875, Merchant Shipping Act 1875 and the Education Act 1876.**

Also important were the **Protection of Property Act, the Public Worship Act and the Enclosure of Commons Act**. There is little evidence to suggest that Disraeli was the author of any of these Acts, but they increased his national standing and enhanced his popularity with the urban working-class voters. The **myth of Tory democracy** developed by Gorst in the late 1860s was therefore employed to great effect by the Disraeli administration. As an electioneering tool this ploy was highly successful, but once the need for even moderate reform had passed, the reforming zeal petered out. Meanwhile the arrival of a new economic trough and problems in foreign affairs caused the administration to dwell less on social problems at home and more on problems abroad.

Sweeping social reform would have raised a storm of protest from stalwarts of individual liberty, yet Disraeli was able to go just far enough to **strengthen working-class Conservatism without losing the vote of the gentry**. It would be fair to argue that there was **little or no discontinuity between the liberal and Conservative administrations of this period**, rather a highlighting of the minor differences for electioneering purposes.

Foreign policy

While Disraeli argued that conservatism was the unifying bond of British society at home, he maintained that the Conservative Party was the only true and capable agent for British interests abroad. In essence it was deemed to be the embodiment of the spirit of British imperialism. Disraeli was **actively interventionist** and subsequently gained the support of those who had earlier supported Palmerston. He opposed Gladstone's attitude which accepted that all states had moral rights and obligations, particularly where this was likely to interfere with British spheres of influence.

The majority of Disraeli's foreign policy was eastward-looking, and it was during this period that the term '**jingoism**' emerged from a contemporary music-hall song. This would seem to indicate that the government's aggressive stance in foreign policy, particularly where Russia was concerned, had permeated all levels of society. Jingoism was thenceforth used by critics to describe Disraeli's aggressive foreign policy. He actively **encouraged imperial expansion** and was prepared to achieve this either by **financial arrangements**, as with the **purchase of the Suez Canal shares** from the Khedive of Egypt, or by **wars, both expansionist and punitive**, as against the **Zulus** or in **Afghanistan** and the **Transvaal**. The other effective measure he adopted was to **allow colonies some rights**. Slavery was eradicated in the Gold Coast in 1874 and India gained Queen Victoria as

Empress. The advantages of the latter may only have been in people's imaginations, however. You should be able to assess how important these individual events were and whether together they amounted to a new spirit of imperialism.

Of continued significance to British foreign policy was the **Eastern Question and the conflict with Russia**. It is important to remember the course of Anglo–Russian rivalry in the Middle and Near East. With the continued decline of the Ottoman Empire and the increase in Balkan nationalism, Disraeli was at pains to **support the Turks and particularly Constantinople against Russian influence**. The chief reason for his support of Turkey was the realization that Constantinople was the **gateway to India**. If the Russians or a power dependent on them were to hold Constantinople, this would leave the way open for a Russian Army to march through the Middle East to India. For this reason Disraeli **rejected the Treaty of San Stefano in 1878** which gave a Russian-backed and much enlarged Bulgaria far greater access to the Black Sea. Both Britain and Austria-Hungary were disturbed by this Treaty, and under their combined pressure Russia agreed to discuss the Balkan situation. For a more detailed analysis of this you should see Chapter 3.

At home Gladstone was busy campaigning against Disraeli's interventionist foreign policy and his inhumanity in supporting the Turks against the Christian Bulgarians. The humanitarian **outrage in Britain over the Turkish massacres in Bulgaria and Disraeli's failure to refute Gladstone's accusations** was one of the major contributory factors to the former's election defeat in 1880. Home affairs also played their part in Disraeli's election failure. The **economic depression worsened** and the formerly protectionist **Disraeli refused to provide aid to Britain's ailing agricultural system**. The **militancy of the Irish politicians in Parliament** also added to the weakening of Disraeli's position. Ill health prevented him from campaigning effectively and the election result saw the Liberals returned with an overall majority of forty-six. Disraeli died in April 1881, almost a year after the election defeat.

Summary

Again, you should be aware of how Disraeli's background was to affect his political development. Of particular importance is his association with the '**Young England**' movement, since it was to some extent a source for the political philosophy which was to develop into Conservative Party policy.

You should examine his opposition to Peel and be able to assess the **extent to which Disraeli was able to manipulate and use public opinion as a weapon**. How successful was Disraeli in creating a political myth regarding Conservative policy based on his own personality?

In his rivalry with Gladstone you should **examine the extent to which Disraeli's policies were a radical expression of public opinion**. You should also consider how far the policies were a tactical and opportunist **reaction to Gladstone's policies**.

Compare the Conservative paternalism of the 1874–80 government with the growth of a strong anti-Liberal middle-class Conservatism opposed to Liberal radicalism after 1870. You should be clear about the **importance of this lower middle-class conversion to Conservatism** and the role it was to play in the 1885 election victory.

The survival of the Conservative Party does, however, owe much to Disraeli's strength of personality. At a time when divisions in society were developing on the lines of class and capital versus labour, Disraeli was able to move the Conservative Party from agrarian preoccupations towards consideration of urban problems.

Chapter 22
Gladstone and Liberalism

Introduction

Gladstone began his career as a reactionary Tory and a staunch Anglican, yet he came to represent the very essence of Victorian liberalism. His great rivalry with Disraeli was to dominate British politics between 1866 and 1881. Their opposition was based upon religious, social, political and personal grounds.

Having originally planned to enter the Church after his successful career at Eton and Oxford, Gladstone soon became interested in the idea of politics as a moral crusade in the best interests of all people. He developed a **policy of politics linked with morality**, feeling that if political decisions were based upon moral correctness they could not be wrong. He developed from staunch Toryism to liberal democracy and was able to **pave the way for the effective transition of power from the aristocracy to mass democracy**.

It is important to be aware of **Peel's influence** on Gladstone's political thinking. It was Peel who taught Gladstone the principle of **using political power to achieve noble aims**, in contrast to Disraeli's pursuit of power for its own sake. Peel's influence extended to Gladstone's time as Chancellor of the Exchequer under Palmerston, when he **attempted to provide indirect social assistance through financial and fiscal control**. Of particular importance were the **free trade budgets** which, though they improved the economy, were costly in terms of the decline in money available for social reforms. As forerunner to his clashes with Disraeli over foreign policy, Gladstone **opposed Palmerston's aggressive stance** on the grounds that it was costing the country too much. He was prepared to support Palmerston's foreign policies when they appeared liberal (as with Italian unification in 1859). When they showed their aggressive side, however, he vehemently opposed such policy, as with the Don Pacifico affair and the Crimean War, over which he resigned.

However, Gladstone's economic policies gained him the **support of the large numbers of middle-class merchants, bankers and industrialists** who were becoming more influential in the new Liberal Party throughout Britain. This stood in good stead when the time came for him to assume the leadership of the Party, first as leader of the Whigs in the Commons and then as leader of the Party.

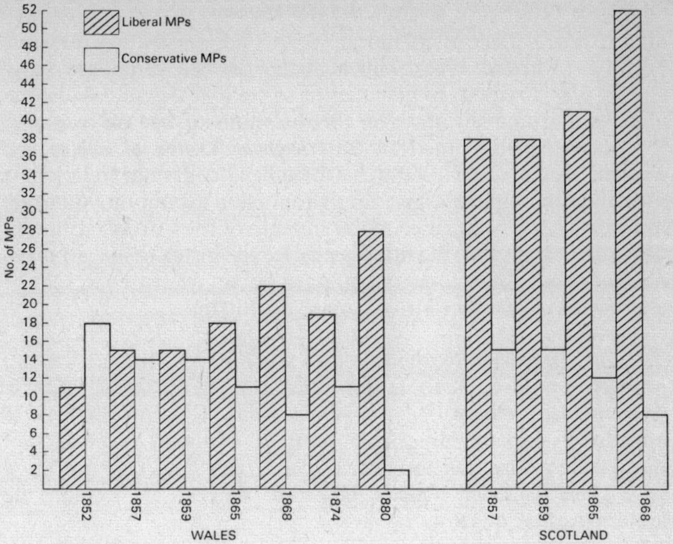

Figure 15. The growth of 'Celtic fringe' liberalism

At the time of Gladstone's rise through the ranks of the parliamentary Whig Party the concept of liberalism was emerging in the provinces. The publication and growth of liberal newspapers aided the expansion of liberal ideals outside of traditional Whig strongholds. This new liberalism had little cohesion in its early stages, being made up of liberal newspaper editors, non-conformist thinkers and members of the trade union labour aristocracy. Gladstone and Bright realized the importance of uniting these diverse groups within the framework of the new Liberal Party. His image as the 'people's William' was cultivated by Bright, who canvassed support for Gladstone's future leadership of the Party. This was particularly true during the **Reform Crisis of 1866** when, despite his speech of 1864 insisting on the right of every man to be within the pale of the constitution, Gladstone only proposed a moderate extension to the franchise. Even Disraeli's passing of a more 'liberal' Reform Act did little to dent Gladstone's popularity and the memory of 1864. It was thus that Gladstone and the Liberals gained office in 1868.

Liberals in power: reform and Ireland

It may be said that the basic tenets of the newly-elected Liberal administration were **progress and improvement**. These applied not only to the British mainland in various administrative reforms, but also to **Ireland**, where much of the new government's early energy was directed. In his attempt to pacify Ireland, Gladstone made important reforms over the questions of **land and religion** in this early period. In 1869 the **Anglican Church of Ireland was disestablished**, i.e. it ceased to be the official church in Ireland. At the same time it had to give up a proportion (about one-quarter) of the wealth it had gained at the expense of the Catholic Church. The move, however, did little to placate the bitter Irish Catholics, nor did it help Gladstone's standing at home, where it was seen as a betrayal of his once strict Anglican principles.

The **First Land Act 1870** attempted to solve one of Ireland's worst problems, namely the **rights of agricultural tenants and the obligations of their absentee landlords**. The loopholes in this Act again did little to appease Irish bad feeling. Historians have tended to see both of these Irish reforms as 'too little too late', and it was the proposed 1873 **Irish University Reform Bill** that helped to defeat the administration in 1874.

Also, Gladstone's reforms at home only appeased those sections of society which had grown in strength within the new Liberal Party. Hence **social reform and material aid for the working classes were ignored in favour of administrative reform**. Forster's **Education Act (1870)** saw the election of School Boards which were empowered to levy a school rate and buy land for the building of new board schools. The Boards were also authorized to make attendance at the elementary schools compulsory. The **Army Regulation Act (1871)** completed Cardwell's reform and modernization of the armed forces in the light of the disastrous performances in the Crimea. The **Civil Service reforms** of 1870 were inspired by the liberal principles of individual self-help, allowing for all Civil Service appointments to be open to public competition. The **University Test Act** opened teaching posts at Oxford and Cambridge to non-Anglicans, while the **Trade Union Act** legalized the existence of unions, protected their funds and gave them the right to strike. At the same time as this legalization of trade unionism, the administration curtailed any union's ability to maintain a strike by outlawing picketing in the **Criminal Law Amendment Act**. In 1872 the secret ballot was introduced in the **Ballot Act**, while in 1873 the **Judicature Act** aimed to rationalize and improve the efficiency of the legal system.

We have seen a number of Acts of Parliament which **increased the unpopularity of the Liberals**: The **Irish legislation** (unpopular on both sides of the Irish Sea); the **Education Act**, which aggravated tensions between Anglicans and Nonconformists who objected to increased rate aid to Anglican voluntary schools; the **Criminal Law Amendment Act**; and, lastly the **Licensing Act** which upset both the breweries and the patrons of Britain's public houses. In 1874 after the general election defeat, Gladstone remarked that the government had been defeated by discontent over the licensing hours. It is certain, however, that, although this may have been an influence on the alehouse voters, the other legislation of this period played its part in the defeat of the Liberals.

Foreign policy

In foreign policy Gladstone was cautious in his approach, tending to concentrate more on domestic affairs. Gladstone was chiefly interested in **maintaining the peace in Europe through negotiation and conciliation**. He rejected the jingoistic approach favoured by Palmerston and **tried to avoid intervening in the affairs of the Empire**. However, **where moral issues were concerned, Gladstone was prepared for diplomatic intervention**, as with the massacres by the Turks in Bulgaria. He was convinced of **the moral right of small states to rule themselves and of the moral obligation of powerful nations to allow them to do so**.

The electorate had become used to Palmerstonian-style foreign policy, and Gladstone's achievement of keeping Britain out of European diplomatic wrangles was seen as failure by the voters. Combined with Ireland, the divisiveness of the administrative reforms (not least the Licensing Act) and the apparently constant concessions in international diplomacy led to an overall majority for the Tories at the 1874 election. Gladstone's policy had been to **maintain neutrality in the Franco–Prussian war** (unless either nation had invaded Belgium), to **accept the International court's ruling that Britain should pay £3¼ million to the USA as compensation for the *Alabama* and to do no more than protest when Russia broke the clauses of the Treaty of Paris** by keeping a navy on the Black Sea and fortifying her naval bases there.

It was Disraeli's promises of an aggressive foreign and imperial policy combined with the myth of Tory democracy and social reform which proved, with the shortcomings of the Liberal legislation, to be Gladstone's downfall.

The **achievements** of Gladstone's first administration are, in retrospect, impressive and comprehensive. However, the reforms disappointed the radical elements within the Party and the non-conformist and trade union supporters within the Liberal Associations. Despite the electoral defeat and the distancing of popular liberalism from the parliamentary Party, Gladstone had managed to shake the foundations of traditional aristocratic privileges by the **encouragement of individualism and advancement through personal merit**. He had also **enabled the middle classes to strengthen their economic position** through his free trade policies as well as allowing them to **gain an element of control in the administration of the country**.

Return to power

Although Gladstone felt that the domestic requirements of liberalism had been achieved, he was sufficiently inspired by the massacres in Bulgaria and Disraeli's mishandling of foreign affairs to come out of political retirement. Many historians have tended to look at the reforming period of the second ministry as somewhat barren, yet several major democratic and social reforms took place during this administration. The **Mundella Act** made elementary education compulsory, while the **Irish Land Act** gave the concessions of fair rents, fixity of tenure and free sale to tenant farmers in Ireland. The **Married Woman's Property Act** gave married women the same property rights as their husbands. The most important democratic reforms of the administration were: the **Third Reform Act** which gave the vote to adult male householders and £10 a year lodgers – this added two million to the electorate; the **Corrupt Practices Act** which set a limit on the expenses that could be used during election campaigns; and, finally, the Redistribution Act which abolished two-member constituencies, with the exception of twenty-three large boroughs and created a larger number of single-member constituencies.

There were major blemishes on the domestic scene. **Ireland** continued to be a problem (see Chapter 23), while the drawn-out **Bradlaugh** affair and the scandal of **Dilke's divorce** added to Gladstone's domestic discomfort, The Party's growing group of influential radicals (notably Chamberlain) were disturbed by Gladstone's refusal to consider state intervention on the scale of their proposed social-liberalism.

Back in power, Gladstone followed through his opposition to Disraeli's imperialism by trying to bring Britain's foreign affairs back to normal. This was far harder in practice than even Gladstone had imagined, for the policy creations of Disraeli's administration proved difficult to dismantle. In trying to solve the problems inherited from Disraeli, Gladstone provided his many critics (Churchill in particular) with ammunition with which to attack him. In the administration's attempted solutions to colonial problems it was continually drawn into positions where intervention or total withdrawal of interests were the only options available. Had the government conceded over **Egypt** in 1881–82 and the **Sudan** in 1883–84, public jingoistic pressure could well have brought about their downfall. As it was, Gladstone was laid open to charges of hypocrisy over his previous non-interventionist stance. In **Afghanistan** he was seen to be putting India at risk by withdrawing General Robert's force and allowing the Russians in, while in the **Transvaal** he was criticized for delaying the restoration of independence to the Boers, which led to the British defeat at Majuba Hill, only to concede at the Convention of London (1884) where once Disraeli might have sent a larger army in.

Gladstonian liberalism

Gladstonian liberalism was more than just Gladstone or the Liberal Party–it was a political ideology. **Civil and religious liberty** played important roles, the latter leading to the Party's involvement in a number of worthwhile causes that sometimes bordered on militancy. The keystones of the Party and the doctrine were **free trade, a non-interventionist foreign policy, equal opportunities through self-improvement** hopefully leading to economic prosperity; though it favoured **political equality, social equality was not to be seen in its policies**.

The **parliamentary Party** was slightly different in that it followed Peel's lead with a **cautious policy of administrative reforms and careful control of fiscal policy**. Dominated still by the Whig aristocracy, it accepted reforms on the grounds of improved efficiency but tended to frown upon the radical measures proposed by Chamberlain. Gladstone still believed that the **aristocracy were the only class in society capable of ruling**, and it is possible to argue that his reforms were aimed at showing the Whig aristocracy in a better light.

Gladstone, however, tended to become **out of touch with political and social developments**, preferring to govern on a grand scale according to his own moral principles. This often disturbed not only the radicals in the Party, but also the Whigs. He became in effect

THE COLOSSUS OF WORDS.

Figure 16. A cartoon depicting the major elements of Gladstonian liberalism

Victorian liberalism, the embodiment of the concept; yet this bore little relation to the direction in which the Liberal Party or Victorian society were moving.

Chamberlain's imperialism and tariff reform

During the depression of 1873–96, the nature of politics was having to change in order to keep pace with changes in society. Trade unionism was becoming more socialist in its outlook, and political divisions were emerging on class grounds. Chamberlain was one of the new style of professional politicians who attempted to bring national and local politics into line with the changing framework of society.

It is worth being aware of Chamberlain's background and political training for examination purposes, particularly his **Nonconformism** and foundation of the **National Education League**, together with his influence in the **National Liberal Federation**. In the former he campaigned for a compulsory, free, universal and secular education system, while in the latter organization he was feared by the Whigs who saw the movement as an attempt to radicalize the Party. In the next chapter we will look at Chamberlain's policy on **Ireland**, but it will suffice to say here that, though he was prepared to offer a large amount of local government autonomy, he refused to consider Home Rule. In fact, from 1886 he split from the Liberals, and with Hartington and Bright and ninety-two other MPs formed the Liberal Unionists, supporting the Conservatives. He was made Colonial Secretary in the Conservative Cabinet in 1895.

Regarding Chamberlain's imperialism, he tended to view the colonies in the same way as he had his home town of **Birmingham**, that is, an area to be improved by careful planning and sound investment. He had turned Birmingham into a model municipality in three years and hoped to achieve similar things in the Empire. He wanted to dispense with the old *laissez-faire* approach to colonial affairs, preferring **direct intervention in the interests of mutual economic improvement**.

To achieve this end, Chamberlain planned to create an **imperial customs union** or *Zollverein* which would benefit financially all those involved in the union. It was hoped that the profits from tariff reform through imperial preference would pay for much-needed and often radical reforms, e.g. the old-age pension. In Britain, Chamberlain tended to see the British Empire not only in trade terms, but also in terms of its becoming a **moderating influence in world politics**. Thus he hoped that the Empire would set an example to other colonial powers through its relatively frequent colonial conferences. However, like Gladstone he was prepared to forsake liberal principles of discussion, conciliation and non-intervention when there appeared to be a threat to imperial interests. Examples of this are his checking of French expansionist policy in **Nigeria** and his implication in the ill-fated **Jameson raid** against the Boers.

When the Cabinet split in 1903 over the question of tariff reform linked to imperial preference and social reform at home, Chamberlain resigned and founded the **Tariff Reform League**, determined to fight the election on the issue of tariff reform. He hoped that he would be vindicated and the Conservatives returned convincingly. However, his action split the Party and allowed the Liberals, inspired by Asquith's dogged campaign against Chamberlain's ideas, to win an overwhelming victory in the 1906 election.

Nearer to trends in politics and society than either Gladstone or Disraeli, Chamberlain perhaps outpaced public opinion, causing his political colleagues much concern. It is certain that he failed to become leader of either party because of his intractable position over **Home Rule for Ireland** and the **Boers**, and over his firm conviction that **tariff reform** was in the best interests of the nation. He was perhaps too aggressive in trying to implement his own moral convictions and in so doing caused major defeats for both parties. Little wonder then that he failed to attain the leadership of either the Liberals or the Conservatives, for which he had at one time appeared destined.

Summary

It is worth keeping in mind **Peel's influence on Gladstone** when answering any questions on the development of Gladstonian Liberalism. Contrast Gladstone's use of office to legislate for the noble aims of the **improvement of British society** with Disraeli's **pursuit of power for its own ends**. You should also be able to chart the growth of English liberalism, particularly its provincial, middle-class and nonconformist nature.

How far were Gladstone's economic and foreign policies liberal? You should **compare** them with those of his rivals and predecessors, which at times appeared liberal when it suited policy decisions for them to do so.

The growth of **middle-class provincial liberalism** is important, as is the emergence of a clearly defined **liberal press**. These were to help liberalism grow beyond traditional Whig strongholds. The growth of a **personality cult around Gladstone** was also vital to the continued support for the man, even when the party seemed at times to be foundering. Like Peel, he was to put national interests before those of the Party. Having placed himself at the head of the radical wing of the Liberal Party, he was determined to carry through a wide ranging series of reforms, particularly in the hope of solving the **Irish problem**.

The **major reforms** of his administrations are worth remembering, as are the **criticisms** that they only aided those groups which had become influential within the new Liberal Party. Note too that much **social legislation was ignored in favour of administrative reforms**. The first ministry saw the **dissolution of the alliance between parliamentary and popular liberalism**. Particularly contentious issues were the **Irish Land Act**, the **Education Act** and the **Irish Universities Reform Bill**.

Having retired after the 1874 election defeat, Gladstone returned to active politics over the issue of the **Bulgarian atrocities**. Despite criticism that the second administration lacked the reforming zeal of the first, a number of important social reforms were to emerge. Most notable was the **second Irish Land Act**. Again, however, Gladstone was **at odds with the radical wing** of the party which called for greater state intervention to alleviate social distress. You should be aware of the **divisions** surrounding the defeat of the second and third ministries, and be able to assess the extent to which these were caused by Gladstone's **failure to keep in touch with political and social trends** in Britain. Central to this is Gladstone's **relationship to the very concept of liberalism** in Britain. As the embodiment of the liberalism of the 1860s and 1870s, was he **unable to adapt** to the changing nature of both the Liberal Party and society in the 1880s?

The growth of **Chamberlain's radicalism** is also important to the course of liberalism in the late nineteenth century, and you should **compare his reaction to the changing nature of British society with Gladstone's**. Examine the similarity of Chamberlain's **ideas for colonial development** with his **achievements in Birmingham**. Assess the reasons for the **failure of his tariff reform movement** and question whether his failure to emerge as leader of either party was caused by **inflexibility** on his part.

Chapter 23
The Irish Problem

Introduction

Throughout the nineteenth and early twentieth centuries the problem of governing Ireland effectively and, what was often more important, peacefully, faced every English administration. Few had much success in either respect, and Irish politics was to play its part in the downfall of a number of administrations and political figures. Few politicians or foreign observers were happy with the way the Irish had been treated, and least of all the Irish themselves. Some politicians, like Disraeli, tried to ignore the problem. Peel had attempted to bridge the sectarian divide, while Gladstone tried to pacify the Irish.

It is important to understand the importance of the **Act of Union 1800** to the Irish problem and its failure to give Irish Catholics adequate representation in Parliament. Stemming from dissatisfaction with the terms of the Act, the ideals of Irish separatism and nationalism grew throughout the nineteenth century. Fired by the success of **Daniel O'Connell** in organizing peasant protest for **Catholic emancipation** in 1829, the **Young Ireland** movement continued the protest into the 1840s. The **famine** between 1845 and 1849 became, as it were, a watershed in Irish political activity; the romanticism of the past faded in comparison with the stark realities of political oppression. American financial support for the Fenians in the 1860s enabled them to take the violent struggle to the English mainland.

Gladstone and Ireland

It was Gladstone's sense of liberal justice which prompted him to confront the Irish problem and achieve a peaceful solution. On his victory in the 1868 election, Gladstone made it clear that his chief aim was to pacify Ireland. One of the crucial elements in the Irish problem was the **conflict of interest between the feelings of Irish nationalism and the interests of English imperialism**. Reform in Ireland was urgently required, yet few Englishmen saw any easy solution to the problem, primarily because of this conflict of interest. No matter how much liberals in England sympathized with Irish nationalism, Ireland was **vital to Britain's security**. The Act of Union also committed Britain to **support the dominant Protestant minority** against the interests (social, economic and political) of the Catholic majority.

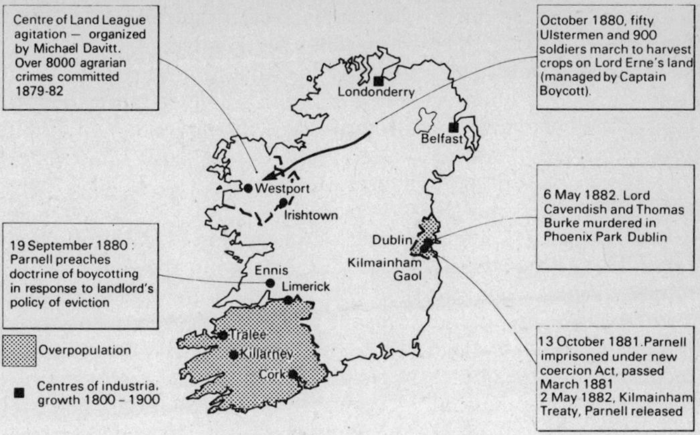

Figure 17. Irish unrest 1879–82

The other major problems were the **lack of effective political representation for the Catholic majority, a lack of religious freedom** and, of course, the **land problem** highlighted in the previous chapter. Most of the land in Ireland was owned by often absent Anglo-Protestant landlords. For many landlords the main interest in their Irish property was to achieve the greatest financial return for the lowest level of investment or maintenance. Large-scale eviction of tenants had exacerbated ill feeling on the part of the Irish peasantry, and the resulting violence and social disorder had led to the **Coercion Acts** and had enabled the growing Irish nationalist movement to develop the conflict between landlord and tenant into one between Ireland and English government. For their part, the Irish nationalists fluctuated between demands for constitutional Home Rule and revolutionary activity in favour of complete separation.

The problem with English rule in Ireland was that it was **seen by the British government in terms of its own domestic and foreign policy and not in terms of the social, economic and political problems exclusive to Ireland**. From the nationalist point of view, British government did not have an 'Irish problem'–rather the Irish were suffering from British mis-government. By 1870 the British government had tried numerous methods of coercing the Irish or conciliating them. Gladstone **accepted that the two Irish grievances of land and**

religion were justified, but felt that calls for separation stemmed from these. He believed that, if these problems were solved, agitation for separation would end. During his first administration and following the Fenian violence in both England and Ireland, Gladstone did much in his attempts to pacify the Irish. You should refer back to the previous chapter to see how Gladstone's legislation fitted in with Liberal ideology.

After Gladstone's defeat in the general election of 1874 (following the defeat of the Irish University Reform Bill), there were three major events which changed the whole nature of Anglo-Irish relations. The first of these was the **depression which caused a disaster in Irish agriculture. Evictions** by the thousand occurred for failure to pay rents, and the **threat of starvation** was very real to many sections of the Irish population. In response to the evictions, Michael Davitt founded the **Land League** which, with financial aid from Irish Americans, proved a successful pressure group against the principles of landlordism.

The second major event was the arrival of **Parnell** on the political scene and the rapid growth of his influence and popularity. As a Protestant landowner, Parnell was an unlikely leader of the Catholic Irish majority, but despite his lack of grounding in Irish tradition he proved an able political organizer and soon succeeded Butt as leader of the Irish MPs in the House of Commons. Parnell saw the need for a **united party of Irish MPs in Parliament** as the only way to achieve Irish aims. If the Irish MPs could hold the balance of power in parliament, it might be possible to gain Conservative support against the Liberals and even Liberal support when there was a danger of Liberal defeat. It was he who convinced Gladstone of the urgent need for reform in Ireland.

The third event was the '**New Departure**' which saw the rapid growth of support for the Land League, funded as it was by the Irish-American Fenians. Davitt succeeded in convincing Parnell that the Land League could be a major force in achieving Home Rule. While Parnell opposed Fenian violence and the Land League's policy for nationalizing the land, he soon accepted that the emotive appeal of the Fenians, combined with popular support over the land question, made his small group of Irish MPs a powerful force in Westminster. The **'New Departure saw the merging of the major influences in Irish nationalism under Parnell's skilful administration**.

THE RIVALS.

Figure 18. The alternative solutions to the Irish problem: peace through the Land Bill or violence through the Land League

A combination of the liberalism inherent in Gladstone's administration and pressure from Parnell's Irish grouping in Parliament saw several legislative attempts at appeasing the Irish. The **second Irish Land Act 1881** aimed to provide the three Fs: **fair rents, fixity of tenure and free sale**. Although the Act stabilized tenant farming in Ireland, it did little to alleviate the problems of the depression, in particular large rent arrears. accompanying this act was the **Coercion Act** aimed at controlling crime and rural disturbances.

The Act was criticized and subsequently denounced by Parnell and acted as a catalyst for increased agrarian violence. Having fought the Act in the courts, many Land League supporters appeared prepared to fight it physically. Those suspected of agrarian violence were imprisoned without trial. Parnell, along with other Nationalist leaders, was imprisoned in Kilmainham Jail. You should be able to **assess the effectiveness of Gladstone's attempts to pacify the Irish and also to what extent Parnell and the Land League had the potential for revolution**. In Parnell's case it may be argued that he only **used Fenianism and the Land League for his own political ends**, discarding them when it was safe to do so. The **Kilmainham Treaty** of 1822 settled the land problem, at least as far as Parnell was concerned, and it was at this point that he and his supporters moved away from social revolution as advocated by the Fenians and the Land League, and created their own **National League** with **Home Rule** as its goal. Be sure that you know the details of the Kilmainham Treaty in order to understand Parnell's conviction that the land problem was settled. Although it was never a written treaty, the agreement is vital to an understanding of Irish affairs.

The election of 1885 saw eighty-six Irish party MPs returned to Westminster. Before the election Parnell had been negotiating with the short-lived Salisbury administration for a system of **devolved government** for Ireland. From this it is clear that the **Tories were quite prepared to use the Irish MPs in the hope of defeating the Liberals**, particularly so in the light of their hurried abandonment of Parnell when news of Gladstone's conversion to Home Rule became clear.

The policy of Home Rule was to split the Liberal Party just as Catholic emancipation had split the old Tory Party in 1829. Debate on the issue now revolved around **religious prejudices and financial and political interests**. Chamberlain and a number of other

Liberals were prepared to accept local self-government for Ireland, but not Home Rule. At the other extreme, Randolph Churchill gave full backing to the Orange groupings in Ulster. At a time when imperialism was still a growing creed, Gladstone's support from the electorate waned. Despite the opposition of a number of Liberal MPs, a **Home Rule Bill** passed through the Commons in 1893, only to fall foul of aristocratic party interest in the Lords, being defeated by 419 to 41. It was after this that Gladstone resigned from the Liberal Party. The failure of this Bill and its more sweeping predecessor of 1886 were clear indications of the inability of the Liberal administrations to solve the Irish problem.

Gladstone took a calculated risk that Home Rule was an issue around which all Liberals could unite, feeling, as Peel had done, that it was an issue which transcended party interests. It is, however, certain that he misjudged the strength of opposition within the Party and failed to accept the need for social reforms as well as Home Rule.

The Easter Rising

By 1910 the Irish nationalist MPs were led by **John Redmond**. In return for Irish support for the controversial People's Budget, the Liberal administration conceded the **Parliament Act** in 1911 which was designed to stop the House of Lords from preventing the passing of a Home Rule Bill and the Home Rule Bill of 1912. The Parliament Act was never in itself designed to placate the Irish, although it certainly helped Anglo-Irish relations; it was primarily an administratvie manoeuvre. The latter was passed by the Commons but rejected by the Lords. Everyone expected and some hoped for the Act to come into force in 1914, but this was interrupted by the war and further delayed by the pressure of the Ulster Protestants upon the Conservatives in Parliament. The Conservatives used Ulster as a weapon against the Liberals. It was as much a convenient stick with which to beat the Liberals as it was an issue of burning concern to right-thinking Conservatives.

The Conservative opposition to Asquith was led by **Bonar Law**, who firmly opposed any idea of an Ulster Protestant minority being ruled by Catholics from Dublin. Between 1912 and 1914, Bonar Law and the Conservatives gave active support to Ulster resistance to the Home Rule Bill. Militant Protestantism developed under **Sir Edward Carson**, who recruited a militia of '**Ulster Volunteers**', smuggled in weapons from Germany and organized half a million signatures on the **Ulster Covenant** which pledged Protestants to defend their right to stay in the Union. The danger of **civil war** in Ireland seemed very real, particularly as Bonar Law's Conservatives seemed ready to support the Protestants to any length; in July 1912 in a speech at Blenheim, Bonar Law reiterated his support for the right to defend their birthright by force if necessary. In 1912 he clearly stated:

> I can imagine no length of resistance to which Ulster will go in which I shall not be ready to support them and in which they will not be supported by the overwhelming majority of the British people.
>
> (Extract from the speech by Bonar Law, 27 July 1912 at Blenheim)

Since 1910 the Liberals and Conservative Unionists had been well balanced, with the former having the support of the Irish Nationalists and the Labour MPs. Formerly the support of the minority groups had been taken for granted; now it had to be worked for. In 1913, Asquith had acquiesced to Unionist pressure for Ulster to be excluded from Home Rule, but in the face of a revolt by Irish Nationalists he left the proposed Bill unaltered. However, Asquith assured the Unionists that use of force of any kind to coerce Ulster was unacceptable to the British government. While the Act of Union 1801 was to be reversed, Asquith's codicil was to thwart any hope of a united self-government to Ireland.

In 1913, the divide between the Irish Nationalist MPs and the popular face of Republicanism widened. Redmond still hoped for Home Rule but was only nominally in control of the growing popoular movement in the south of Ireland. The **Irish Volunteers** were formed in response to Carson's Ulster Volunteers and came under the control of the **Irish Republican Brotherhood**. Another development was the **growing support for Connoly's socialist ideals**.

At the outbreak of World War I the new Home Rule Bill was suspended until the end of hostilities, while Redmond persuaded his followers to enlist in the British Army. The radical element under Connolly and the IRB meanwhile planned an **armed uprising**.

The remaining Irish Volunteers had continued to train, drill and openly promote revolt. The Irish Secretary, Birrell, felt unable to disarm them, as the Ulster Volunteers had not been disarmed before the war when they had talked of rebellion. In Germany Sir Roger Casement had unsuccessfully attempted to recruit an Irish legion from amongst prisoners of war. A rising had been planned for **Easter Sunday 1916** in the anticipation of receiving German aid. When Casement returned, not with German arms or an Irish legion, but with a warning to abandon the rising, he was captured within hours of landing, but there was time for MacNeill to call off the rising on Sunday. On Monday, however, **a group in Dublin took the General Post Office**, proclaiming the Irish Republic as they did so. After four days of hostilities, four hundred and fifty Irish and one hundred British soldiers had died. By the Friday after Easter the first Provisional Government of the Irish Republic had surrendered. The action had been unsupported by other Republican groups in Ireland, yet during World War I, of the European states it was ironically only Britain, the guarantor of Belgian neutrality, and, in the popular press, the defender of freedom, which experienced a national rebellion.

Ulster and the Irish Free State

Initially public reaction in Ireland was against the extremist action, even after the execution of some of the leaders of the movement. However, it is certain that there was a **growing popular feeling in support of the nationalistic ideals** of the martyrs. **Asquith** was aware of this on his visit to Dublin and hoped to forestall any further unrest by instituting Home Rule immediately. However, he lacked the political creativity necessary to solve the problem. **Lloyd George**, attempting to eclipse Asquith in the Liberal Party, negotiated with Carson and Redmond over a possible settlement whereby twenty-six counties would receive Home Rule, the other six from Ulster to remain in the United Kingdom. This achievement created disarray in the Unionist ranks and saw Law, Balfour and F. E. Smith accept the proposals. However, when the Unionist landowners and aristocracy protested, Asquith **shelved the plans, effectively destroying the Irish constitutional party and making the use of force the only solution** available to all parties. The extreme Republican elements, which had been discredited earlier, began achieving by-election success, while the Irish nationalists at Westminster seceded in all but formal declaration.

By 1918, the Sinn Fein had almost swept Redmond's party from the political scene, and at the Dail in 1919 demanded **complete withdrawal of British forces** from all of Ireland and the establishment of an **Irish Republic**. The original Sinn Fein plan for non-violent separation (simply by ignoring British authority) was thwarted by the **commencement of hostilities by the IRB** and its re-formed National Volunteers (renamed the **IRA**) in a war of liberation against the British.

The ensuing guerrilla war saw a three-year conflict in which neither side was able to achieve a military victory. In 1920 the **Government of Ireland Act** was introduced (incorporating much of what had been agreed between Lloyd George, Carson and Redmond), but this allowed for **separate parliaments in Dublin and Belfast**. Both parts were to retain **some representation at Westminster**, while representatives from both Irish parliaments were to form a **council of Ireland**, thus retaining some semblance of unity.

The Sinn Fein rejected the southern parliament and attended it only to elect a new Dail. The guerrilla war continued in the south while Lloyd George and **De Valera** wrangled over terms for Irish Home Rule, unification and separation. Rejecting the offer of dominion status, De Valera, having ended hostilities, demanded once again **complete independence for a united Ireland**. Lloyd George was prepared to offer the **inclusion of Ulster in Irish dominion status for a trial period**, but the threatened return of Bonar Law from retirement to lead a Unionist revolt led Lloyd George instead to **threaten De Valera with war**. At the same time, Lloyd George hinted that border changes by the Boundary Commission would make Ulster unworkable and would lead to Irish re-unification.

It is important to note that, having made little progress with De Valera, Lloyd George continued to **negotiate with the moderates**, Griffith and Collins. De Valera was excluded from the final meetings, and it was under the influence of the moderates that the Dail accepted the terms on 7 January 1922 by a narrow margin. De Valera resigned as President of the Irish Republic, and a bitter civil war commenced between the **rival Sinn Fein factions** which continued until April 1923. The Dail survived the hostilities and managed to draft a constitution acceptable to Westminster which was accepted on 5 December 1922, one year after the signing of the peace treaty. On the very next day, Ulster formally cut itself off from the Republic in the south. In forty-eight hours, therefore, Ireland received Home Rule and was at the same time irrevocably partitioned. Be sure that you are aware of the **details of the treaties** which gave the Republic its independence through initial dominion status. For Ulster, the separation did little, but made it **more dependent upon the British treasury**. As the subsidies to its agriculture and industry grew, so economic ties with the south became harder to maintain.

The Ulster government did little to ease existing tensions between the religious and political groups. The Protestant majority, by rigging elections and constituencies and using special police powers, created and maintained what was termed a 'Protestant State for a Protestant People', despite one-third of its population being Catholic. The solution in Ireland was, in its final form, advantageous to the Conservatives, who, by the addition of the province's Unionist MPs, regularly gained ten or so seats in the Commons. Previously, the Irish nationalists had tended to swell Liberal and radical ranks by eighty or so. The revival of extreme Protestantism saw **increases in violence** and **a lack of effective trade union representation for Catholic workers**. The militant political Protestantism of the Ulster working class also **slowed the growth of a Labour Party** in the Province. The problems of Ireland were therefore only solved in theory. They were to emerge once again as the problems of Ulster.

Summary

A grasp of the background of Irish problems is essential to any understanding of this topic: the **failures of the Act of Union** to give adequate parliamentary representation to the Catholics in Ireland and the **economic and social deprivations** of the mass of the population combined with **political dissatisfaction** to fuel ideas of **nationalism and separatism**. **Landlordism** and **religious discrimination** did little to alleviate tensions, while **fear in Britain about the dangers of another Catholic state nearby** helped the opposition to Home Rule.

You should revise thoroughly the rise of Irish nationalism and should be able to **compare it with contemporary nationalist and Romantic movements elsewhere in Europe**. The growth of support for the Fenians and their carrying of the conflict to the British mainland was to have its effect on the policies of the British government.

Gladstone's chief aim after the 1868 election victory was to achieve the pacification of Ireland, and a prevailing sense of injustice regarding British treatment of the Irish problem added to Gladstone's electoral support. Gladstone felt that if the grievances over land and religion were solved, then separatist agitation would disappear.

It is important to remember the three major events which were to alter the nature of Anglo-Irish relations: the **worsening of the depression, the emergence of Parnell**, and finally the development of the **'New Departure'**. The concessions of the **Land Act** and the **Kilmainham treaty** saw a movement towards conciliation between the two parties. Further progress was prevented by the **Phoenix Park**

murders and for this reason Parnell was to **split with Davitt and the Irish National League** in favour of a **negotiated settlement** with either Liberals or Conservatives. Following an inconclusive election result, the Conservatives were to drop any alliance with the Irish Party, while the split within the Liberal Party over Home Rule meant that Irish MPs were forced to give their support to a weakened Liberal Party if Home Rule was to be achieved.

Parnell's divorce scandal did little to help the cause, and Gladstone insisted that the IPP choose either Parnell or continued support for Home Rule.

Be clear about the **religious, political and economic interests** surrounding the question of Home Rule, as it is important to be able to explain the **motives** of British and Irish politicians in their various maneouverings, particularly where the '**Orange card**' was brought into play.

Gladstone's failure to achieve Home Rule was seen as a noble one, but it did little to lessen Irish agitation. Out of this, further political divisions were to emerge. With Irish support, Asquith was able to challenge the power of the House of Lords successfully, yet not even this was to alleviate tensions in Ireland, as can be seen from the determination of Unionists to play the Orange card and similarly the extreme nationalist elements in the south (the IRB) to plan an armed insurrection.

You should have a sound understanding of the **course taken by negotiations before and after the Easter Rising of 1916** and of the important role which **Lloyd George** was to play in these. Try to account for **Asquith's shelving of the agreement** in the face of relatively minor opposition and note the growth of **support for extreme republicanism**. The **course of the conflict in Ireland** and the subsequent **civil war in the Irish Free State** are important elements, as is the continued growth of entrenched **Unionism** and **Protestant extremism** in the north. For a problem which has seen the proposal and rejection of any number of solutions, political and religious unrest remains in Ireland to this day.

Chapter 24
New Liberalism 1906–14

Introduction

Despite the numerous reforms in this period of Edwardian new liberalism and the creation of the forerunner to the modern Welfare State, the Liberal governments of the Edwardian period faced conflict rather than consensus. The reforming liberals were confronted by **unrest from 'women's rights' groups, trade unions, Ulstermen** and also the **House of Lords**. Instead of optimism resulting from the progress in social administration, there emerged a mood of pessimism and political violence.

By the turn of the century the principles of *laissez faire* capitalism, along with Britain's industrial lead and its imperial interests, were being threatened at home and abroad. There was a **growing belief that Britain's economy could only be revitalized by tackling the nation's social welfare problems**. From the late 1880s to 1905 the Conservatives had done little to confront Britain's social problems, despite Chamberlain's efforts, and this was to play its part in their crushing defeat in the 1906 election, when Campbell Bannerman won a massive majority. The Liberal victory had as much to do with the non-conformist vote against Conservatism and the Education Act 1902 as it did with support for the Liberals. Labour and the trade unions were also to play their part in the vote against the Conservatives, returning around twenty MPs each. As much as anything, the electoral result indicated a massive rejection of Conservative protectionism. Be sure that you have, at the very least, a basic comprehension of the **successes and failures of Lord Salisbury's various administrations in the late 1880s in order to be able to compare these administrations with those of the 'New Liberals'**.

'New Liberalism' and Labour

The victors of 1906 were in effect **representatives of a variety of political forces**, Liberals and traditional radicals, Labour supporters and trade unionists, and dissident nonconformists. With such diverse support, the Party was often **in danger of being torn in different directions**. There was always the possibility that reforms to appease one group would outrage another.

While a good many Liberals were determined to adhere to traditional Liberal ideals of Gladstonian economics, free trade and nonconformist moral codes, Lloyd George and Churchill did their utmost to bring the Party into line with twentieth-century industrial society. They hoped to forestall any rapid growth in support for the Labour Party by convincing the electorate that the Liberals represented the best interests of the industrial working classes. **Lloyd George**, first at the **Board of Trade** and later at the **Treasury**, **Asquith** as **Chancellor of the Exchequer** and then **Prime Minister**, and **Churchill** as a replacement for Lloyd George at the **Board of Trade** were the politicians chiefly **responsible for the sweeping social reforms of the Liberals**. They were to introduce legislation governing trade disputes, old age pensions, conditions of employment and health insurance. All reflected the growing importance of the independent working-class voter. Asquith's reformers were constantly reiterating the progressive nature of Liberalism despite some Liberals' determination to adhere to *laissez faire*.

Owing much to Fabianism, Chamberlain and other reform groups of the late nineteenth century, Lloyd George and Churchill were fortunate in that theirs were the first reforms actually to enact the creative social thinking of their predecessors. The surveys of Booth and Rowntree had made clear the urgent need for reform, showing atrocious living conditions amongst one-third of the population, while recruiting stations for the army during the Boer War discovered that more than half of the volunteers were unfit for service. The advances of German industry under Bismarck were seen as a result of improved efficiency through effective social welfare. A combination of **competition with Labour at home and Germany abroad** gave New Liberalism the incentive for reform. Churchill declared that unlike socialism's plan to pull wealth down to the level of the poor, Liberalism aimed to '**raise up poverty**', in other words to create a lower limit below which wages, living and working conditions would not be allowed to fall.

During this reforming period the Labour Party seemed satisfied merely to play a supporting role in the House of Commons in return for trade union concessions. The General Election in January 1910, while showing that the Liberals could still win working-class voters away from socialism, indicated through their reduced majority people's dissatisfaction with its current piecemeal approach to reform. It has been argued that 1910 was the high point of this period of Liberalism, when Liberal ideals offered a realistic alternative to socialism.

For its part, **socialism** had developed comparatively rapidly between 1880 and 1900. A number of groups emerged during this period, often centred upon small political groups which either drew their inspiration from traditional radical sources, Chartism and trade unionism, or more directly from the writings of Marx. Groups such as the **Social Democratic Federation**, the **Socialist League** formed by William Morris in 1884 after he left the SDF, the **Fabians** who hoped to persuade both major parties to reform and create a peaceful passage for socialism. Blatchford and the *Clarion* were influential in educating working-class readers to socialism. The organization of **Labour clubs and local Labour parties** followed Hardie's success in the 1892 election. A conference between representatives of these and the SDF met in 1893 and saw the **formation of the independent Labour Party**. Although Hardie and Burns both lost their seats in the 1895 election, membership of the ILP continued to grow.

Between 1895 and 1900 there were numerous **calls for the large, well-organized and well-funded trade unions to support the ILP**. However, successive TUC conferences rejected the call until 1899, when leaders of the skilled unions began to realize that for the conditions of their members to be improved, they had to have effective political representation. In 1900 several trade unions, the Fabians, the SDF and the ILP met to form the **Labour Representation Committee**. Opposition to the **Taff Vale judgment** led a number of skilled craft unions to join the Committee in 1902–3 (although they had voted against Hardie in 1899).

In 1903 the LRC entered an electoral pact with the Liberals and, as we have seen, won twenty-nine seats in 1906, with the miners' federation returning twenty-four MPs. In the early years of the alliance **it was unclear whether the newly renamed Labour Party was merely a representative of trade union interests, part of the radical liberal movement or a revolutionary party in its own right**. By 1910, however, Liberal reforms to appease the Labour Party were beginning to peter out.

The reforms

A number of reforms followed the 1906 electoral victory. Some were aimed mainly at satisfying Labour and trade union demands, e.g. the **Trade Disputes Act** which reversed the Taff Vale decision of 1901 whereby trade union funds had been liable to damages actions in the courts. The **Workmen's Compensation Act** obliged employers to pay compensation to workmen injured during the course of their employment. Other Acts limited the working day in various industries and fixed minimum wages, e.g. the **Trade Board Act** which applied to the sweated trades such as tailoring and lace-making. Social reforms included the **Old Age Pension Act**, of course, and also the **School Meals Act**, allowing local authorities to finance and provide school meals.

Despite losing their overall majority in the Commons in the 1910 election, the Liberals scored two electoral victories over the Conservatives and Unionists and, more importantly, achieved an impressive legislative victory over the House of Lords. The Dangerfield thesis has shown this constitutional struggle as a major victory for Asquith and the Liberals, but has posed the question as to **whether such policy was indicative of the death throes of Liberalism in the face of the growing popularity of the Labour Party**. While we can conclude that the Liberals had not ceased to govern effectively, it is certain that the **constitutional battles were largely a defensive measure** used by Liberalism in decline.

While some of the reforms were designed to appease the working classes, others were aimed at placating the Irish nationalists. In return for supporting the Liberals over the Parliament Act 1911, Redmond's nationalists demanded Home Rule. The **Parliament Act** itself was designed to prevent the Lords stopping budgetary Bills already passed by the Commons, only allowing them to delay legislation. Other Acts after 1910 were the **National Insurance Act**, the **Trade Union Act 1913**, reversing the Osborne Judgement of 1909 and allowing trade unions to raise a political levy. Finally in September 1914 the **Home Rule Act for Ireland** was passed, although it was suspended until the end of hostilities.

You should keep in mind the **extent to which Asquith and Lloyd George undertook intricate political manoeuvring and compromises in order to achieve their own ends**, as with some of the social legislation and also with Ireland. It is necessary to know of the tactics employed by **Balfour and the Conservatives**, namely **using their strength in the House of Lords to thwart selected pieces of Liberal legislation, though avoiding conflict with Labour by passing the social administration**. The Conservatives, with no hope of defeating the Liberals in the Commons, had to use the Lords to provide any effective opposition. Within two years of their 1906 election victory, the Liberals began searching for **an issue on which to challenge the Conservatives in the Lords**. That issue turned out to be the **People's Budget** which was to increase income tax and and death duties and introduced a land tax in order to fund old age pensions and a naval building programme. As we have seen, a combination of Irish nationalists, Liberals and Labour MPs helped defeat the Conservatives on the Parliament Act in 1911.

Decline and rise: political fortunes of the Liberal Party

We have seen the gradual **rise of Labour influence** in British politics and also the continued importance of the **Irish Question**. During this period the Conservatives were shown to be out of favour because of their failure to keep in touch with social trends. By 1910 the Liberals too were beginning to decline in popularity despite their reforming successes. Elements of the Liberal-voting **working class became dubious about the ability of the Liberals to look after their interests**, particularly when price increases began to outpace wages. It gradually became clear that many of the social reforms were a means to an end, this being the maintenance of the Liberals in power. Of course, because of the diverse make-up of the Liberal Party, it was difficult for Asquith and Lloyd George to provide legislation to satisfy all its various conflicting interests.

For their part, **middle-class Liberal supporters** were beginning to feel that there was a distinct **danger from socialism through the Party's social reforms**. Free trade seemed to be losing its appeal, while the Conservative and Unionist policy of protection seemed to offer benefits for all groups. The increase in government spending on the armed forces, though strictly limited by Haldane, appeared to contradict for many members of the Party the traditional Liberal principle of non-intervention abroad. We have already seen that the government was under pressure from all parties in **Ireland**, both nationalist and Unionist, the latter exerting pressure in the House of Lords.

Unrest at home came from the **women's suffrage movement** which, failing to gain any concessions inside Parliament, advocated, like the Unionists, extra-Parliamentary activity. Their militancy in the face of Liberal intransigence and political manoeuvring (the government feared women would vote Conservative) led to violent confrontation between 1912 and 1914. The chief source of unrest was, however, the **Labour movement** which, influenced by the growth in syndicalism and what was seen as the failure of Liberal reforms to go far enough, waged a **campaign of industrial strike action**. Between 1911 and 1914 trade union membership doubled and it seemed that an independent Labour Party was inevitable. The

Lib – Lab pact was precarious, and there seemed little the Liberals could do to prevent a Conservative victory if the pact did collapse.

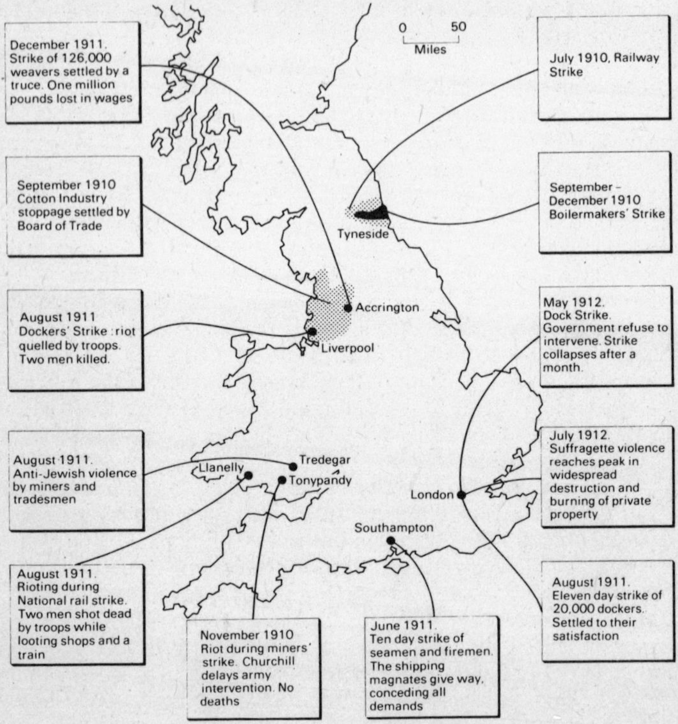

Figure 19. Labour unrest in Britain 1910 – 12

War

The social conflicts at home and in Ireland certainly played an important part in the decline of Liberalism, although it is certain that **World War I** 'finished off' traditional Liberal principles. The government was **forced to discard free trade, retrenchment and reform and to follow a policy of massive state intervention**. Britain's **foreign policy** also played its role in effecting the decline of the Party. **Intervention was seen as a direct contradiction of Liberal principles**. The naval race and the determination to maintain imperial and economic spheres of influence saw an exacerbation of Anglo – German rivalry. After the war, continued pressure from the dissatisfied political groupings in British society saw to it that the final years of Liberalism were ones of unrest.

Summary

It is important to be aware of the **developments in the Liberal Party** up to 1914, particularly the **causes of the various splits** in the Party, e.g. **Home Rule and the Boer War**. Also of importance is the **decline in support for the Liberals amongst the middle classes**, who were beginning to switch their allegiance and, more importantly, their financial support to the Conservatives. Because of middle-class dissatisfaction it became difficult for the Liberals to adopt working-class parliamentary candidates for fear of further alienating the middle class. Despite attempts by Herbert Gladstone to make the Party machine more efficient, it still found it **difficult to compete with the highly-organized Conservative Party**.

The difficulty of getting working-class candidates into Parliament within the Liberal framework, combined with the growth of socialist and social democratic movements, saw the emergence of a **far more independent Labour Party**. The development of the Gladstone–MacDonald pact in 1903 enabled the Labour Party to gain its own foothold in Parliament after the 1906 election. For their part, Liberal MPs were **uncertain how to react to the Labour Party**. They were fearful that on its own it might steal traditional Liberal working-class support but were equally wary of giving support to a Labour faction within the Liberal Party which it was feared they would not be able to control.

The 1906 landslide for the Liberals has been seen conversely as an indication of the development of New Liberalism and the strange death throes of Gladstonian Liberalism. There was certainly a determined effort to **revitalize the Liberal Party** under Asquith, Rosebery and Grey, this being continued and extended under Lloyd George and Churchill. There was a positive move towards **increased state intervention in the economy in order to improve national efficiency**. Campbell-Bannerman's and Asquith's administrations saw the emergence of a number of **sweeping social reforms**, and you should know what these were. You should also understand the background and details of the constitutional crisis surrounding the **People's Budget**, the **Parliament Act** and the use of **Ulster** as a political weapon.

Do not forget to study these areas in conjunction with Liberal handling of the **Irish problem**, as they are inextricable. While the unrest in Ireland and Ulster continued to occupy much of the government's energies, there was also not inconsiderable **industrial unrest** at home, along with various **tensions in international affairs**. While the government handled industrial affairs with firmness, there was much division and indecisiveness over the question of **women's suffrage**. You should assess the **Dangerfield thesis** regarding this strange death of Liberal power.

Chapter 25
Britain between the Wars

Introduction

A tremendous strain was placed upon the British economy during World War I, for, as we have seen, massive state intervention was required to maintain British society during this period. In the previous chapter it became clear that British Liberalism was in decline, along with British industrial efficiency, and had been so for a number of years. The decline had started as far back as the 1870s during the initial economic challenge posed by the United States and Germany. The USA, in particular, had the added economic advantage over Britain of larger home markets, making mass production in larger quantities more cost-effective. The fact that Britain's industry had expanded rapidly at the beginning of the century meant that it was still using **out-of-date techniques and machinery** in contrast to the new plant and technology employed in the **USA** and **Germany**. British industry was geared to the **old heavy industries**, whereas its competitors were already investing in new technology and plant to deal with the growing petro-chemical, car and electrical industries.

Britain before World War I was already beginning to suffer economically because of its tendency towards preference of imperial trade from 1870 onwards. Although Chamberlain had been unable to introduce imperial preference in a tariff sense, **British industry had become geared to the demands and production capacities of the Empire**. **Inflation and unemployment** followed, and government policy seemed unable to provide any workable solutions, After the war, the growing influence of the Conservatives prevented any hope of an increase in government expenditure to solve the nation's economic problems: instead, protectionist principles became hardened in government circles.

Effects of World War 1

The war created a **false boom** in the British economy by increasing the demand for **heavy industrial goods, munitions and agricultural produce**. As a consequence a temporary period of full employment existed during the war years. The boom continued after the war until around 1920, when demand for war products, heavy industrial output and high agricultural yields fell. While both politicians and electors still retained some optimism that

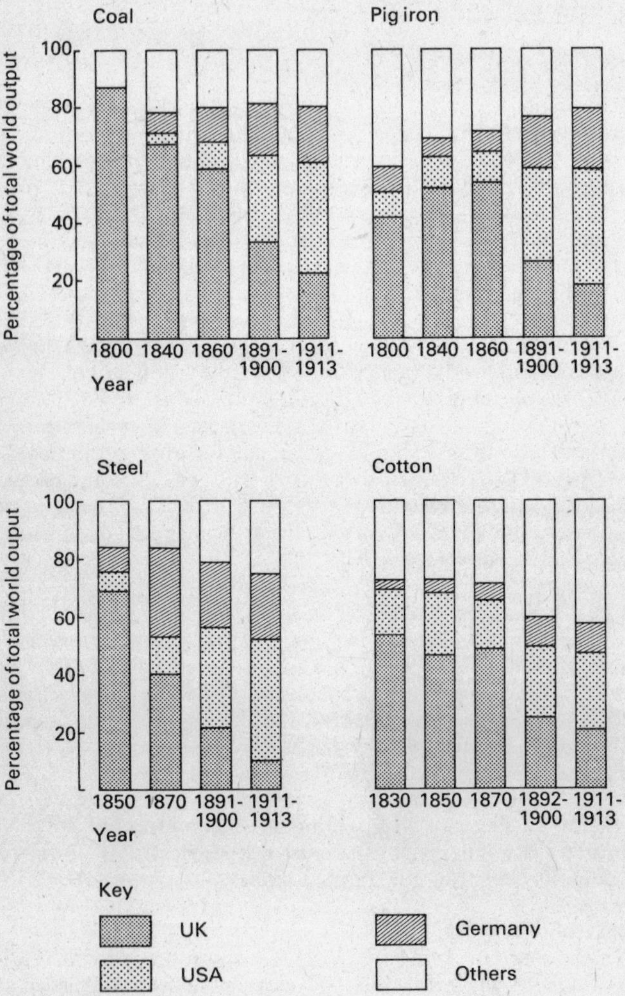

Figure 20. A comparative analysis of Britain's industrial output. You should be able to analyse the causes of the steady decline.

economic affairs would return to normal, **industrial unrest** grew, and this was reflected in **trade union and Labour Party growth**.

During the war years traditional British customers were obliged to find alternative sources for their imports. Two nations which were quick to take full advantage of the economic vacuum were **Japan** and the **USA**. They were able to expand their overseas trading concerns with the opposition. Those customers who were not won over to American or Japanese products had either to produce the goods themselves or find alternatives. Many of the allies to whom Britain had formerly exported were forced to reduce their import levels in order to pay back **war loans** to both the USA and Britain itself. In order to protect their own ailing economies, they began introducing **protective tariffs** which had a further detrimental effect on the competitiveness of British goods.

The inter-war economy

As has already been seen, the nature of British manufacturing and the type of goods produced were changing rapidly, yet Britain's staple industries had not modernized, nor had new industries been developed at the same rate as those of its competitors. After the war the markets for heavy industrial output (coal, iron, steel, textiles and shipbuilding) declined. It is certain that capital investment in new plant could have been made available, but, as we have seen, politicians and industrialists were convinced that pre-war normalcy would return. Subsequently, both were prepared to accept lower profit margins for what they fully expected to be only a relatively short period. The ensuing rapid decline in these staple industries led to increased unemployment, an increase in the growth rate of **depressed areas** where the staple industries had been situated and an overall decline in the national income.

The depressed areas (the North-East, South Wales, Lancashire and south-western Scotland) contributed almost a half of Britain's total of unemployed, though only making up a third of the nation's population. Such a clear indication that the divisions of wealth and class were as great as ever led to considerable **disillusion with Conservative claims that protection would improve the lot of all**.

The **return to the gold standard** in 1925 and the subsequent **revaluation of the dollar** to a level of $4.25 to the pound had the effect of increasing the cost of British exports in markets where the USA was the chief competitor. At the same time, the cost of American imports was reduced to the extent that home-produced commodities began to fail. Uncompetitiveness in the home market and overseas, where British exports were maintained at an artificially high level, led to further industrial decline and unemployment. Despite Keynes' insistence that the return to gold would lead to more deflation and unemployment, the Conservative economists refused to put the nation's economic decline down to anything more than a period of bad luck.

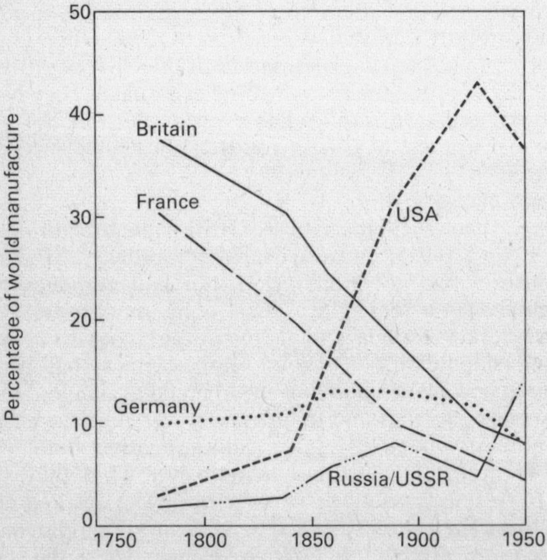

Figure 21. Britain's percentage of world manufacture

The **coal miners**, badly hit by the depression and faced with the loss of government subsidies and a cut in wages, went on **strike** in April 1921. However, unsupported by the rail and transport unions, they were forced back to work within three months. Though some historians have deemed that the moderation of the transport and railway workers in not striking was a more realistic approach to industrial relations, the net result of the miners' defeat was a **fall in wages in all the staple heavy industries**. The industrial unrest was to take its toll on the popularity of Lloyd George who was already Prime Minister in a Conservative-dominated coalition. For a number of years he had attempted to convince the working class that the Liberals, whether with a majority in Parliament or in a coalition, were the most effective representatives of working-class interests.

By 1922 Bonar Law (who had returned from retirement) and the Conservative majority in the coalition were ready to abandon Lloyd George and the Liberals in an attempt to gain their own majority in Parliament. One of the major reasons for this, from the **Conservative** viewpoint, was **dissatisfaction with Lloyd George's Home Rule settlement**. From the position of the **working-class voters** it is clear that, despite the legislation to improve social conditions, the **unpopularity of the 'Geddes axe'** and the apparent **failure of the coalition to deal effectively with depression and rising unemployment** were at the root of opposition to Lloyd George.

There are **major problems in historical thinking** to be tackled when looking at the economic problems of this inter-war period. There are **problems over definitions of the depression**, in particular when examining unemployment and economic decline. With the latter, **different pictures emerge of the economic state of Britain depending on the different dates which may be used** in any analysis, and also depending on **which industries are examined**. If we look at the growth rates of selected industries, the impression is one of growth, particularly where these industries are producing consumer goods, e.g. plastics, synthetic fibres and electrical goods. Other areas of apparent growth were in the service industries and retail. As late as 1930, however, the products of these newer industries made up only 16 per cent of Britain's exports (60 per cent coming from the well-established staple industries) and only employed around 8 per cent of Britain's working population. As we have said, the economic state of Britain may appear different depending on the year taken as a starting point. 1918 to 1920 were boom years, whereas those from 1920 to 1937 were most certainly depressed. Rearmament at the end of the 1930s also tends to lead to a distorted picture as it created another false boom. **Comparison of output with competing countries in Europe also tends to create false impressions**, for although productivity increased in relation to capital investment and overheads, it was at the expense of large sections of the workforce.

Unemployment was possibly the most serious problem facing the inter-war administrations, the national average for the period as a whole being 14 per cent. This figure takes into account the discrepancies between those workers who were uninsured as well

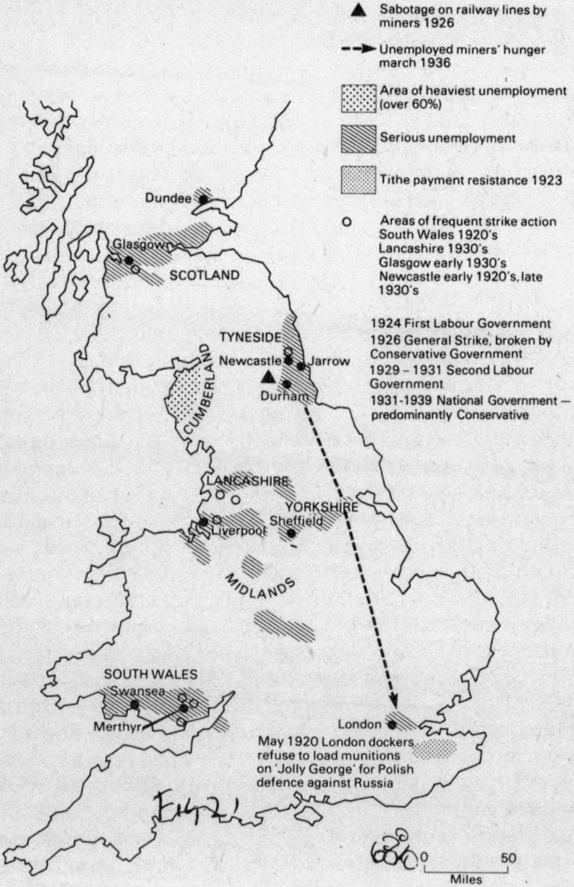

Figure 22. Unemployment and unrest in the inter-war years

as those who were insured. The figure in the latter group reached 21 per cent in 1931, while the rate of unemployment amongst uninsured workers was only 15 per cent in the same year. The **different types of unemployment (cyclical and structural)** also play their part in creating a different image. The first of these is caused by a sharp decline in an economy (affecting all sectors), as in 1921 and after the Wall Street Crash in 1932. The second type occurs when a particular industry (and its dependents) is in the process of contraction. This can be seen in the traditional heavy industries in Britain between the wars. When both cyclical and structural unemployment occurred simultaneously, few recommended solutions appeared to have much chance of success. In the next section we will look at government responses or their failure to respond effectively to these economic problems.

Inter-war politics

Just as World War I had a profound effect upon Britain's economy so it also provided a test for the very nature of British politics and society. In its wake came a number of **fundamental changes in the political structure**, not least being the **demise of the Liberals and their replacement by the Labour Party** as one of Britain's two main political parties.

For a time it seemed possible that a new and moderate centre party would emerge from the three-party conflict. But by 1919 it became apparent that the Lloyd George coalition had lost its reforming zeal. A combination of considerable working-class unrest over unemployment, the Geddes axe on services and Conservative dissatisfaction with the pre-war Home Rule Act led the Conservatives to 'ditch' Lloyd George and his Liberal minority from the coalition. The onset of economic depression following the immediate post-war boom seemed to paralyse the economic thinking of the administration.

The rapid growth of the Labour Party, drawing support as it did from the trade union movement, and the eventual disintegration of the Liberal Party as a force in Parliament **changed little in economic terms**. By the time that the power struggle was between only Labour and Conservatives **the rhetoric of class struggle had given way to one of social stability** amongst the leadership of the Labour Party. Both Baldwin and MacDonald wanted social and political stability combined with economic recovery, yet neither could formulate constructive plans for this recovery. It has been argued that the policy of stability at any price prevalent among the leadership of the two major parties was what prevented total collapse (economic and political) on the lines of some other European states.

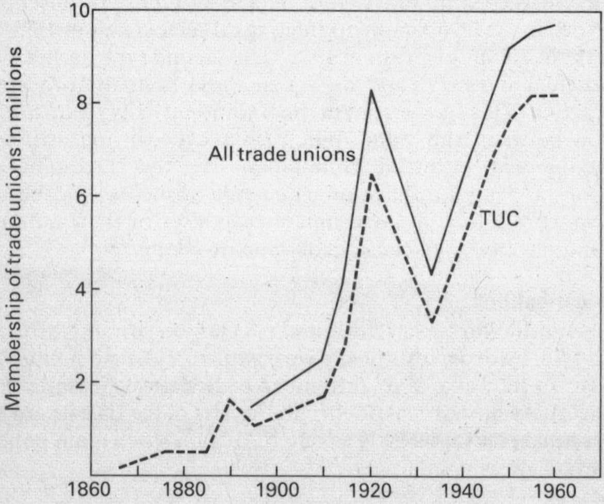

Figure 23. Trade union growth in Britain

Trade union agitation had continued in 1918 from where it had left off in 1914. In 1919 the pre-war triple alliance of railway, transport and mineworkers was resurrected and the **threat of a general strike** appeared once more. Various elements of the alliance were, however, subdued, first the **miners** by the promise of the Sankey Commission and later the **railway workers** who, threatened with wage reductions, went on strike in September 1919 (Lloyd George, having initially allowed provocation of the railway men to go ahead eventually settled on the railwaymen's terms). Likewise, the **transport workers** were allowed a commission of inquiry which granted them improved conditions. Whereas the **miners continued a head-on class struggle** with the owners **over nationalization of the mines**, the other two unions, led in 1921 by J. H. Thomas and Ernest Bevin, were prepared for **compromise**, but through **discussion**, and with **strike action only as a last resort**. During the early 1920s the Labour movement was beginning to grow, as was the strength of the trade union movement. Between 1918 and 1922 Labour increased their number of MPs to 142, while the trade unions under the new type of leadership of Thomas and Bevin reached a peak membership of eight million. It is clear from the results of the 1922 election that the strength of anti-Lloyd George feeling amongst trade unionists played a significant role in the Liberal decline.

Labour in power

Knowing that the defeat of the Liberals could best be achieved by the Labour Party, Baldwin allowed a **minority Labour government** into office after the **1923** election. He felt it was better to have a Labour government that could restrain the unions than either a Labour Party in radical opposition and supportive of union action or a Lib–Lab opposition. Their dependence upon Liberal support in the Commons goes some way to explain the growth of Labour animosity towards the Liberal Party. Despite their relatively short time in office, the first Labour administration created a good impression abroad. Like their Conservative counterparts, however, they **lacked any positive ideas on how to tackle Britain's economic problems**.

The fact that the Labour government was a minority tends to explain their cautious approach. They could quite easily have lost power far sooner than they did had they either gone against the support of the Liberals or seemed inclined towards extremism. The moderate nature of their policies, particularly their inability to take positive action on economic problems, brought the administration into confrontation with many members on the left of the party and with trade unionists. For the purposes of the examination, you should be able to **assess the demise of the Liberals and growth of the Labour party, from voice of trade unionism to potential government**. Was it as a result of **growing class awareness and conflict** during this period, or was it due to a **combination of these**, together with **Conservative stage-management** and the **collapse of the Liberal *laissez-faire* economy**? It is certain that these are merely a few ways of interpretating this issue. Be sure that you are aware of others and are able to compare them with the above.

Stanley Baldwin, like MacDonald, was interested more in stability and conciliation than in the political dynamism offered by characters such as Lloyd George or Churchill. While political and economic extremism were common in Europe, Baldwin aimed at achieving a **balance between Labour's class analysis of Britain's problems and radical Liberalism on the one hand, and the right wing of his own Party who called for sterner measures in imperial and fiscal policy**. His administration lacked any new ideas, however, for dealing with the economic crisis, and it was this rather than any particular failure in policy which brought about the downfall of the administration.

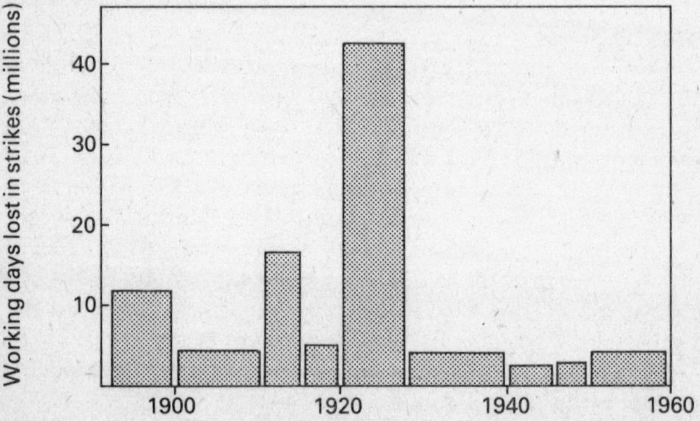

Figure 24. Working days lost through strikes in Britain

The **General Strike** during Baldwin's administration has been **interpreted in a number of different ways** by historians, depending largely on their political views. It has been argued that few unionists wanted the Strike, and that it was forced upon them by Baldwin's refusal to continue negotiations. For the unions' part, we have already seen the intransigence of the mineworkers illustrated in 1921. The government was, however, comparatively well prepared for the Strike, since it had been planning for such eventualities since 'Red Friday' in May 1925. For both parties the strike had its successes: the **government managed to keep all essential services running**, while the unions, despite their unpreparedness for the Strike, received **overwhelming support from the majority of trade unionists**.

Trade unionists tended to see the Strike as an **economic lever to force the government back into negotiation**. Baldwin, however, saw it as **extremist action to usurp Parliament**. Because of their own policy weakness and fear of a communist take-over of the Strike and the government's stubbornness, the TUC terminated the strike action on 12 May, although the miners stayed out until December. Though technically defeated, the TUC had given due warning to employers and government of its political and economic power.

Having **extended the franchise to women** on the same terms as men in **1928 (Representation of the People (Equal Franchise) Act)**, the Conservatives added around five million voters to the electoral roll (the 'flapper vote'). Historians have often assumed that the Labour Party was the chief beneficiary of the enlarged voting population, and while it almost certainly took a percentage of this vote, a large proportion of the increase probably came from the dissatisfied Liberal voters. Even so the Liberals actually increased their vote. MacDonald returned to power in June 1929, but brought with him very little in the way of new policies. The same **paralysis in the face of economic depression** possessed the second Labour administration as had possessed all of its predecessors since the end of the war. Despite Lloyd George's attempts to turn unemployment into a crisis issue around which to rally the Liberals, the rest of Parliament seemed to regard the issue in a rather fatalistic way.

Foreign policy rather than home affairs tended to preoccupy the Labour government. While their foreign policy decisions were innovative, especially with regard to **disarmament**, fiscal policy was nothing if not orthodox. And when this orthodoxy demanded cuts in public expenditure it caused a major **political crisis** – apart that is from the **financial crisis caused by foreign investors withdrawing funds** and causing the Bank of England to lose £2½ million per day. The proposed cuts were rejected by Henderson and his supporters, and in the face of revolt among nine members of the Cabinet as well as the TUC, MacDonald decided that political power was preferable to party division. He accepted, therefore, the suggestion of Herbert Samuel (Liberal leader during Lloyd George's illness) that a **National Government** be formed with him (MacDonald) as head.

Summary

There are three important areas to look at when studying Britain between the wars. The first is the **effect of World War I** on Britain in general, the second is the **nature of the economy** during this period, and the third is the **course taken by British politics**. You should be aware of the **historical influences** upon inter-war Britain, and these ought to encompass cultural and social as well as economic and political factors. Look at the **decline of British Liberalism** and the **rise of the Labour Party** and compare their fortunes with those of the **Conservatives**. You should also look at the way in which the **role of the state in the economy** altered during World War I and **why British industry was in decline** before the war. Analyse the **effects of the war** on industry and society, and note the creation of a false boom.

Where the economy is concerned, you should study the **changing nature of British industry**, particularly the **conflict between new and staple industries**, along with Britain's **need to compete in the world market**. Did the growth of new industries indicate an **economic recovery** or were they merely part of traditional **cyclical upswings** in the economy? It is therefore important to try to **differentiate** between economic fluctuations in the short term, and long-term structural revitalization. **Consider the argument that the relative recovery between 1924 and 1939 was a defensive move** and not an indication of aggressive economic planning, the assessment being that there was a substantial withdrawal from highly competitive international markets towards protection in home and Commonwealth markets. It is important to note that, while per capita income increased, so too did unemployment and social deprivation. You should **examine regional patterns of unemployment**, with reference in particular to the **depressed areas**. At the same time, it is important to **assess the role played by industrial unrest** in the course of inter-war British politics.

As has already been said, the increasing **shift from Liberalism to the Labour Party among working-class voters** is an important element in British politics. It is important to be aware of the **changing fortunes of all three major parties**, particularly the **lack of effective leadership** for long periods within the **Liberal Party**. Make sure that you are aware of the **ways in which the Labour Party grew in strength** and are able to assess the **extent to which the Conservatives were able to use the Labour Party** as a means of defeating the Liberals.

Assess the approach of the **minority Labour government** and be able to argue for the **necessity of such a cautious approach**, given their tenuous hold on power. To what extent was British politics in the inter-war period dominated by the **preoccupation with conciliation and stability** of both Baldwin and MacDonald? It is arguable that, of the major parties, only **Lloyd George and the Liberals** with their proto-Keynesianism offered any constructive policy for dealing with the dual problems of **economic decline and unemployment**. Assess the argument that the **prevailing mood in domestic politics was one of orthodoxy**.

Chapter 26
The National Governments

Introduction

The political crisis of 1931, aggravated as it was by the financial collapse in Central Europe, brought about a Conservative-dominated National Government. The Conservatives were predominant at ministerial level in the new administration and it has been argued that the government's policies between 1931 and 1935 were only **barely disguised Conservative-Party policies**. The same economic problems existed in 1931 as had existed ten years earlier. The country was still in the grip of an economic depression and unemployment continued to remain high, reaching three million at its peak.

MacDonald had not wanted to go to the polls on the issue of National Government, but was forced to do so by the Conservatives in October 1931, and a large majority was secured. The deflationary measures adopted by the government, inspired by the Conservatives, did little to solve the fundamental problems of the British economy or of British society. Government spending was reduced, and ostensibly the economic balance sheets looked healthier, but they did little to help the mass of unemployed or to improve Britain's standing in the international financial markets.

Origin and value

Between 1921 and 1931 no British government had dealt adequately with the problems of unemployment brought about by the depression. As we have seen from the last chapter, the second Labour government under MacDonald was forced into a position where a strict budget was required. As a minority administration, MacDonald and Snowden had little option but to accept Opposition demands for cuts in unemployment relief in return for their supporting the budget. The Cabinet revolt led MacDonald, at Samuel's suggestion, to negotiate with the other Party leaders and form a national administration. As we have seen, many historians have regarded this as a thinly-disguised Conservative administration. However, **one of the problems of British politics that was solved by the creation of a National Government was that of the effective operation of three parties in a two-party ('first past the post') electoral system**.

The most pressing concern for the new administration was financial. There was an urgent requirement to **instill confidence in sterling among foreign investors**. Snowden has often been criticized for his extreme fiscal orthodoxy at the Treasury, but both he and MacDonald firmly believed that for socialist policies to be effective in redistributing wealth from capitalist industry, those industries had to be made successful in the first instance. The only way for successful industries to emerge was through investor confidence, and that required **orthodox policies**.

After a short period when the economy appeared to be reviving, the confidence in sterling inspired by orthodoxy suddenly collapsed. The money markets panicked after the **Invergordon mutiny** and left the economy in at least as bad a condition as it was before the National Government. Britain's optimism seemed to continue as it had done since 1920, and the National Government won a resounding victory in the 1931 election. The nation, it would appear, trusted the administration, even if it was a government of national unity in name only. By 1932 the **Conservative majority** was beginning to force through their **traditional policies of protection and imperial preference**. The **Ottawa agreements** brought the ideal of free trade in the Empire closer to reality.

Unemployment and the depression

Throughout the lives of the inter-war national governments unemployment continued at a high level, never dropping below one million four hundred thousand and reaching a peak of three million in 1932. As we saw in the previous chapter, the picture of unemployment and economic depression varies depending on the area of the country under examination. North-east England and South Wales show a massive percentage of the workforce as being unemployed, while London and the Home Counties were, by comparison, only mildly affected.

Because of the **regional nature** of mass unemployment, linked as it was to the staple industries, national politics conveniently ignored the problem. Alternatively, they considered the problem to be unsolvable and therefore only produced limited measures with which to combat it.

Throughout the 1920s and 1930s the government response to unemployment was predictable and cautious in its approach. In 1934 the National Government instituted the **Unemployment Insurance Act**. This was designed to administer unemployment

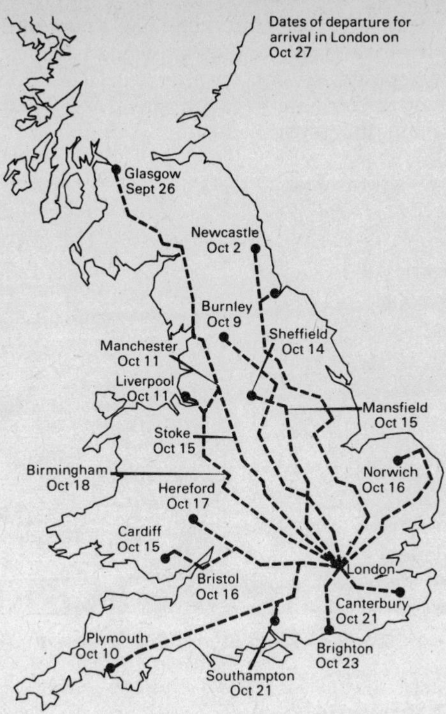

Figure 25. The National Hunger March on London, 1932

relief, responsibility for the welfare of the unemployed having been accepted by the government. The aim of the Act was to create a minimum standard of living which those who were unemployed could expect. Other than this, however, the responses of the National Government were minimal or had minimal effect. Attempts to **rationalize industry** were encouraged, as was **job creation in the depressed areas**, but lack of funds meant few positive achievements. It was not until the advent of **rearmament** at the end of the decade that any return to an acceptable level of employment was achieved.

Rearmament planning began in about 1933 and, in the face of strong pacifist feeling, made little headway until 1936, when even some Labour MPs were beginning to change their position. It should be noted that the influx of Jewish immigrants from the continent, while adding to unemployment figures, probably helped change public opinion towards rearmament, in that news of Nazi activity in Germany began to spread. 1937 saw the British public criticizing the government for rearming too slowly.

Figure 26. Rearmament and the distressed areas

Baldwin and MacDonald

From late 1932 onwards MacDonald had been little more than a figurehead in the government, a token perhaps to the ideas of national unity. In 1935 **Baldwin** succeeded MacDonald, who became Lord President of the Council. Possibly the most significant thing about both men is their mediocrity of ideas on the home front when compared to their **preoccupation with foreign and imperial affairs**. Both are inextricably linked with **appeasement** and equally with the traditional Conservative policy of **imperial preference** and **tariff reform**. In foreign affairs the chief aim, as it had been from the days of Castlereagh, was to protect British imperial interests. Therefore, as **Japan** and not Germany was seen as the chief threat to the Empire, Britain's policy did not stretch to confronting potential rivals in Europe. Thus the **Hoare–Laval pact** would have allowed Italy two-thirds of Abyssinia. Public outrage forced Hoare's resignation, but the scandal hardly affected Baldwin who soon regained any standing he may have lost through his handling of Edward VIII's abdication.

Baldwin was replaced by **Chamberlain**, who conducted domestic affairs in much the same way as his predecessors. While **confrontation abroad was avoided** in the hope that somehow the British economy could be saved through conciliation, Chamberlain adopted a far **more active foreign policy**. In the face of National Government consensus, albeit a Conservative version of it, there developed in Britain a **politically extreme opposition of both left and right**. This occurred because, since before the outbreak of World War I, governments had failed to respond effectively to Britain's social and economic problems. Both communism (which had already achieved some romantic popularity) and fascism were successful in creating relatively large and well-organized followings. Although it is important for you to know some of the details of the activities of both the Communist Party and the British Union of Fascists, it is clear that public opinion of the government never declined enough to allow more than a fraction of the population to be disillusioned with their token of national unity. However, even if the governments since 1920 had adopted more dynamic policies as proposed by Lloyd George, Churchill and the like, it is not certain either that the economy would have fared any better or that extremism would have been unnecessary.

Chamberlain and appeasement

As shown above, Britain's policy of appeasement is far more complex than it is often portrayed. There was certainly a consensus of opinion in Britain which was opposed to war, and the governments of the 1930s reflected this feeling. In the aftermath of many comments by Churchill, the term 'appeasement' has become almost an insult. This tends to ignore the fact that Chamberlain was an early advocate of rearmament, both for Britain's defence and as an aid to reduce unemployment in depressed areas.

With their policy of imperial preference as a means of stimulating the British economy, the National Governments were obliged to **avoid confrontation with more than one of Britain's potential enemies**. While **Germany** posed a threat to European peace and stability, **Italy** posed a threat in Africa and **Japan** in the Far East. To a certain extent, it might be argued that British appeasement attempted to 'play off' various states against each other. Britain had helped fund German recovery after World War I and it is clear that, while fearing German destabilization of Europe, Chamberlain also feared a **Soviet** threat in Eastern Europe and the Middle East, in particular to British oil interests in the Persian Gulf.

In the light of some of the **economic implications** of appeasement, make sure that you are able to **reassess the traditional simplistic interpretation**. When studying the area of appeasement, check that you have clear in your mind the **course of events leading to war**. Look at the way in which British **defence and imperial policy** were closely linked. In turn they were to play a major part in the creation of the Stresa front and the Hoare–Laval pact.

Where **Germany** was concerned, Chamberlain feared not only the **economic and political consequences** of the war on Europe but also realized that it would almost certainly mean the **break-up of the British Empire**. The course of events between the *Anschluss* and the outbreak of war are well documented and indicate that Chamberlain, fearing a war possibly on three fronts, was prepared to renege on obligations and convince France to act in a similar fashion.

Britain's rearmament, slow as it was in starting, had speeded up by 1939, yet Chamberlain understood perfectly that with the possible exception of the navy, Britain's armed forces were not geared to offensive warfare. The services in 1939 were equipped not for a war on the European continent in defence of Eastern European states but rather for national self-defence. Appeasement had therefore enabled the extent of rearmament to reach a level which would allow the armed forces to undertake both functions. Up until the German–Polish crisis, Chamberlain had hoped for a negotiated settlement with Hitler, but after the fall of Czechoslovakia Parliament's attitude had hardened and guarantees were given to Poland, Romania and Greece. By August 1939 it was clear to the British and French governments that little could be gained from further appeasement. With no further room for diplomatic manoeuvring, war was declared on 3 September 1939.

Summary

You should understand the **background to the formation of the National Government**, particularly the political crisis of 1931. Look at the extent to which the first of the National Governments was **used by the Conservatives** as a means of maintaining their concept of political and economic orthodoxy. Do not forget that the same **economic problems** were still facing the country as had done ten years earlier, and you should try to account for the apparent **reluctance or inability** of the government to come to terms with these. Why, in the light of the failures of such orthodoxy should a **mood of optimism** have continued to prevail nationally? It is worth noting that the mood of optimism was perhaps following the same lines as regional unemployment, although it is clear that at least in the early years of the National Governments, support was on a national level. You should consider the **effect that rearmament was to have on the depressed areas** and their staple industries and be able to assess whether this accounts for continued support for the National Government in these regions.

Consider the **mediocrity in domestic affairs** displayed by both MacDonald and Baldwin when compared to their **innovations in foreign policy**. Assess the role played by traditional Conservative ideals of **imperial preference** in the development of British foreign policy during this period, and be able to indicate why this was to be so influential where **appeasement** was concerned. It is worth **comparing Chamberlain with both of his predecessors** at the head of the National government, noting the continuation of **domestic orthodoxy** and the growth of a far **more active foreign policy**. You should look also at the growth in Britain of **political extremism** in opposition to such orthodoxy.

Assess the importance of **appeasement** to British foreign policy aims and be able to analyse whether the aims and even their execution were greatly different from **traditional British foreign policy from the days of Castlereagh**. It is important to note the **economic benefits of rearmament** to the British economy and also the **dangers of war to the economic and political structure of the Empire**.

Chapter 27
Labour Majority 1945–51

Introduction

Major changes in Britain's political structure and in the political expectations of the electorate were brought about by World War II. The appearance of the Labour Party had changed by the end of the war. It apparently offered a new dynamism not seen in British politics since Lloyd George's victory after World War I. The Labour Party also differed radically from the one which had taken office in either 1924 or 1929. The Party achieved a majority of 146 over all other parties and, unlike their predecessors under MacDonald, had a large number of ministers who had already gained experience and proved their worth in Churchill's War Cabinet.

The first post-war Labour government was faced with huge problems both at home and abroad, but unlike its Conservative counterpart it had a clear **policy document** in *Let us Face the Future*. The collectivism of the war years had proved to be popular (just as faith in the Government of National Unity under both MacDonald and Baldwin had proved popular), and unlike the situation at the end of World War I there was to be no going back to pre-collectivist policies and no alternatives from the opposition.

Reasons for victory

In 1944 in the face of renewed industrial unrest the coalition government accepted responsibility for maintaining full employment after the war. And while Churchill was preoccupied with affairs of war, a number of Cabinet members began planning openly for reconstruction. The **Conservatives**, in the face of growing pressure, agreed to implement the **Beveridge Report** with its plan for universal social security. However, the electorate, sensing that wartime promises are easily forgotten, gave the **Labour Party** a mandate to represent and realize the aspirations of the moderately socialist consensus in Britain.

Labour policies were based upon planning on a national level and upon effective local administration. Government **intervention in social welfare** and **nationalization of industry** were keystones of Labour policy. Labour emphasized the need for **co-ordinated planning in**

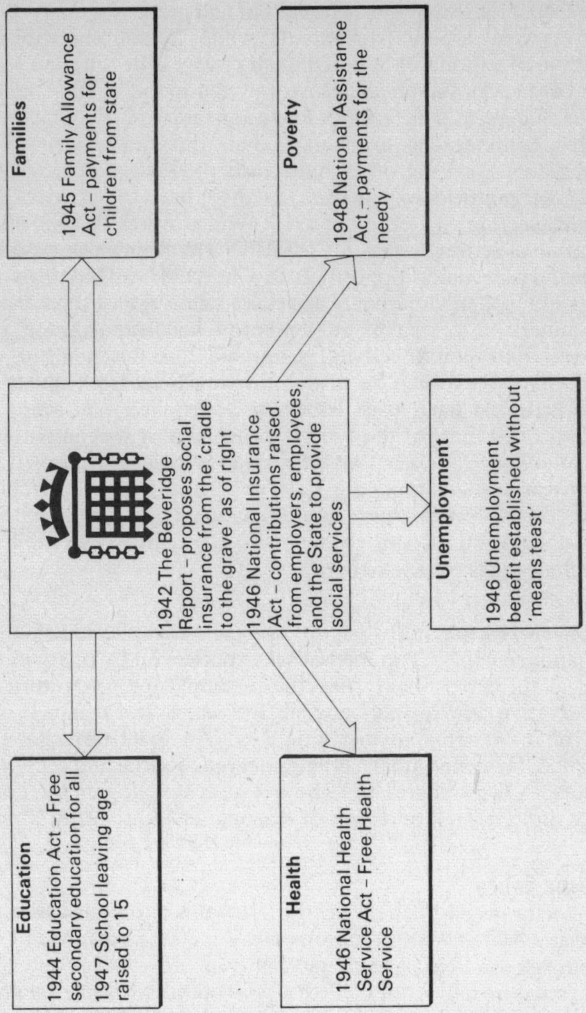

Figure 27. Labour in power and the creation of the Welfare State 1945–51

domestic affairs, while Churchill was prepared to limit himself largely to stressing the importance of foreign affairs. Labour's *Let us Face the Future* was well thought out and more systematic than the Conservative policy documents, while the policies, with the exception of nationalization of industry, were little different from those of the Conservatives. However, the mood of the country was for change, and the Labour Party appeared to have a far more positive commitment to change than did their rivals. The Conservatives, on the other hand, accepted social reform as a matter of political expediency as they had Lloyd George's 'coupon election' in December 1918. While Churchill retained his appeal as a **wartime leader**, his **popularity with the working class had declined**. Trade union opposition to Churchill was based on his earlier outspoken and openly **aggressive stance against strike action**. The miners in particular remembered his intransigence and opposition to union activity. Churchill also lost out in the popularity stakes when he turned his **vitriolic speeches against the Labour Party and trade union leadership**. 'Vitriolic' may seem an emotive word, but for the Labour movement it was an emotive issue. Language such as that which had once been reserved for Hitler was turned upon the Labour movement in Churchill's attacks on the Soviet Union and the dangers posed by socialism. The moderation of Attlee seemed, to many, preferable to Churchill's aggressive stance.

The **effect of the war** on British urban society also played its part in the Labour victory. The **deprivations** experienced by many in the 1930s determined them that there should be no return to Conservative inaction as between the wars. The war had also brought its benefits to urban society. An **egalitarian spirit** had prevailed, bringing with it a greater degree of social and economic equality. A large degree of Labour's success rested on the belief that it offered a continuation of wartime egalitarianism.

Domestic policy

The electorate had experienced the **benefits of collectivization and government intervention** and therefore had high expectations of the Labour government. Members of the Liberals and progressive Conservatives had examined the possibilities of social welfare before the end of the war, but it was only Labour who made clear their determination to **implement the 1942 Beveridge Report**. The idea of a **Welfare State** was enthusiastically received, and while the Conservatives disliked the structure of the NHS, nothing about

Labour's Welfare State was revolutionary. In actual fact, Labour policy was little more than an **extension of wartime pragmatism**.

An increase in **council house building** was another important element of Labour's domestic policy, although progress in this area was slow, due largely to shortages of materials. **Unemployment benefit and pensions** were also increased at a time when unemployment was not a problem. This was evidence for many that the Labour victory had been a positive gain.

Nationalization was the most controversial element of the new Labour government's programme, and the approach to the problem, rather than being on the grounds of ideological necessity, was based largely upon the **need for efficiency**. The **Bank of England** was the first institution to be placed under public ownership and this was possibly the least radical of the moves towards nationalization, as most western countries had state-controlled national banks. The various British **national airlines were amalgamated for** efficiency of operation.

As had happened with earlier governments, Labour faced the problem of continued **demands for nationalization from the coal, rail and transport unions**. Later on in the term of office the administration would also be pressured by the steel unions for nationalization. The difficulty with all of these industries was that their fundamental problems had existed for decades and could not be improved other than by a very slow process. The **unpopularity** of Labour, caused by fuel shortages in the severe winter of 1946 (following the nationalization of coal) could have been avoided, although little had been done to increase coal production. Nationalization of the **railways** did little to help Labour's image, for the traditional criticisms of the rail network were now transferred to the Labour government. Public ownership of **road haulage** brought fierce opposition from the influential hauliers and from the Conservatives, while nationalization of the **steel** industry created such divisions in the Labour government that the Conservatives had little opposition when they came to denationalize steel on their return to power after the 1951 election.

Foreign policy

Britain's severe economic problems after the end of World War II had been inherited from the crises of the 1930s. The war had merely postponed the problem and led to an increased **dependence, economically and politically, on the USA**. Foreign policy was geared to

reflect American international interests and was in return for American financial aid to Western Europe.

The Labour government continued to **increase spending on defence** despite their being committed to an extensive policy of social reform at home. In fact, Britain was beginning to spend proportionally more on defence than any other country in Western Europe. There are several reasons for this: American commitment to the **defence of the 'free world' against Soviet aggression** and Britain's commitment to the continuation of the **military alliance with the USA**, Britain's continued overseas obligations in the **Empire** and the **Commonwealth**, and the conviction that Britain still had a **role to play as a world power** in international affairs. Attlee and Bevan were convinced, as Churchill had been, that if Britain were to play an influential role in world politics, they would have to remain in an alliance with America. They felt, perhaps rightly, that survival through an alliance on American terms, but from a position of independence and military strength, was preferable to isolation and economic collapse.

After the crises of Berlin and Korea, **NATO** was formed in 1949, while in 1950 rearmament increased at a greater rate in Britain. This final commitment to American policy saw a clear division between the West and the Soviet bloc which has remained intact ever since.

In order to finance some of the rearmament, the administration proposed the introduction of health service charges, a move which led to the resignation of Wilson and other left-wingers. **Imperial policy** was determined as much by **Labour's anti-colonialism** as by **American anti-imperialism** or, when it suited, **anti-communism**. For example, while Britain relinquished control over India and Palestine with little conflict, the USA held on to Malaya in order to prevent the spread of communist influence in the region.

Attlee and defeat

Attlee was the successor as party leader to the pacifist Lansbury in 1935, and few saw him as being either strong or capable enough to eventually become Prime Minister. Despite the view that his was a temporary appointment, Attlee's leadership was never under serious threat from either extreme of the Party. His success was in moderation: he prevented any major divisions in the Party and ensured that the ideological differences between left and right had to come together in order for Labour to work as a government. He rejected ideological dogmatism in favour of a pragmatic approach to Britain's social and economic problems.

Despite Attlee's uninspiring appearance alongside some of the more dynamic political leaders, both in his own party and in the Conservatives he was successful in carrying through his policy of **moderation** and in effecting the **radical social reforms** promised in the Labour manifesto. The economic record of the government was as good as could be expected given the harsh post-war economic climate, but, as with nationalization, people expected the improvements to be immediate.

Even though the Labour Party polled more votes than ever before in the 1951 election, they lost their majority. The defeat, however, was not surprising, as the Party's resources had been drained by the 1950 election when their majority had been reduced to seven. Internal differences were beginning to surface, and policies had seemingly lost their earlier dynamism.

In spite of the election defeat, Labour's term of office had had a profound and continuing effect upon British society and also on political and economic thinking. The policies of both parties differed drastically only over the principle of **nationalization** in the post-war period, there having emerged a new **political consensus** based upon the **Welfare State and a mixed economy** at home, and **collective defence with the USA and decolonization** in foreign policy. Although nationalization itself was not as far-reaching as some trade unionists wanted, there was little the Conservatives could do to reverse the process. Out of the deprivations of the war years there had emerged, through the unity of purpose of the Labour Party, a change in the nature of British politics and in British society.

Summary

As a starting point it is important to have a sound grasp of the **way in which the Labour Party had developed** up to World War II. Of particular relevance is the **creation of a 'broad left' Labour Party** during the 1930s out of a combination of the ethical socialism of **Stafford Cripps** and the Fabian realism of **Morrison**. Essential to the successful growth of the Labour Party was the **pragmatic planning of policies**, particularly those regarding **nationalization of industry** and

state intervention in both the economy and society. The **intellectual mood** is also worth some investigation, for example the growth of the Left Book Club.

You should be able to assess the reasons for **Labour's victory** in the 1945 election with reference to the above factors, while it is important to note the view that Labour offered a new **dynamism** to British politics, a move away from the ineffectual orthodoxy of the National Governments. There also appeared to be a **moderately socialist consensus** in post-war Britain, a consensus that preferred the quiet efficiency and economic planning of Attlee and the Labour Party to Churchill's aggressive posturing and the disastrous economic record of the Conservatives during the 1930s when Baldwin's orthodoxy prevailed. The **collectivism** of the war proved to be more popular than an offer of a return to pre-war normalcy.

It is worth having an understanding of the contents of Labour's *Let us Face the Future* and of being able to examine how far the outlined policies actually differed from those of the Conservative planners. Within the Labour government you should be able to examine the **balance of power at Cabinet level** and be able to assess what effect this had on Labour **policies**.

You should assess whether the **high expectations** of the electorate under the Labour government were realized; in particular, look at the extent to which the **revival in economic fortunes** compensated for the **hardships of austerity and rationing**. It is of course vital to have a sound understanding of **Labour's economic and social welfare programmes** and to be able to examine how the **nationalization programme** caused great divisions within the Party.

Where **foreign policy** is concerned you should be able to account for the movement of the Labour Party to a **pro-American stance**. Dependent as it was on economic loans from the USA, to what extent was the Labour Party able to carry out a **socialist foreign policy**? You should, of course, be able to assess the **extent to which the policies of this first post-war government were socialist** at all. It is vital to look at the Labour Party's attitudes to **imperial affairs** and also its views on **proposed European unity**.

When analysing the **defeat** of the Labour Party, you should look at the dissatisfaction with the **continuation of austerity**, the divisions over the **nationalization** programme, particularly the general

unco-ordinated nature of the policy and the controversies over providing adequate **compensation** and the nationalization of the **road haulage industry**. Within the Party it is necessary to look at the **dissatisfaction with Attlee as leader** and the plans by Cripps and Dalton to replace him with **Bevan**. Compare the divisions within the Labour Party with the newly-found **organizational improvements of Lord Woolton in the Conservative Party** and the emergence of progressive Conservatives such as **Butler** and **Macmillan**.

Chapter 28
Conservative Rule 1951 – 64

Introduction

If there had been a turning point in the fortunes of Attlee's Labour government, it was in 1950. Divisions had already crept into the Labour leadership over defence spending, and, despite the fact that Labour had not lost a by-election since coming to power, and their vote had increased in 1950, they were losing ground to the Conservatives. Many middle-class voters who had supported the Labour Party in the consensus of moderate socialism prevailing at the end of the war had turned back to the Conservatives. There was a general feeling that rationing and economic restrictions had continued long enough and that the middle classes were now beginning to be legislated against in order to maintain the improved living standards of the working class.

By the time of the 1951 election further divisions had emerged in the Labour administration, particularly over the effect that the **Korean War** was having upon the economy, leading as it had done to an **increase in British imports** and subsequently a problem with the nation's **balance of payments**. Wilson and Bevan had resigned over Gaitskell's plans to fund **increased defence spending at the expense of the Welfare State**, and in particular some of the free services offered by the NHS. Foreign policy was meanwhile in tatters following Morrison's **inability to prevent Mossadeq nationalizing the Anglo – Iranian Oil Company**. Having seen the successes of Labour's well-planned radical social policies in 1945, the Conservatives, inspired by Butler and Lord Woolton (who had revitalized Conservative Party machinery) produced a series of policies aimed at convincing the electorate that Conservatism did not mean an end to the Welfare State, but rather an end to rationing and the creation of a healthier economy.

Conservative return to power

On their return to power in 1951, the Conservatives, far from attempting to undo all of Labour's works, **changed very little**. The **Iron and Steel Act 1949 was repealed**, although its original enactment had been far from unanimously welcomed by the Labour Party. Some public control was, however, retained over steel, particularly in the areas of prices and raw materials.

In the 1951 election the Conservatives had promised to 'set the people free' from the unacceptable and undesirable restrictions of rationing and socialism. While there was no further denationalization under Churchill other than that already mentioned, those industries that had already been nationalized under Labour were reorganized and, in several instances, rationalized. Plans were drawn up for **inefficient coal mines to be closed** and for the introduction of **increased mechanization**. At the same time the nationalized **electricity company** was provided with a large programme of **capital investment** to enable it to provide double the amount of electricity to the National Grid within ten years. The **rationalization of the railway network** under the now famous Beeching Report was to follow later in this period of Conservative domination.

In foreign policy, Churchill promised a more vigorous approach than that which had allowed the Labour government to lose Britain's lucrative oil interests in Iran. Yet with the closing stages of the Korean War and the beginnings of withdrawal from the Empire, his claims seemed hollow.

At home, meanwhile, by 1953 the promise of 'Tory freedom' seemed to be working. The balance of payments deficit inherited from the Labour government had been settled. **Increased export revenue** and new **capital investment in the 'new industries'** (a policy that should have been adopted in the 1930s) led to a healthier economy. The remaining **nationalized industries also received investment**, although, as we have seen, this was accompanied by rationalizing measures. The **welfare services also received cash boosts**, as did the **building programme** under Macmillan between 1952 and 1955. There was a 50 per cent increase in home building during this period, which also saw more scope for building in the private sector. The result of this was that around 300 000 houses were being built every year.

Eden and Suez

Full employment and a foreign policy that drew away from international conflict meant that there was little drain on government funds. The economy was healthy and the government popular. Thus, when Eden succeeded Churchill as leader, having for several years been the Foreign Secretary and his logical successor, he sought his mandate from the electorate. The result gave Eden a sixty-seven seat majority over Labour. This working majority allowed Conservative policy to move away from the established orthodoxy in domestic affairs and to a **more positive stance in foreign policy**.

At home, inflation was beginning to rise because of increases in the price of imports, rising wage settlements and higher indirect taxation such as Purchase Tax. An increased demand for imported goods had helped push up inflation and, although export figures were healthy, there was a requirement for increased quantities of raw materials in order to meet export needs. As a result there was a serious balance of payments deficit throughout the mid- and late fifties.

A number of policies were introduced in an attempt to cure the double problem of **inflation** and **balance of payments deficit**. The most significant of these were attempts to limit the money supply by **credit squeezes**. Higher interest rates would increase the cost of loans to borrowers and hopefully therefore reduce home demand for imported goods. Other legislation included **increased Purchase Tax**, which only added to inflation and the **alteration of hire purchase agreements**, forcing debtors to repay loans over reduced periods. Abroad, Eden was drawn into the ill-fated **Suez expedition**, firstly by a determination to **assert Britain's great power status** in response to American domination of British policy decisions, and secondly to **protect British Gulf oil interests**.

The Suez invasion in alliance with the **French** and **Israelis** had been prompted by different facets of Nasser's policies. The British claimed to be representing international interests by stopping any Egyptian attempt to close the Canal. The French hoped to end Egyptian support for Algerian nationalists, while Israel's motives need little explanation in the light of previous and future events.

The anticipated international backing for the operation did not, however, materialize. Pressure from both the USA and the Soviet Union forced an end to the fighting and a withdrawal of forces to make way for a United Nations' peacekeeping force. Eden's attempts to break the moulds of economic and political orthodoxy had ended in failure. He resigned due to ill-health.

Macmillan and prosperity

On Eden's resignation, Macmillan, as new Party leader, was faced with two major problems inherited from Eden's miscalculated attempt to move away from orthodoxy. The first task was to **reunite the badly divided Conservative Party** which was split over Suez. The second was to **regain electoral confidence by a return to economic and political orthodoxy** in domestic affairs. This would be a pre-requisite for defeating Gaitskell and the Labour Party, whose popularity with the middle classes was growing.

With the Party divisions healing, Macmillan turned to the economy. When **Thorneycroft**, who was Chancellor of the Exchequer, offered his resignation on the issue of Macmillan's rejection of his balanced budget, the Prime Minister was prepared to let him go. Thorneycroft had asked in 1957 for further spending cuts and financial controls, or alternatively an increase in taxation. Both policies would have lost the party electoral confidence and support, and would quite possibly have allowed the Labour Party to gain more ground on the government.

Thorneycroft's successor as Chancellor was Heathcote Amory who, as a firm believer in Macmillan's return to orthodoxy, implemented a series of policies which were aimed at achieving a **budget deficit**. **Interest rates were lowered** in order to increase the supply of money, likewise **hire purchase regulations were relaxed** after having been toughened under Eden. A budget deficit enabled government spending to increase without the need for increased taxation to pay for it. The subsequent boom between 1958 and 1960 was to have its effect on **working-class voting**, as in 1959 the Conservatives increased their majority over the Labour Party in the Commons to 107. The results of the boom, however, were similar in nature to the Conservative relaxation of interest rates and HP agreements – **all the gains had to be paid for at some stage**. The boom had drawn many more **immigrants** and **women** into the workforce, but this too was to have its effect upon government spending and social welfare.

Between 1960 and 1963 the **balance of payments deficit** continued to grow, while **inflation** similarly continued to rise. The boom and an improved flow of cash to the consumer had led to an **increased demand for imported goods**. In particular the emergence of mass media advertising had helped create a huge demand for **consumer durables**. British manufacturers began to find the **competition** difficult, both at home and abroad. Meanwhile, trade unions used the arguments of 'Tory freedom' to claim **large wage settlements**.

Growth at home was sluggish when compared to Britain's European competitors who had instituted effective long-term planning for economic growth. Although Macmillan had created a boom by a return to Labour-style orthodoxy, it would appear that planning had been neglected in favour of political expediency.

In 1961, fearing economic collapse, Macmillan made three major changes in Conservative policy. The government made Britain's **first application to join the EEC** in the hope of being part of the Community's economic success. The second policy change was to introduce the NEDC (**National Economic Development Council**) which was to provide a forum for government, unions and employers to plan the future of the economy. The final new development was the creation of a **National Incomes Commission** whose aim was to regulate and determine the parameters for wage increase in the future. It would appear, however, that Macmillan's attempts to improve economic planning were **too late** to alter the outcome of the 1964 election.

Figure 28. The move from Conservative freedom to a planned economy. Selwyn Lloyd begs a lift down the same road as Labour's Harold Wilson.

Britain was **refused entry to the EEC**; the **NEDC**, although producing plans with great potential, **effected little positive change before the 1964 election**. The **agreements of the NIC were ignored by the Chancellor** (Selwyn Lloyd), who had returned to a policy of **credit squeeze** in an attempt to draw in money to balance the economy. He also imposed a **wages freeze on government employees**, advising the private sector to follow suit.

Challenges to the policy came initially from the state-controlled **electricity industry**, where power workers threatened strike action in support of their pay claim. Meanwhile, **unemployment** was rising as a direct result of cuts in government spending. **By-election defeats** and **spy scandals** led Macmillan to retire in 1963. The attempts to inspire new confidence in the government by Maudling as Chancellor in Alec Douglas Home's administration centred upon **reduced interest rates and cuts in taxation**. This was in the hope that investment in industry would follow as a consequence. The moves were, however, too little and too late in the face of Wilson's promises to get the country back to work. Labour subsequently achieved an overall majority of four in the 1964 general election.

Summary

Compare the **improved organization** of the Conservative Party with the at times **bitterly divided** Parliamentary ranks of the Labour Party. You should look at the **change in middle-class attitudes towards Labour policies** and the national **dissatisfaction** with the failings of **foreign** and **imperial policies**, particularly where these began to have detrimental effects upon the British economy. One of the most important elements in the Conservative election victory in 1951 was their ability to convince the electorate that it was possible to have **all the benefits of Conservative government** (private ownership, firm government at home and a strong foreign policy) **without losing the advantages of the Welfare State**. As you will have seen, the Conservatives **changed very little** of their predecessors' legislation. Indeed, it is arguable that the denationalization programme was necessary in those industries where nationalization had been poorly planned and executed, resulting in industrial plans that were unworkable.

Conservative freedom had been the key concept of the 1952 election, and it is vital that you understand what was meant by the **Conservative promise to 'set the people free'**. By 1953 Conservative freedom still retained its popularity, the economy was healthier, and a large capital investment programme in industry and the welfare services served to maintain Conservative popularity.

Eden's succession to Churchill saw a change in both domestic and foreign policies. At home, inflation was rising and numerous **'squeeze' measures** were adopted in an attempt to limit the money supply, yet all were to end in failure, as was the disastrous policy of **intervention in Suez**. Eden's failings seem to have been the failure to **plan new domestic economic policies effectively** before dispensing with established orthodox practices, and failing to **assess accurately international opinion in foreign affairs**.

Macmillan's job as new leader was to **reunite** the Conservative Party after the splits caused by Suez and to convince the electorate that, once there was a return to orthodoxy, **Conservative economic policies were as sound as ever**. Macmillan was determined not to lose an election on the issue of high taxation, increased spending cuts or poor economic planning. It is important that you understand the implications for the economy of **Thorneycroft's proposals**, and **how far the policies actually adopted by Macmillan and Heathcote Amory differed from these**.

The increase in government spending was to have an effect on **working-class voting behaviour** beneficial to the Conservatives, but this economy, based upon the principle of 'live now, pay later', needed to be paid for at some stage. The **economic problems** faced by the Conservatives in the early 1960s and their inability to deal with them effectively may be seen as directly responsible for their election defeat in 1964. Despite attempts to stave off disaster, **Macmillan's three-point change in Conservative policy had come too late to save the election result**. None of these major policy developments was seen to work effectively. Later attempts by **Douglas Home** to inspire confidence in Conservative policies also failed, proving to be **not positive** enough measures to prevent Labour and Harold Wilson from achieving an overall majority in the election of 1964.

Revision and examination hints

Revision

There is a great difference between revising for Ordinary- and Advanced-level history, and you should be clear as to what these differences are. At O level, simple recall of important facts (names, dates and events) and an understanding of how the events relate to one another could well have gained you a reasonable pass. At A level, however, simple recall is not enough. Recollection of the course of events and their relation to one another is still of importance, but of far greater importance are:

1. the ability to analyse the causes of such events;
2. the ability to think out and express well-balanced arguments to support or refute your analysis;
3. the ability to call upon source material (both primary and secondary) to illustrate your arguments..

At O level, your revision may well have been merely a re-reading exercise; at A level, however, you should use revision as an opportunity for a thorough reassessment of your class notes, course work and reading material. If, at the end of your revision, you find yourself asking more questions than when you started, this is a clear indication that you are beginning to understand what the study of history is really about.

When you come up against new questions in your revision, you should attempt to answer them in note form in order to gain practice in answering questions from different perspectives. It will also be useful to draft essay plans in order to gain practice in creating balanced arguments for your examination answers. Make a series of headings and list in note form the essential arguments, analysis and evidence that you will need to use for each point. Try at all times to be relevant to the problem in question – therefore any narrative that you decide to use should relate directly to your analysis. While the narrative should not overshadow the analysis, do not expect the examiners to assume that you are aware of all of the relevant information if you have not stated it.

Try to gain as much practice as you can in answering examination-type questions under examination conditions. Test and time yourself as often as possible in order to gain confidence in answering questions in the time allowed.

Your revision should be planned effectively and, while this is best achieved as an ongoing process in conjunction with your class and coursework, you should work out a schedule for final revision in the run-up to the A-level examination. If your examinations are in June, your revision should be planned for every week from Easter onwards. It is better to allocate a set period each day for revising particular subjects, as opposed to studying one subject for several days at a time. It would be best to aim to revise thoroughly about two topics per day rather than quickly scanning half a dozen. Scanning is of far more use as a final memory-jogger a few days before the examination.

Plan your revision properly and there will be no need for panic or last-minute cramming. If you follow these very basic principles and have studied the course and background reading thoroughly, you should be able to approach the examination with confidence.

The examination

Much of what follows will seem obvious and you may well have been told all of it before, but remember that neglect of any of these points could possibly mean the difference between a poor pass and a good grade.

1. Make sure that you have read and understood the instructions on the exmination paper and its constituent parts. Examination papers are often subdivided, so be sure that you answer the correct number of questions from the relevant sections.

2. Read the questions carefully and be absolutely clear that you understand what each question you propose to answer is asking. Beware the pitfalls of confusing terms such as 'examine', 'assess', 'explain' and 'discuss'.

3. Read through the paper carefully and mark the questions you feel able to tackle. Hopefully, you will be able to answer more than the number required, thus giving yourself some choice.

4. Do not spend too much time on the early questions to the detriment of the later ones. Try to spend an equal amount of time on each question – if you have practised timing yourself during your revision, this should present few problems.

5. Be careful when you answer questions with more than one part. If you are asked to 'compare and contrast' the careers of any

two of a list of politicians or thinkers, make sure that you actually choose two. Do not supply an analysis of one or all of them. Errors like this are very easy to make under pressure, so beware.

6. As we have said elsewhere, be relevant to the question asked and not the question you would have preferred to answer.

7. Try to avoid making conclusions which merely repeat the core of your answer. It is far better to show the examiner that you have thought about the problem by highlighting new questions in your conclusion.

8. Plan your answers and aim to produce a balanced argument. You should practise this during your revision.

9. Do not be vague when dealing with factual references, but avoid filling your answer with unnecessary factual information in the hope of hiding your inability to answer the question that was actually asked.

10. Document questions often appear, and you should have practised analysing these in your revision. Do not be misled into considering these as an easy option, as they require as much and sometimes more thought than straight essay questions.

11. Allow time at the end of the examination to re-read your answers and to make any necessary alterations; hopefully these should be minimal.

Chapter 1 The Concert of Europe

Basic texts

Thomson D., *Europe since Napoleon* (Penguin, 1977)
Wood A., *Europe 1815–1945* (Longman, 1975)

Background reading

Albrecht-Carrié R., *The Concert of Europe* (Harper and Row, 1968)
Artz F. B., *Reaction and Revolution 1814–32* (Harper and Row, 1968)
Holbraad C. *The Concert of Europe* (Longman, 1970)
Seaman L. C. B., *From Vienna to Versailles* (Methuen, 1972)

Further reading

Crawley C. W. (ed), *The New Cambridge Modern History*, Vol IX (Cambridge University Press, 1974)
Kissinger H. A., *A World Restored: Metternich, Castlereagh and the Problems of Peace 1815–22 (Gollancz, 1973)*

Chapter 2 Restoration and Revolution 1815–48

Basic texts

Glenville J. A. S., *Europe Reshaped 1848–78* (Fontana, 1976)
Thomson D., *Europe since Napoleon* (Penguin, 1977)
Wood A., *Europe 1815–1945* (Longman, 1975)

Background reading

Hobsbawm E. J., *The Age of Revolution, Europe 1789–1848* (Sphere, 1977)
Langer W. L., *Political and Social Upheaval 1832–52* (Harper and Row, 1972)

Further reading

Namier L. B., *1848–The Revolution of the Intellectuals* (Oxford University Press, 1962)
Postgate R., *Story of a Year: 1848* (Greenwood, 1976)

Chapter 3 The Eastern Question

Basic texts

Grenville J. A. S., *Europe Reshaped* (Fontana, 1976)
Thomson D., *Europe since Napoleon* (Penguin, 1977)
Wood A., *Europe 1845–1945* (Longman, 1975)
Woodward E. L., *War and Peace in Europe 1815–70* (Cass, 1963)

Background reading

Anderson M. S., *The Eastern Question 1774–1923* (Macmillan, 1966)
Crawley C. W. (ed), *The New Cambridge Modern History*, Vol IX (Cambridge University Press, 1974)
Seaman L. C. B., *From Vienna to Versailles* (Methuen, 1972)

Further reading

Clayton D., *Britain and the Eastern Question from Missolonghi to Gallipoli* (University of London, 1971)
Taylor A. J. P., *The Struggle for Mastery in Europe* (Oxford University Press, 1971)

Chapter 4 The Unification of Italy

Basic texts

Grenville J. A. S., *Europe Reshaped* (Fontana, 1976)
Thomson D., *Europe since Napoleon* (Penguin, 1977)
Wood A., *Europe 1845–1945* (Longman, 1975)
Woodward E. L., *War and Peace in Europe 1815–70* (Cass, 1963)

Background reading

Holt E., *The Risorgimento; the Making of Italy 1815–70* (Macmillan, 1970)
Mack Smith D., *The Making of Italy 1796–1870* (Harper and Row, 1970)
Seaman L. C. B., *From Vienna to Versailles* (Methuen, 1972)

Further reading

Procacci G., *A History of the Italian People* (Penguin, 1973)
Ridley J., *Garibaldi* (Constable, 1974)

Chapter 5 France 1848–70

Basic texts

Grenville J. A. S., *Europe Reshaped* (Fontana, 1976)
Thomson D., *Europe since Napoleon* (Penguin, 1977)
Wood A., *Europe 1845–1945* (Longman, 1975)
Woodward E. L., *War and Peace in Europe 1815–70* (Cass, 1963)

Background reading

Bury T. P. T., *France 1815–40* (Methuen, 1969)
Cobban A., *History of Modern France*, Vol 2 (Penguin, 1970)
Seaman L. C. B., *From Vienna to Versailles* (Methuen, 1972)
Thomson J. M., *Louis Napoleon and the Second Empire* (Blackwell, 1969)

Further reading

Guerard A., *Napoleon III* (Greenwood, 1979)

Chapter 6 The Unification of Germany

Basic texts

Grenville J. A. S., *Europe Reshaped* (Fontana, 1976)
Thomson D., *Europe since Napoleon* (Penguin, 1977)
Wood A., *Europe 1845–1945* (Longman, 1975)
Woodward E. L., *War and Peace in Europe 1815–70* (Cass, 1963)

Background reading

Böhme H., *The Foundation of the German Empire* (Oxford University Press, 1971)
Medlicott W. N., *Bismarck and Modern Germany* (English Universities Press, 1965)

Further reading

Pflanze O., *Bismarck and the Development of Germany 1848–71* (Princeton University Press, 1963)
Simon W. M., *Germany in the Age of Bismarck* (Allen and Unwin, 1968)
Taylor A. J. P., *Bismarck* (New English Library, 1974); and *The Struggle for Mastery in Europe* (Oxford University Press, 1971)

Chapter 7 Russia 1855–1917

Basic texts

Grenville J. A. S., *Europe Reshaped* (Fontana, 1976)
Thomson D., *Europe since Napoleon* (Penguin, 1977)
Wood A., *Europe 1845–1945* (Longman, 1975)
Woodward E. L., *War and Peace in Europe 1815–70* (Cass, 1963)

Background reading

Charques R., *The Twilight of Imperial Russia* (Oxford University Press, 1965)
Kochan L., *The Making of Modern Russia* (Penguin, 1970)
Seton-Watson H., *The Russian Empire 1801–1917* (Oxford University Press, 1967)

Further reading

Carr E. H., *Studies in Revolution* (Cass, 1962)

Chapter 8 The Origins of the First World War

Basic texts

Joll J., *Europe since 1870* (Pelican, 1976)
Roberts J. M., *Europe 1880–1945* (Longman, 1967)
Thomson D., *Europe since Napoleon* (Penguin, 1977)
Wood A., *Europe 1815–1945* (Longman, 1975)

Background reading

Hale O. J., *The Great Illusion* (Harper and Row, 1971)
Taylor A. J. P., *The Struggle for Mastery in Europe* (Oxford University Press, 1971)
Turner L. C. F., *The Origins of the First World War* (Edward Arnold, 1976)

Further reading

Balfour M., *The Kaiser and his Times* (Penguin, 1977)
Fischer F., *Germany's Aims in the First World War* (Chatto, 1975)
Lafore F., *The Long Fuse* (Weidenfeld and Nicolson, 1975)

Chapter 9 The Peace Treaties and International Restraint

Basic texts

Joll J., *Europe since 1870* (Pelican, 1976)
Roberts J. M., *Europe 1880–1945* (Longman, 1967)
Thomson D., *Europe since Napoleon* (Penguin, 1977)
Wood A., *Europe 1815–1945* (Longman, 1975)

Backgroung reading

Nicolson H., *Peacemaking 1919* (Methuen, 1964)
Sontag R., *A Broken World 1919–39* (Harper and Row, 1971)
Wiskeman E., *Europe of the Dictators* (Fontana, 1973)

Further reading

Carr E. H., *The Twenty Years' Crisis 1919–39* (Macmillan, 1981)

Chapter 10 Russia 1917–19

Basic texts

Joll J., *Europe since 1870* (Pelican, 1976)
Roberts J. M., *Europe 1880–1945* (Longman, 1967)
Thomson D., *Europe since Napoleon* (Penguin, 1977)
Wood A., *Europe 1815–1945* (Longman, 1975)

Background reading

Carr E. H., *The Bolshevik Revolution*, Vol 1 (Macmillan, 1980)
Kochan L., *The Making of Modern Russia* (Penguin, 1970)

Further reading

Deutscher I., *Stalin* (Penguin 1972)
Laqueur W., *The Fate of the Revolution: Interpretations of Russian History* (Weidenfeld and Nicolson, 1967)

Chapter 11 Mussolini and Italian Fascism

Basic texts

Joll J., *Europe since 1870* (Pelican, 1976)
Roberts J. M., *Europe 1880–1945* (Longman, 1967)
Thomson D., *Europe since Napoleon* (Penguin, 1977)
Wood A., *Europe 1815–1945* (Longman, 1975)

Background reading
Cassels A., *Fascist Italy* (Routledge, 1969)
Procacci G., *A History of the Italian People* (Penguin, 1973)

Further reading
Chabod F., *A History of Italian Fascism* (Cedric Chivers, 1974)
Nolte E., *The Three Faces of Fascism* (Mentor Books, 1969)
Woolf S. (ed), *European Fascism* (Weidenfeld and Nicolson, 1970)

Chapter 12 The Weimar Republic and the Rise of Hitler

Basic texts
Joll J., *Europe since 1870* (Pelican, 1976)
Roberts J. M., *Europe 1880–1945* (Longman, 1967)
Thomson D., *Europe since Napoleon* (Penguin, 1977)
Wood A., *Europe 1815–1945* (Longman, 1975)

Background reading
Grunberger R., *A Social History of the Third Reich* (Pelican, 1974)
Hiden J. W., *The Weimar Republic* (Longman, 1974)
Nicholls A. J., *Weimar and the Rise of Hitler* (Macmillan, 1979)

Further reading
Bracher K. D., *The German Dictatorship* (Penguin, 1973)
Bullock A., *Hitler: a study in tyranny* (Penguin, 1968)
Fest J. C., *Hitler* (Penguin, 1977)
Nolte E., *The Three Faces of Fascism* (Mentor Books, 1969)
Shirer W. L., *The Rise and Fall of the Third Reich* (Pan, 1968)
Speer A., *Inside the Third Reich* (Weidenfeld and Nicolson, 1970)

Chapter 13 The Path to War: the Failure of Appeasement

Basic texts
Joll J., *Europe since 1870* (Pelican, 1976)
Roberts J. M., *Europe 1880–1945* (Longman, 1967)
Thomson D., *Europe since Napoleon* (Penguin, 1977)
Wood A., *Europe 1815–1945* (Longman, 1975)

Background reading

Carr W., *Arms, Autarky and Aggression: Study in German Foreign Policy 1933–39* (Edward Arnold, 1972)
Taylor A. J. P., *The Origins of the Second World War* (Penguin, 1963)
Thorne C., *The Approach of War 1938–9* (Macmillan, 1976)

Further reading

Bullock A., *Hitler: a study in tyranny* (Penguin, 1968)
Robertson E. M., *The Origins of the Second World War* (Macmillan, 1971)

Chapter 14 From Co-operation to Conflict: the Cold War

Basic texts

Joll J., *Europe since 1870* (Weidenfeld and Nicolson, 1973)
Laqueur W., *Europe since Hitler* (Weidenfeld and Nicolson, Penguin, 1970)
Stuart Hughes H., *Contemporary Europe: A History* (Prentice Hall, 1976)
Thomson D., *Europe since Napoleon* (Penguin, 1977)

Background reading

Fontaine A., *History of the Cold War*, Vols, 1 and 2 (Vintage Books, 1970)
Halle L. J., *The Cold War as History* (Harper and Row, 1975)

Further reading

Deutscher I., *Stalin* (Penguin, 1972)
Mowat R. C., *Ruin and Resurgence 1939–65* (Blandford, 1966)

Chapter 15 Moves to European Unity

Basic texts

Joll J., *Europe since 1870* (Weidenfeld and Nicolson, 1973)
Laqueur W., *Europe since Hitler* (Weidenfeld and Nicolson, Penguin, 1970)
Stuart Hughes H., *Contemporary Europe: A History* (Prentice Hall, 1976)

Background reading

Vaughan R., *Twentieth Century Europe: Paths to Unity* (Croom Helm, 1979)

Further reading

Crozier B., *De Gaulle: the Statesman* (Methuen, 1974)
Grosser A., *Germany in our Time* (Pall Mall, 1971)
Mowat R. C., *Ruin and Resurgence 1939–45* (Blandford, 1966)
Ryder A. J., *Twentieth Century Germany from Bismarck to Brandt* (Macmillan, 1973)
Urwin D. W., *Western Europe since 1945* (Longman, 1968)

Chapter 16 Britain in 1815

Basic texts

Briggs A., *Age of Improvement* (Longman, 1959)
Webb R. K., *Modern England* (Allen and Unwin, 1980)
Wood A., *Nineteenth Century Britain* (Longman, 1960)

Background reading

Ashton T. S., *The Industrial Revolution* (Oxford University Press, 1969)
Brock W. R., *Lord Liverpool and Liberal Toryism 1820–27* (Cass, 1967)
Cookson J. E., *Lord Liverpool's Administration: the Crucial Years* (Scottish Academic Press, 1975)
Hilton B., *Corn, Cash, Commerce: The Economic Policies of the Tory Government 1815–30* (Oxford University Press, 1977)
Hobsbawm E. J., *Industry and Empire* (Pelican edn, 1969)
Hobsbawm E. J., *The Age of Revolution* (Weidenfeld and Nicolson, 1962)
Mitchell A., *The Whigs in Opposition 1815–30* (Oxford University Press, 1967)

Further reading

Anderson P., Origins of the Present Crisis *New Left Review*
Hollis P., *Class and Conflict in 19th Century England 1815–50* (Routledge and Kegan Paul, 1973)
Stevenson J., *Popular Disturbances in England 1700–1870* (Longman, 1979)
Thomis M. I., and Holt P., *Threats of Revolution in Britain 1789–1840* (Macmillan, 1977)
Thompson E. P. *The Making of the English Working Class* (Gollancz, 1963)
Thompson E. P., 18th Century English Society: Class struggle without class? *Social History* Vol. 3 No 2 1977

Chapter 17 The Whig Reforms

Basic texts

Briggs A., *Age of Improvement* (Longman, 1959)
Webb R. K., *Modern England* (Allen and Unwin, 1980)
Wood, A., *Nineteenth Century Britain* (Longman, 1960)

Background reading

Brock M., *The Great Reform Act* (Hutchinson, 1983)
Gash N., *Reaction and Reconstruction in English Politics* (Oxford University press, 1965)
Llewellyn A., *The Decade of Reform: The 1830s* (David and Charles, 1972)
Marshall J. D., *The Old Poor Law 1795–1834* (Macmillan, 1974)
Rose M. E., *The Relief of Poverty 1834–1914* (Macmillan, 1972)
Southgate D., *The Passing of the Whigs 1832–86* (Macmillan, 1962)
Ward J. T. (ed), *Popular Movements c. 1830–1850* (Macmillan, 1970)

Further reading

Hollis P., *Class and Conflict in 19th Century England 1815–50* (Routledge and Kegan Paul, 1973)
Stevenson J., *Popular Disturbances in England 1700–1870* (Longman, 1979)
Taylor A. J. (ed), *The Standard of living in Britain in the Industrial Revolution* (Methuen, 1975)
Thompson E. P., *The Making of the English Working Class* (Gollancz, 1963)

Chapter 18 Chartism and the Anti-Corn Law League

Basic texts

Briggs A., *Age of Improvement* (Longman, 1959)
Webb R. K., *Modern England* (Allen and Unwin, 1980)
Wood A., *Nineteenth Century Britain* (Longman, 1960)

Background reading

Briggs A., *Chartist Studies* (Macmillan, 1959)
Cole G. D. H., *Chartist Portraits* (Macmillan, 1941)
Hobsbawm E. J., *The Age of Revolution* (Weidenfeld and Nicolson, 1962)
McCord N., *The Anti-Corn Law League* (Allen and Unwin, 1958)
Read D., *Cobden and Bright* (Arnold, 1967)

Further reading

Hollis P. (ed), *Pressure from without in Early Victorian England* (Arnold, 1974)
Hollis P. (ed), *Class and Conflict in 19th Century England 1815–50* (Routledge and Kegan Paul, 1973)
Jones D., *Chartism and Chartists* (Allen Lane, 1975)
Royle E., *Chartism* (Longman, 1980)
Stevenson J., *Popular Disturbances in England 1700–1870* (Longman, 1979)

Chapter 19 Peel and the Conservative Party

Basic texts

Briggs A., *Age of Improvement* (Longman, 1959)
Webb R. K., *Modern England* (Allen and Unwin, 1980)
Wood A., *Nineteenth Century Britain* (Longman, 1960)

Background reading

Blake R., *The Conservative Party from Peel to Churchill* (Fontana, 1972)
Gash N., *Peel* (Longman, 1972)
Gash, N., *Politics in the Age of Peel* (Harvester, 1977)

Further reading

Machin G. I. T., *Politics and the Churches in Great Britain* 1832–68 (Oxford University Press, 1978)
Stewart R. M., *The Foundations of the Conservative Party 1830–67* (Longman, 1978)
Stewart R. M., *The Politics of Protection: Lord Derby and the Protectionist Party 1841–52* (Cambridge University Press, 1971)

Chapter 20 British Foreign Policy 1815–65

Basic texts

Briggs A., *Age of Improvement* (Longman, 1959)
Webb R. K., *Modern England* (Allen and Unwin, 1980)
Wood A., *Nineteenth Century Britain* (Longman, 1960)

Background reading

Anderson A., *A Liberal State at War* (Macmillan, 1967)
Barlett C. J., *Castlereagh* (Macmillan, 1966)
Dixon P., *Canning, Politician and Statesman* (Weidenfeld and Nicolson, 1976)

Hobsbawm E. J., *The Age of Revolution* (Weidenfeld and Nicolson, 1976)
Ridley J., *Lord Palmerston* (Constable, 1970)
Seaman L. C. B., *From Vienna to Versailles* (Methuen, 1955)

Further reading

Bourne K., *The Foreign Policy of Victorian England* (Oxford University Press, 1970)
Joll J. (ed), *Britain and Europe 1793–1940* (Oxford University Press, 1967)
Southgate D., *The Most English Minister . . . the Policies and Politics of Palmerston* (Macmillan, 1966)

Chapter 21 Disraeli and Conservatism

Basic texts

Webb R. K., *Modern England* (Allen and Unwin, 1980)
Wood A., *Nineteenth Century Britain* (Longman, 1960)

Background reading

Adelman P., *Gladstone, Disraeli and Later Victorian Politics* (Longman, 1970)
Blake R., *Disraeli* (Methuen, 1966)
MacDowell R. B., *British Conservatism 1832–1914* (Faber, 1959)
Smith P., *Disraelian Conservatism and Social Reform* (Routledge and Kegan Paul, 1967)

Further reading

Cowling M., *Disraeli, Gladstone and Revolution* (Cambridge University Press, 1967)
Eldridge C. C., *England's Mission, The Imperial Idea in the Age of Gladstone and Disraeli* (Macmillan, 1973)
Smith F. B., *The Making of the Second Reform Bill* (Cambridge University Press, 1966)

Chapter 22 Gladstone and Liberalism

Basic texts

Webb R. K., *Modern England* (Allen and Unwin 1980)
Wood A., *Nineteenth Century Britain* (Longman, 1960)

Background reading

Adelman P., *Gladstone, Disraeli and Later Victorian Politics* (Longman, 1970)
Browne H., *Joseph Chamberlain: Radical and Imperialist* (Longman, 1974)
Feuchtwanger E. J., *Gladstone* (Allen Lane, 1975)
Hamer D. A., *Liberal Politics in the Age of Gladstone and Roseberry* (Clarendon Press, 1972)
Jones A., *The Politics of Reform, 1884* (Cambridge University Press, 1972)
Lowe C. J., *The Reluctant Imperialists* (Routledge and Kegan Paul, 1967)
Magnus P., *Gladstone* (John Murray, 1954)
Vincent J., *The Formation of the Liberal Party 1857–68* (Constable, 1966)

Further reading

Barker M., *Gladstone and Radicalism* (Harvester Press, 1975)
Chamberlain M. E., *The New Imperialism* (Historical Association, 1970)
Hanham H. J., *Elections and Party Management: Politics in the time of Disraeli and Gladstone* (Longman, 1959 1978)
Judd D., *Radical Joe* (Hamish Hamilton, 1977)
Louis W. R., *Imperialism: The Robinson and Gallagher Controversy* (New Viewpoints, 1976)
Robinson R. and Gallagher J., *Africa and the Victorians* (Macmillan, 1961)

Chapter 23 The Irish Problem

Basic texts

Webb R. K., *Modern England* (Allen and Unwin, 1980)
Wood A., *Nineteenth Century Britain* (Longman, 1960)

Background reading

Beckett J. C., *The Making of Modern Ireland 1603–1923* (Faber, 1966)
Hamer D. A., *Liberal Politics in the Age of Gladstone and Roseberry* (Clarendon Press, 1972)
Hammond J. L., *Gladstone and the Irish Nation* (Cass, 1964)
Lyons F. S. L., *Ireland since the Famine* (Collins, 1971, 1973)
Lyons F. S. L., *Charles Stewart Parnell* (Collins, 1977)

Further reading
Lee J., *The Modernization of Irish Society 1848–1918* (Gill and Macmillan, 1973)
Solow B. L., *The Land and the Irish Economy 1870–1903* (Harvard University Press, 1971)

Chapter 24 New Liberalism 1906–14

Basic texts
Lloyd T. O., *Empire to Welfare State* (Oxford Universty Press, 1970)
Webb R. K., *Modern England* (Allen and Unwin, 1980)
Wood A., *Nineteenth Century Britain* (Longman, 1960)

Background reading
Adelman P., *The Rise of the Labour Party 1880–1945* (Longman, 1945)
Cook C., *A Short History of the Liberal Party 1900–1976* (Macmillan, 1976)
Morgan K. O., *Lloyd George* (Weidenfeld and Nicolson, 1974)
Morgan K. O., *The Age of Lloyd George* (Allen and Unwin, 1971)
Read D., *Edwardian England* (Harrap, 1972)

Further reading
Dangerfield G., *The Strange Death of Liberal England* (Paladin, 1936, 1970)
Phelps Brown E. H., *The Growth of British Industrial Relations* (Macmillan, 1965)
Rover C., *Women's Suffrage and Party Politics 1866–1914* (Routledge and Kegan Paul, 1967)
Thompson P., *The Edwardians* (Paladin, 1975)

Chapter 25 Britain between the Wars

Basic texts
Lloyd T. O., *Empire to Welfare State* (Oxford University Press, 1974)
Seaman L. C. B., *Post-Victorian Britain* (Methuen, 1966)
Webb R. K., *Modern England* (Allen and Unwin, 1980)

Background reading

Aldcroft D. H., *The Interwar Economy: Britain 1919–39* (Batsford, 1973)
Blake R., *The Conservative Party from Peel to Churchill* (Fontana, 1972)
Cook C., *A Short History of the Liberal Party 1900–1976* (Macmillan, 1976)
Farman C., *The General Strike*, (Hart-Davis, 1972)
Glyn S., and Oxbarrow J, *Interwar Britain, A Social and Economic History* (Allen and Unwin, 1976)
Lyons F. S. L., *Ireland Since the Famine* (Collins, 1971, 1973)
Mowat C. L., *Britain Between the Wars* (Methuen, 1955)
Pollard S., *The Development of the British Economy 1914–67* (Arnold, 1962, 1968)
Taylor A. J. P., *English History 1914–45* (Oxford University Press, 1965)
Williams L. J., *Britain and the World Economy 1919–70* (Fontana-Collins, 1971)

Further reading

Constantine S., *Unemployment in Britain Between the Wars* (Longman, 1980)
Lovell J., *British Trade Unions 1875–1933* (Macmillan, 1967)
Middlemas R. K. and Barnes A. L., *Baldwin, a Biography* (Weidenfeld, 1967)
Middlemas R. K., *Politics in Industrial Society* (André Deutsch, 1979)
Marquand D., *Ramsay MacDonald* (Jonathan Cape, 1977)
Skidelsky R., *Politicians and the Slump* (Macmillan, 1967)
Stevenson J. and Cook C., *The Slump* (Jonathan Cape, 1977)

Chapter 26 The National Governments

Basic texts

Lloyd T. O., *Empire to Welfare State* (Oxford University Press, 1970)
Seaman L. C. B., *Post-Victorian Britain* (Methuen, 1966)
Webb R. K., *Modern England* (Allen and Unwin, 1980)

Background reading

Constantine S., *Unemployment in Britain between the Wars* (Longman, 1980)

Feiling K., *The Life of Neville Chamberlain* (Macmillan, 1946, 1970)
Medicott W. N., *British Foreign Policy since Versailles* (Methuen, 1968)
Mowat C. L., *Britain Between the Wars* (Methuen, 1955)
Richardson H. W., *Economic Recovery in Britain 1932–39* (Weidenfeld & Nicolson, 1967)
Stevenson J. and Cook C., *The Slump* (Jonathan Cape, 1977)
Taylor A. J. P., *English History 1914–45* (Oxford University Press, 1965)
Taylor A. J. P., *The Origins of the Second World War* (Penguin, 1964)
Thorne C., *The Approach of War 1938–39* (Macmillan, 1967)

Further reading

Benwick T., *The Fascist Movement in Britain* (Penguin, 1972)
Howell D., *British Social Democracy* (Croom Helm, 1976)
Middlemas R. K., *Politics in Industrial Society* (André Deutsch, 1979)
Miliband R., *Parliamentary Socialism* (Merlin Press, 1964, 1973)
Rock W. R., *British Appeasement in the 1930s* (Edward Arnold, 1977)

Chapter 27 Labour Majority 1945–51

Basic texts

Lloyd T. O., *Empire to Welfare State* (Oxford University Press, 1970)
Seaman L. C. B., *Post-Victorian Britain* (Methuen, 1966)
Webb R. K., *Modern England* (Allen and Unwin, 1980)

Background reading

Barry E. E., *Nationalization in British Politics* (Jonathan Cape, 1965)
Beer S., *Modern British Politics* (Faber, 1965, 1969)
Eatwell R., *The 1945–51 Labour Governments* (Batsford, 1979)
Fraser D., *The Evolution of the British Welfare State* (Macmillan, 1973)
Williams L. J., *Britain and the World Economy 1919–1970* (Fontana–Collins 1971)

Further reading

Birch R. C., *The Shaping of the Welfare State* (Longman, 1974)
Cook C. and Ramsden J. (eds), *Trends in British Politics since 1945* (Macmillan, 1978)
Miliband R, *Parliamentary Socialism* (Merlin Press, 1964, 1973)
Middlemas R. K., *Politics in Industrial Society* (André Deutsch, 1979)
Northedge F. S., *Descent From Power: British Foreign Policy 1945–73* (Allen and Unwin, 1974)

Chapter 28 Conservative Rule 1951–64

Basic texts

Lloyd T. O., *Empire to Welfare State* (Oxford University Press, 1970)
Seaman L. C. B., *Post-Victorian Britain* (Methuen, 1966)
Webb R. K., *Modern England* (Allen and Unwin, (1980)

Background reading

Beer S., *Modern British Politics* (Faber, 1965, 1969)
Northedge F. S., *Descent from Power: British Foreign Policy 1945–73* (Allen and Unwin, 1974)
Williams L. J., *Britain and the World Economy 1919–1970* (Fontana-Collins 1971)

Further reading

Cook C. and Ramsden J. (eds), *Trends in British Politics since 1945* (Macmillan 1978)
Leys C., *Politics in Britain* (Heinemann 1983)
Middlemas R. K., *Politics in Industrial Society* (André Deutsch 1979)

Index

British

Other study aids in the **Keyfacts** series

KEY FACTS CARDS

Additional Mathematics
Algebra
Arithmetic & Trigonometry
Biology
Chemistry
Computer Studies
Economics
Elementary Mathematics
English Comprehension & Précis
English Language and the Examination Essay
French
General Science
Geography
Geography, British Isles
German
British History (1815-1914)
British History (1914–1951)
Human Biology
Modern Mathematics
New Testament
Physics
Technical Drawing

KEY FACTS COURSE COMPANIONS

Additional Mathematics
Algebra
Arithmetic & Trigonometry
Biology
Chemistry
Economics
English
French
Geography
Geometry
Modern Mathematics
Physics

KEY FACTS A-LEVEL BOOKS

Biology
Chemistry
Physics
Pure Mathematics

KEY FACTS O-LEVEL AND CSE PASSBOOKS

Biology
Chemistry
Computer Studies
Economics
English Language
French
Geography
Geography, British Isles
German
History (Political and Constitutional)
History (Social and Economic)
Human Biology
Modern Mathematics
Physics
Technical Drawing

KEY FACTS O-LEVEL AND CSE MODEL ANSWERS

Biology
Chemistry
Computer studies
English Studies
French
Geography
History (Social and Economic)
Modern Mathematics
Physics

KEY FACTS REFERENCE LIBRARY

Biology
Chemistry
Geography
History
Physics
Traditional and Modern Mathematics

KEY FACTS A-LEVEL PASSBOOKS

Applied Mathematics
Biology
Chemistry
Economics
Geography
Physics
Pure Mathematics
Pure and Applied Mathematics

KEY FACTS A-LEVEL WORKED EXAMPLES

Applied Mathematics
Biology
Chemistry
Economics
Geography
Physics
Pure Mathematics
Pure and Applied Mathematics

KEY FACTS DICTIONARIES

Biology
Chemistry
Economics
Geography
Mathematics
Physics